CATHOLIC EAST ANGLIA

Catholic East Anglia

A History of the Catholic Faith
in Norfolk, Suffolk, Cambridgeshire
and Peterborough

edited by

Francis Young

GRACEWING

First published in England in 2016
by
Gracewing
2 Southern Avenue
Leominster
Herefordshire HR6 0QF
United Kingdom
www.gracewing.co.uk

ISBN 978 085244 887 8

Typeset by Word and Page, Chester, UK

Cover design by Bernardita Peña Hurtado

CONTENTS

TABLES

Abbreviations

Bd	Blessed (beatified)
CJ	Companions of Jesus (formerly Institute of the Blessed Virgin Mary)
Fr	Father
HMSO	His/Her Majesty's Stationery Office
Mgr	Monsignor
OCD	Carmelites (Discalced)
ODNB	*The Oxford Dictionary of National Biography* (Oxford: Oxford University Press, 2004), 60 vols
OFM	Franciscans
OP	Dominicans
OSA	Augustinians
OSB	Benedictines
SJ	Society of Jesus (Jesuits)
sm	Society of Mary
Sr	Sister
Ven.	Venerable (cause for canonisation declared open by the Pope)

FOREWORD

'Remember all those holy confessors, bishops and
kings, all those holy monks and hermits, all those holy
virgins and widows who made this once an Island of
Saints, illustrious by their glorious merits and virtues.'
This prayer, recited at Benediction every Sunday in
every church in England for over a hundred years,
could easily be a description of the kingdom of East
Anglia.

This book is both a record of past heroic achievements and abundant blessings, and a stirring challenge
for the future: God calls us, each and every one, to be
holy, saints indeed, and to encourage each other in our
pursuit of holiness as together we journey towards the
Kingdom of God.

May this work hearten and encourage us, then, 'so
that we may be strengthened in our inner being with

power through his Spirit ... as we are being rooted and grounded in love ... so that we may comprehend, with all the saints ... to know the love of Christ that surpasses knowledge, and ... be filled with all the fullness of God' (*cf.* Ephesians 3.16–19).

+ Alan. Hope

The Right Reverend Alan S. Hopes
Bishop of East Anglia

PREFACE

Catholic East Anglia celebrates the fortieth anniversary of the creation of the Diocese of East Anglia out of the Diocese of Northampton in 1976, which gave East Anglian Catholics, for the first time since the Reformation, their own bishop. However, this book also celebrates over 450 years of the continuous survival of the Catholic faith in East Anglia, after Catholicism was outlawed by Queen Elizabeth in 1559. Without the witness of the men and women who cherished the Catholic faith during centuries of persecution, discrimination and marginalisation, the present Diocese of East Anglia could never have come into being. This book tells the story of the Catholics of East Anglia since the Reformation. Some of them have been much studied, others not at all, but their collective story has never before been the subject of a dedicated volume.

The idea of this book was first suggested to me by Anne Parry, who was then a trustee of the Diocese of East Anglia, at a study day I delivered on East Anglian Catholic families at Sutton Hoo, near Woodbridge, in March 2014. On that occasion we discussed suitable ways to commemorate the fortieth anniversary of the establishment of the Diocese in 2016, and Anne suggested that I consider editing a diocesan history. Later the same year I met with Prof. John Morrill and Frs Russell Frost and Tony Rogers to discuss the project. They introduced me to Fr Derek Lance's excellent history of the Diocese of Northampton, *The Returning Tide* (2000). However, rather than following the model of Fr Lance's book, *Catholic East Anglia* consists of a series of chapters by different historians, chronologically arranged, which I hope will not only illuminate each historical period but will also offer different perspectives and emphases.

I am very grateful to the Rt Revd Alan Hopes, Bishop of East Anglia, for supporting this project and for writing a Foreword to the book. I thank all the authors for their contributions and I am especially grateful to John Morrill and the other members of the informal 'publication committee', Russell Frost and Tony Rogers, who kindly offered their insight and advice on the text and the structure of the volume. I also acknowledge with thanks information provided by Chris Larsen on East Anglian bishops. It is my hope that this book will stimulate more research into East Anglia's Catholic history, which represents a fertile field of enquiry with many rich repositories of original source material.

Ely, Cambridgeshire
March 2016

Catholicism in East Anglia:
A Timeline of Key Events

1559   The Act of Uniformity outlaws the Mass

1561   St Robert Southwell born at Horsham St Faith, Norfolk

1565   Dr William Allen (later Cardinal) composes *Certain Brief Reasons concerning Catholic faith* while hiding in the Duke of Norfolk's Palace at Norwich

1569   Thomas Howard, 4th Duke of Norfolk, flees to Kenninghall

1570   Sir John Appleyard attempts a Catholic rebellion in Norwich

1572   The Duke of Norfolk executed for treason and the dukedom attainted

1578   Queen Elizabeth's East Anglian progress; Bd Montford Scott arrested in Cambridge

1580   The first priests are sent as prisoners to Wisbech Castle

1588   Recusant gentlemen imprisoned at the Bishop's Palace, Ely

1589   John Gerard SJ begins his East Anglian mission

1591   Martyrdom of Bd Montford Scott

1595   Martyrdom of St Henry Walpole; Martyrdom of St Robert Southwell; St Henry Morse born at Brome, Suffolk

1597   Recusants released from the Bishop's Palace, Ely

1600   Priests moved from Wisbech Castle to Framlingham Castle

1605   Ambrose Rookwood supplies the horses and gunpowder for the Gunpowder Plot

1606   Ambrose Rookwood executed

1616   Martyrdom of Bd Thomas Tunstall in Norwich

1633   Lord Petre establishes the Jesuit College of the Holy Apostles to serve Norfolk, Suffolk, Cambridgeshire and Essex

1642   Stour Valley Riots target Catholics in Essex and Suffolk; martyrdom of St Alban Roe

1645   Martyrdom of St Henry Morse

1648   Catholics involved in Royalist risings at Linton and Bury St Edmunds

1655   James Mumford SJ arrested in Norwich

1657   Benedictine mission founded at Flixton, Suffolk

1662   Dukedom of Norfolk restored

1672   James, Duke of York defeats the Dutch in the Battle of Sole Bay, off Southwold, Suffolk (with his chaplain Thomas Downes SJ)

1678   'Popish Plot' scare; many East Anglian Catholics forced into exile

1685   The Jesuit College of the Holy Apostles moves into the Abbot's Palace in Bury St Edmunds

1687   James II's Declaration of Indulgence; public Catholic chapels in Norwich, Bury St Edmunds, Cambridge and elsewhere; East Anglia placed under the jurisdiction of the Vicar Apostolic of the Midland District

1688   Rioters destroy chapels in Norwich, Bury St Edmunds, Cambridge and elsewhere

1696   Ambrose Rookwood executed for planning to assassinate William of Orange

1710   The Duke of Norfolk abandons his Palace in Norwich as a residence

1715   Catholics are obliged to register their estates

1745   Catholics are obliged to register their estates and hand in horses and firearms

1751   John Joseph Hornyold appointed Coadjutor to Bishop Stonor, with responsibility for the eastern half of the Midland District

1752   Publication of Anselm Mannock's *The Poor Man's Catechism*

1753   Fr Alban Butler becomes chaplain to the Duke's Palace chapel in Norwich

1761   Fr John Gage SJ opens East Anglia's first public chapel since 1688 in Bury St Edmunds

1764   New chapel opened next to the Duke's Palace in Norwich

1773   Pope Clement XIV suppresses the Jesuits

1778   First Catholic Relief Act

1784   François de la Rochefoucauld visits East Anglia

1786   Closure of Duke's Palace chapel

1791   Second Catholic Relief Act; Maddermarket Chapel opens in Norwich; publication of Elizabeth Inchbald's *A Simple Story*

1793   England declares war on France; Fr Louis Pierre Simon establishes Ipswich mission

1794   East Anglia's first post-Reformation convents established at Bodney Hall and Hengrave Hall

1809   Great Yarmouth mission founded

1811   Fr Pierre Louis Dacheux establishes King's Lynn mission

1813   William Eusebius Andrews founds *The Orthodox Journal*

1820   Frederick Husenbeth appointed chaplain at Costessey, Norfolk

1824   Jerningham family inherits the Barony of Stafford

1829   Third Catholic Relief Act (Catholic Emancipation)

1840   Eastern District created; William Wareing appointed Vicar Apostolic

1841   St Andrew's Catholic church opened in Cambridge

1842   Bishop Wareing moves into Giffords Hall, Suffolk and establishes Seminary of St Felix

1844   Seminary of St Felix closes

1847   First Catholic mission opens in Peterborough

1850   Restoration of the hierarchy; East Anglia incorporated into the Diocese of Northampton

1859   Church of St Mary and St Thomas, Northampton becomes a cathedral

1861   Church of St Pancras founded at Ipswich

1880   Church of Our Lady and St John the Evangelist founded at Sudbury

1881   Church of Our Lady Star of the Sea founded at Lowestoft

1889   Churches founded at Felixstowe and Southwold

1890   Church of Our Lady and the English Martyrs completed in Cambridge

1895   Church of Our Lady of Refuge founded at Cromer

1897   Church of Our Lady of the Annunciation, King's Lynn becomes a papal shrine

1904   Slipper Chapel at Walsingham taken over by Diocese of Northampton

1934   Slipper Chapel at Walsingham becomes National Shrine of Our Lady

1957   Consecration of the Church of St John the Baptist, Norwich

1969   Alan Clark appointed Bishop of Elmham, assistant bishop in the Diocese of Northampton

1975   Bishop Charles Grant of Northampton petitions Pope Paul VI to create a Diocese for East Anglia

1976   Creation of the Diocese of East Anglia by the decree *Quod Oecumenicum*; Alan Clark enthroned as first Bishop; St John's becomes a cathedral

1995   Peter Smith appointed second Bishop of East Anglia

2001   Bishop Smith appointed Archbishop of Cardiff

2002   Death of Bishop Alan Clark

2003   Bishop Michael Evans appointed third Bishop of East Anglia

2011   Death of Bishop Michael Evans

2013   Bishop Alan Hopes appointed fourth Bishop of East Anglia

2015   Pope Francis elevates the National Shrine of Our Lady at Walsingham to the status of a minor basilica

2016   The Diocese of East Anglia celebrates its fortieth anniversary

Introduction

Francis Young and Rachel Young

THE DIOCESE OF EAST ANGLIA came into being on 13 March 1976, when the counties of Norfolk, Suffolk and Cambridgeshire (then including the present Peterborough Unitary Authority) were separated from the jurisdiction of the Diocese of Northampton. One of the justifications given for the creation of the new diocese was the 'natural unity' of the territory, and indeed the new diocese assumed the name of an ancient Anglo-Saxon kingdom. The sea coast of Norfolk and Suffolk bounded the diocese to the north and east, while the River Stour, the ancient boundary between East Angles and East Saxons, separated East Anglia from the Diocese of Brentwood. To the west, where in centuries past great earthworks such as Devil's Dyke and the long-since-drained waters of the Fens had demarcated the edge of a kingdom, now the county boundary of Cambridgeshire separated East Anglia from its neighbouring dioceses.

The Diocese of East Anglia is at once something very modern—a product of the Second Vatican Council and a fast-growing post-war Catholic population—and very ancient, a long-established territory with an unbroken Catholic heritage. This book, which tells the story of the Catholic faith in these easternmost counties of England since the Reformation, seeks to reflect the reality of a modern diocese in an ancient land. The East Anglia encountered by the first missionaries to the Anglo-Saxons was in many ways very different from that of the present day. The undrained Fens still cut off East Anglia, which was almost a peninsula jutting into the North Sea, while a great estuary broke into eastern Norfolk, so that the site of present-day Norwich was on the water's edge. In other ways, however, East Anglia has changed comparatively little. It remains now, as it was then, a primarily agricultural region. Cities such as Norwich, Peterborough, Cambridge and Ipswich have grown up, but East Anglia still lacks conurbations and a network of motorways, and retains a rural feel. Norfolk and Suffolk are still noticeably more sparsely populated than nearby counties in London's orbit.

East Anglia's people have a distinctive character too. They are traditionally regarded, and regard themselves, as independent-minded and stubborn, wary of pretensions of authority, and perhaps more interested in their own local concerns and civic pride than in national matters. The Reformation was welcomed eagerly in East Anglia, where Lollardy had flourished in the late Middle Ages, and the cloth industry fostered the development of a literate class with a taste for dissent. The University of Cambridge and south Suffolk became heartlands of Puritanism, where communities sought to take the Reformation even further than the Tudor and Stuart state. This led eventually to an exodus of 'godly pilgrims' to the New World, where the names of the cities, towns and villages of New England still bear witness to East Anglia's huge contribution to early America. On the outbreak of Civil War, East

Anglia's communities sided firmly with Parliament and the Puritan cause against Charles I.

In no part of England was Protestantism (and indeed Puritanism) more deeply rooted than in East Anglia. Yet, as Joy Rowe has argued, the very same spirit of 'stiff-necked independence and conservatism' that sustained East Anglia's godly Puritan communities also contributed to the survival of a small yet 'perdurable' Catholic minority, especially in Norfolk and Suffolk, throughout the years when Catholicism was a proscribed religion (1559–1829).[1] Although East Anglian Catholicism has been immeasurably strengthened by the contribution of Irish, French, Polish and other Eastern European immigrants since the end of the eighteenth century, many of today's parishes owe their existence to a small but determined number of recusant families who kept the Catholic faith alive. The parishes of Sawston, Lawshall, Costessey and Withermarsh Green all trace their origins to secret chapels in nearby recusant houses, and the cathedral parish of St John the Baptist can be traced to a congregation that met in the chapel of the Duke of Norfolk's Palace in Norwich. St Edmund's, Bungay, is the direct descendant of a Benedictine mission established at Flixton Hall in 1657, while the church of St Edmund, King and Martyr, in Bury St Edmunds incorporates the oldest post-Reformation Catholic chapel in the diocese, founded by John Gage and his mother Elizabeth Rookwood in 1761. The diocese's oldest continuously functioning church, St Mary's, Thetford, was built in 1824 but gave a permanent home to a much older 'riding mission' originally centred on Bacton.

East Anglia was the scene of many significant events in the post-Reformation history of Catholic England.

Here the loyal Catholic gentry rallied to Queen Mary in July 1553, helping her defeat the Duke of Northumberland's attempt to put Jane Grey on the throne, and ushering in England's short-lived Counter-Reformation. It was in the Duke of Norfolk's Norwich Palace, in 1565, that William Allen conceived the idea of a network of continental seminaries to sustain the English mission. From 1580, Wisbech Castle in north Cambridgeshire became an internment camp for captured priests, and it was here in the 1590s that the 'Wisbech Stirs' defined and divided English Catholic identity. John Gerard's mission at Coldham Hall in 1589–91 re-converted key figures among the East Anglian gentry, and Ambrose Rookwood, a teenager at the time of Gerard's stay, provided the gunpowder and horses for the terrorist attack on Parliament in November 1605.

Of the Forty Martyrs of England and Wales canonised by Pope Paul VI in 1970, four are East Anglians: the Jesuit martyrs St Henry Walpole (*c.* 1558–93), St Robert Southwell (1561–95) and St Henry Morse (1595–1644), and the Benedictine St Alban Roe (d. 1642). East Anglia's beatified martyrs include the secular priests Montford Scott (d. 1591)[2] and Thomas Benstead (d. 1600), the Franciscans Bd Arthur Bell (1591–1643) and Bd Henry Heath (1599–1643) and the secular priest and Benedictine postulant Bd Thomas Tunstall (d. 1616). East Anglia's last martyrs were the Jesuit Venerable Thomas Downes (alias Bedingfield) (1617–78), and the layman Bd Edward Colman (1636–78), both executed during the 'Popish Plot'. While St Henry Walpole was perhaps the most venerated of these martyrs, the best known today is undoubtedly St Robert Southwell, widely considered the greatest of Elizabethan Catholic poets and the equal of Spenser, Sidney and even Shakespeare.

Other Catholics in East Anglia also made significant contributions to English Catholic culture, and brief accounts of the lives of eighty of them are given in Appendix 1. Alongside three bishops, an abbot and a multitude of priests and religious, they include spiritual writers, translators, publishers, a famous moral theologian, poets, novelists and playwrights, as well as doctors, diplomats, courtiers, colonists, explorers, antiquaries, a scientist, a sculptor, the first Catholic Cabinet minister since the seventeenth century and even a famous brick-maker. The East Anglian Catholic community produced rogues as well, and several convicted traitors and a notorious perjurer came from the region. Apart from those who achieved fame or notoriety, over two hundred East Anglian men entered the Catholic priesthood between 1559 and 1800, and a large number of women from the region entered religious houses on the Continent as nuns. Few of the latter achieved fame, but their quiet witness was another factor that ensured Catholicism endured in this corner of England during dark years of persecution. In this book, eight authors tell the story of the Catholic faith in East Anglia, from the Elizabethan Act of Uniformity in 1559 to the founding of the Diocese of East Anglia in 1976, and beyond that to the present time. It is not—and is not meant to be—a definitive study of the subject. Rather, the editor and authors hope that *Catholic East Anglia* will introduce an aspect of England's religious history still little understood to East Anglians, whether Catholic or not, who want a deeper knowledge of their heritage. However, since the chronology covered by this book begins in 1559, it is necessary in this introduction to return to an earlier era and set the post-Reformation history of the region in context: the Diocese of East Anglia is, after all, heir to Anglo-Saxon and medieval dioceses as well as the turmoil of the Reformation.

The Diocese of East Anglia: old and new

The title of the Diocese of East Anglia may only date from the 1970s, but it is an evocative one that recalls the earliest days of English Christianity. We know less about early Christianity in East Anglia than in other parts of England, which is due partly to Viking depredations in the ninth century and partly to poor curation of manuscripts in the Middle Ages.[3] Most of what we do know comes from Bede's *Ecclesiastical History of the English People* (731), but Bede was a Northumbrian and not primarily concerned with the history of the East Anglian Church.[4] The Angles were a Germanic people who came from a region in northern Germany and southern Denmark, and were among the first invaders to reach Britain after the withdrawal of the Romans, settling the coast of Lincolnshire and Yorkshire as well as East Anglia. They may have co-existed for a time with the Christian inhabitants of the former Roman *civitas* of the Iceni (with its capital at *Venta Icenorum*, now Caister St Edmund), but the archaeological evidence suggests that within a short while Romano-British Christianity and Romano-British culture were replaced by the pagan ways of the Angles.

When St Augustine arrived in Kent in 597, England was divided into numerous small kingdoms, and the success or failure of the Christian mission depended on the co-operation of regional kings. One of the most important of these was Rædwald (d. *c.* 624), king of the East Angles, who also happened to be high king of the English at the time. Rædwald was baptised in

Canterbury, probably in around 604,[5] and returned to his court, which was probably at Rendlesham in Suffolk, where he supposedly maintained a Christian church alongside a temple to the pagan gods. Bede's story about Rædwald's non-committal attitude to Christianity led archaeologists to speculate that the splendid Sutton Hoo ship burial discovered in 1939, with its mixture of pagan and Christian elements, was Rædwald's last resting place, and this remains a popular theory. Richard Hoggett has argued that Rædwald was only ever a nominal Christian, on the grounds that Christianity made no discernible progress during his reign and no attempt was made to set up a diocesan structure.[6] Certainly, on Rædwald's death the kingdom of East Anglia fell back into paganism until the accession of St Sigebert, who was either a son or stepson of Rædwald, in around 629.

Sigebert seems to have spent some time on the Continent and was already a Christian when he became king, and his lasting achievement was to invite a Burgundian monk, St Felix, to set up an episcopal see in East Anglia. Felix was already Bishop of Châlons, and crucially he was sent to East Anglia by Archbishop Honorius of Canterbury,[7] meaning that the mission to East Anglia was under the authority of the Roman Church. Felix followed established practice in England at the time by choosing an old Roman fort as a fortified mission station. This was probably Walton Castle, now submerged beneath the North Sea but then known as *Dommoc* (the old association between Dommoc and Dunwich is no longer accepted by most scholars).[8] One early mission station of this kind still survives a few miles further south in Essex, the seventh-century church of Othona established by St Cedd at Bradwell-on-Sea.

Together, Sigebert and Felix established East Anglia's first school,[9] beginning the tradition of Christian education that, centuries later, would culminate in the founding of Cambridge University. Felix was soon joined by another missionary, St Fursey, who came to East Anglia from Ireland, via the other Anglian kingdom of Northumbria. Fursey was part of a simultaneous and parallel movement to convert the English from Ireland, and introduced ascetic Celtic spirituality to East Anglia. Fursey founded another important early Christian site in the region called *Cnobheresburh*. Its site, like that of Dommoc, is no longer known with certainty, although it may have been Burgh Castle.

The early Anglo-Saxons were not an urban people, and Felix and Fursey's mission stations may have been similar to the old Franciscan missions of Texas and New Mexico. They were bases of operations for missionary activity rather than parish churches, and Felix was 'Bishop of the East Angles', associated with the people rather than with a particular place. Just as the king of the East Angles would have travelled from hall to hall to secure his kingdom, so Felix probably went from place to place to secure the faith. As a result, he lent his name to the port of Felixstowe and to two villages, both called Flixton, in northeast Suffolk. By a strange historical irony, one of these Flixtons (near Bungay) became the centre of the oldest post-Reformation Catholic mission in East Anglia. Like Felix's original mission, it was led by monks and still endures to this day as the parish of St Edmund, King and Martyr in Bungay. Felix may also have founded another episcopal centre at Soham in the Cambridgeshire Fens. He died at Dommoc in 647, although centuries later his body was moved to Soham, and later still to Ramsey Abbey in Huntingdonshire.[10]

In around 640 the pagan King Penda of Mercia attacked East Anglia, having heard that Sigebert had retreated to a monastery (possibly at *Beodericesworth*, the future Bury St Edmunds). The East Angles compelled Sigebert to lead them into battle but he refused to bear arms, and was killed while carrying only a staff. Penda did not conquer East Anglia, however, and the Church there continued to grow. Gipeswic, the future Ipswich, was a thriving emporium for international trade and Christianity was seen by many as a mark of sophistication, just like the luxury goods that were being imported from the Continent. In around 654 St Botolph founded his monastery at Iken Hoo,[11] and another important foundation followed at *Medehamstede* (later called Peterborough) by a monk called Seaxwulf.[12] In 673, a daughter of King Anna of the East Angles, Æthelthryth (better known by her Latinised name St Etheldreda) fled her husband Ecgfrith, king of Northumbria, and returned to the island of Ely, which had been granted to her as part of her dowry on her first marriage. Here she established a double monastery of monks and nuns that became one of the most important in the region.

In around 676, at the Council of Hertford, Archbishop Theodore of Canterbury divided the East Anglian diocese into two smaller dioceses, which probably corresponded to present-day Suffolk (the 'South Folk') and Norfolk (the 'North Folk'). The seat of the southern bishop remained at Dommoc, while a new see was established for the northern diocese at *Helmham* This may have been either present-day North Elmham or South Elmham; there are ruins of Anglo-Saxon minsters at both sites. In Stephen Plunkett's view, the proximity of South Elmham to Flixton (which was probably one of Felix's early mission sites) counts in its favour,[13] while Richard Hoggett favours North Elmham on the grounds of its subsequent relationship with the monastery at Norwich.[14]

In the late eighth century, the kingdom of East Anglia fell under Mercian dominion, but the Church continued to flourish, for example in the monastery at Brandon which produced beautiful works of art at this time.[15] By the 790s, the East Angles had their own king under Mercian overlordship, Æthelberht. In 794 Æthelberht travelled to the court of the powerful King Offa of Mercia to seek the hand of Offa's daughter in marriage, but according to legend Offa had him beheaded. Æthelberht was subsequently acclaimed a saint and the cult of St Ethelbert was established at Hereford, as well as in the dedication of numerous East Anglian churches. St Ethelbert became East Anglia's second royal martyr, after St Sigebert.[16]

In the early ninth century, at the Council of Clofesho in 803, the East Anglian Church resisted Mercian attempts to make Dommoc and Elmham suffragans to Lichfield, and Bishop Tidfrith of Dommoc affirmed his loyalty to the see of Canterbury.[17] From the 820s onwards, the East Anglians gradually began to release themselves from Mercian suzerainty, and East Anglian kings began to assume the title *Rex Anglorum* ('King of the Angles') on their coinage. However, in 840–1 a new threat emerged as Vikings attacked East Anglia from the sea for the first time. It seems likely that they targeted the trading centres of Gipeswic (Ipswich) and Northwic (the future Norwich) on the River Wensum. In 845, Bishops Wilred of Dommoc and Hunberht of Elmham attended a meeting with Archbishop Ceolnoth in London to discuss the Viking threat.[18] One remarkable relic of this period is the seal matrix of a Bishop Æthelwald, presumably of Dommoc, which was dug up near Eye church in Suffolk by the child of a labourer in around 1822 and is now in the British Museum.

The Vikings invaded again in force in the autumn of 865. They made peace with the locals and set up winter quarters, moving into Mercia, where they clashed with the Northumbrians. Then, in the autumn of 869, the Vikings returned to East Anglia, where the king of the East Angles, Eadmund, met them in battle. According to *The Anglo-Saxon Chronicle*, Eadmund was slain in battle, but in around 985 a monk named Abbo of Fleury recorded a story which apparently came from the mouth of the man who was Eadmund's armour-bearer in the battle. Realising that the Vikings would go after him and spare his people, Eadmund headed for a place called Hægglisdun, where the Vikings soon caught up with him, offering him the position of an under-king if he renounced Christianity. Eadmund refused, and was tied to a tree while the Viking archers used him as target practice. Still alive after being pierced by so many arrows, Eadmund was finally beheaded by the Vikings and, to further desecrate his body, the pagans threw his head into the undergrowth. According to legend, Eadmund's Christian followers later found his head cradled between the paws of a wolf and rejoined it to his incorrupt body.

The martyrdom of Eadmund, the last East Anglian king, on 20 November 869 marked the end of the old kingdom of East Anglia. The Viking destruction of churches and monasteries was so great that we cannot even be certain of the locations of many of the places mentioned in pre-Viking records, and religious life apparently ceased for a time. However, St Eadmund's incorrupt body quickly became the centre of a cult that began to convert the pagan Vikings, a development shown by the fact that Viking imitations of Eadmund's coins (the so-called 'memorial coinage') were being minted in East Anglia within a few years of his death. St Eadmund became the unifying figure who bound together the new East Anglia, which was now part of the Danelaw and ruled by a Viking king. By the time Edward the Elder of Wessex reconquered East Anglia in the early years of the tenth century, it is likely that most of the Vikings were already Christians.

Edward's reconquest marked the reconstruction of an organised Church in East Anglia, although only the see of Elmham was restored, and the subsequent Bishops of Elmham styled themselves 'Bishop of the East Angles'.[19] Elmham remained the seat of a bishop with a diocese more or less co-extensive with the present-day Diocese of East Anglia until 1075, when in the aftermath of the Norman Conquest the see was moved to Thetford. It moved to Norwich in 1094 and in 1109 the diocese was divided when the Diocese of Ely was created out of the westernmost districts of the Diocese of Norwich (present-day Cambridgeshire and West Norfolk). The Diocese of Peterborough came into being in 1541, when Henry VIII decided to turn the old monastic church at Peterborough into a cathedral for a new diocese carved out of the enormous Diocese of Lincoln; Peterborough briefly became a Catholic cathedral when England was reconciled to Rome under Queen Mary (1553–58).

It is unclear how much historical reflection went into choosing the name 'Diocese of East Anglia' when the Church in Norfolk, Suffolk, Cambridgeshire and Peterborough was separated from the Diocese of Northampton in 1976, but there are many parallels with the history of the first East Anglian diocese. Like the East Anglian Church under Mercian influence,

East Anglian Catholics had to wait for many years for their institutional independence from first the Midland District, then the Eastern District, and finally the Diocese of Northampton. William Wareing, the first Vicar Apostolic of the Eastern District, dedicated the region's short-lived seminary to St Felix in 1843 and lived among the seminarians as a missionary bishop. And like his predecessor St Felix, Bishop Alan Clark found himself serving a widely dispersed and scattered Catholic population when he became the first Bishop of East Anglia. Furthermore, the missionary work of St Fursey was echoed in the contribution of immigrant Catholics to the life of post-Reformation Catholicism in East Anglia: Irish immigrants from the 1780s onwards, then French refugee priests in the 1790s and, since the Second World War, Catholics from Eastern Europe and even further afield, who have immeasurably enriched the Catholic life of the diocese.

Local Mass centres in rural areas remain a significant (and somewhat distinctive) feature of life in the Diocese of East Anglia, just as they were throughout the penal era and, indeed, the days of Felix and Fursey, when communities were served by priests travelling from a central minster church. The Diocese of East Anglia has inherited a name that recalls Felix's original mission, but it is also the spiritual heir of that mission, which sought to plant the Catholic faith in the wide fields and close-knit communities of this culturally distinctive English region. Catholicism in East Anglia is characteristically tolerant, collaborative and ecumenical in outlook, mindful that Catholics are a fairly small minority who must look beyond differences with their Christian neighbours, celebrating instead what they share with them. The celebration of Mass in Anglican churches is not uncommon in the diocese, and the joint

Catholic and Anglican foundations of All Saints' Inter-church Academy in March and St Bede's in Cambridge well express this spirit of ecumenical cooperation.

The Reformation in East Anglia

Medieval East Anglia was home to two of the great cathedrals of England — Norwich and Ely — and two of the greatest monastic churches, at Bury St Edmunds and Peterborough. It was also the home of England's first and most important Marian shrine, at Little Walsingham. The shrine at Walsingham is tradition-ally said to have been founded in 1061 after a vision in which the Virgin Mary instructed a local woman, Richeldis de Faverches, to build a replica of the 'holy house' in which the holy family lived at Nazareth. This early manifestation of Marian devotion was charac-teristic of East Anglia, where the monasteries at Bury St Edmunds and Ramsey continued the Anglo-Saxon tradition of celebrating the Feast of the Conception of the Virgin Mary on 8 September. At Bury, the nephew of St Anselm of Canterbury (also called Anselm), abbot 1121–48, especially promoted the cult of the Virgin Mary, and Bury and one other East Anglian monastery were the only places in England where the Feast of the Annunciation was celebrated on 18 December — a feast day that would eventually become the Solemnity of the Immaculate Conception on 8 December.[20]

In the late Middle Ages, Norwich became England's second city as an economic boom, based on wool and the weaving of cloth, turned East Anglia into one of England's wealthiest regions. The legacy of this period of plenty remains, in the hundreds of lavish churches built in Norwich and the villages of Norfolk and Suffolk in the fifteenth century, many of them far larger than necessary for the communities that worshipped in them. Pilgrims flocked to Our Lady at Walsingham, St Edmund at Bury, St Audrey (Etheldreda) at Ely, the holy rood at Bromholm Priory and many other shrines, both small and great. Schools of Christian art flourished at Bury and Norwich, England's second university was established at Cambridge in 1209 and Julian of Norwich gave voice to a powerful new form of spirituality that emphasised a personal relationship with the crucified Christ.

In his 1992 book *The Stripping of the Altars*, Eamon Duffy drew on the still-surviving material evidence of East Anglian churches to challenge the long-accepted view that late-medieval Christianity was ignorant, unsophisticated and oppressive of the laity. Duffy showed that late-medieval East Anglians were well informed about their faith, often literate and interested in the latest developments in spiritual literature. Shrines such as Walsingham and Our Lady of Grace at Ipswich were at the forefront of a more personal and reflective spirituality in the late Middle Ages. While ancient saints like St Edmund and St Audrey commanded royal devotion and the interest of those seeking healing from specific illnesses, Walsingham was the most popular shrine in the region at the dawn of the Reformation, perhaps because it offered the faithful the chance to encounter Mary and Jesus as fellow human beings by visiting what was supposed to be a replica of their house. Both before and after the Norman Conquest, the number of religious houses in East Anglia was huge and exceeded that of any other region, and at the time of the dissolution there were no less than 117 houses, with a high proportion of Benedictine and Augustinian foundations.

Storm-clouds, however, were gathering on the horizon. In Germany, Martin Luther's break with the Church inspired radical thinkers in Cambridge to contemplate whether the English Church, too, was in need of this new evangelical 'reform'. Cambridge University became the main springboard from which reformed theology spread to the court of Henry VIII and some of the clergy. However, the early stages of the English Reformation were driven, first and foremost, by Henry VIII's desire to establish a national Church of which he was head. The first major impact of the Reformation on East Anglia was the dissolution of the lesser religious houses in 1536, which saw the closure of many monasteries. Even so, a majority survived, along with the great abbeys of Bury St Edmunds and Peterborough and the cathedral priories of Ely and Norwich.

When these great abbeys and minsters were finally dissolved in 1539, East Anglia was changed for ever; not just because the monasteries were the 'welfare state' of their time, but also because they formed a patchwork of local spiritual and temporal jurisdictions that were suddenly swept away at a stroke. Ordinary people were at the mercy of secular landlords, intent on making as much money as possible from the land, and the landlords themselves were no longer shielded from royal authority by the intervening jurisdictions of abbots and priors. But the greatest change was, perhaps, to the lived experience of worship for ordinary East Anglians.

By the end of the 1540s, even chantries and Masses for the dead were gone, and under Edward VI a plain English liturgy was imposed instead of the Mass. In his recent book, *Saints, Sacrilege and Sedition* (2012), Duffy has explored the impact the Reformation had on one Norfolk church, Salle, which was transformed in a short while from a colourful, brightly illuminated space proclaiming the village's communal identity into an austere, whitewashed preaching house where the authority of the state was paramount. The royal arms replaced the rood loft and the doom painting behind it, and in 1552 the state confiscated everything from churches apart from one surplice, one chalice and one paten.[21] Although stained glass lasted a little longer, partly because glass was so expensive to replace, the aesthetic changes were profound.

The Reformation in East Anglia has received sustained attention from some of the twentieth century's greatest historians of the Reformation, including Eamon Duffy, Patrick Collinson and Diarmaid Mac-Culloch, partly because it was an area in which the Reformation was 'successful', and partly because the physical evidence of the Reformation is especially well preserved in hundreds of churches. Many people in the Dioceses of Norwich and Ely undoubtedly welcomed the Reformation, and they later became heartlands of Puritanism, the movement within English Protestantism that wanted to take the Reformation even further and get rid of the last trappings of Catholicism: bishops, diocesan government, surplices and prescribed liturgy.

However, this was not the whole story, and a considerable minority in East Anglia opposed Reformation changes. In 1537, in response to the suppression of the pilgrimage to Walsingham and inspired by the 'Pilgrimage of Grace' in the north, the sub-prior of Walsingham, Nicholas Myleham, and a group of Norfolk yeomen began to discuss a rising in Norfolk against Henry VIII's religious policies. However, the men were arrested before they had the chance to carry out any of their plans, and nine of them were hanged at Norwich,

Great Yarmouth and King's Lynn while the sub-prior and another accomplice were hanged at Walsingham, in a place later called the 'Martyrs' Field'.[22]

Other acts of defiance were less dramatic but equally striking. In 1536, Abbess Elizabeth Throckmorton surrendered the Poor Clare Abbey of Denny, just outside Ely, but she and two other nuns returned to her family home of Coughton Court in Warwickshire and continued to observe the rule and wear the habit of St Clare until their deaths.[23] When the prior and monks of Ely surrendered their monastery on 18 November 1539, the incorrupt body of St Etheldreda was removed from her shrine but the saint's left hand was somehow removed and preserved until its discovery on the Duke of Norfolk's estate in Arundel in 1811, enclosed in a seventeenth-century reliquary and now preserved at St Etheldreda's church in Ely.[24] Similarly, an oral tradition survived among the English Benedictines that the body of St Edmund was hidden by monks shortly before or after the dissolution.[25]

We can never know how many parish priests, in the reign of Edward VI, carried on saying the Latin Mass alongside the new English service, but when Catholicism was restored in 1553–8 the majority of the population acquiesced, even though the Diocese of Norwich saw many Gospellers put to death under the revived heresy laws. One of the most influential conservative voices in the reigns of Henry VIII, Edward VI and Mary was Stephen Gardiner, Bishop of Winchester, a native of Bury St Edmunds. When Edward died it was to East Anglia and its gentry that the Lady Mary naturally turned to uphold her claim to the throne, suggesting that she trusted the loyalty of East Anglians both to her and to the faith she intended to restore.

Catholicism restored: Queen Mary's reign

Mary was at Greenwich Palace on 3 July 1553 when she was forewarned that her brother's death was imminent. She immediately left for Norfolk, stopping at Sawston Hall in south Cambridgeshire to stay with the Huddlestone family. Mary went next to Hengrave Hall in Suffolk, the home of John Bourchier, Earl of Bath, and his teenage stepson, Thomas Kitson, and then on to Euston Hall, the home of the Rookwood family. On 9 July she arrived at her own house at Kenninghall in Norfolk. For the next five days a stream of local gentry arrived to show their support, and Mary rode south with them to Framlingham Castle, raised her standard and rallied the gentry and commons of East Anglia to her claim. By 19 July she had been proclaimed Queen in London, and the Duke of Northumberland, who had arrived in Cambridge to confront her supporters, was forced to concede defeat.[26]

In later years, Mary's ride from Kenninghall to Framlingham acquired an almost mythical significance within the East Anglian Catholic community, and having an ancestor who rode with Queen Mary was a source of immense pride. The list of gentry who supported Mary that summer is a roll-call of later Elizabethan recusant families: the Huddlestones of Sawston, the Kitsons of Hengrave, the Sulyards of Haughley, the Rookwoods of Euston, the Jerninghams of Costessey, the Cornwallises of Brome, Sir William Drury of Hawstead, and William Petre of Ingatestone in Essex. Diarmaid MacCulloch argued that nostalgia for the abbey at Bury St Edmunds could have motivated local gentry to support Mary's Suffolk-based bid for the throne,[27] while Peter Wickins pointed to 'the comparative absence of dissent' in Suffolk during

Mary's reign—connected, perhaps, to the fact that the Duke of Norfolk, a key figure of the Marian regime, was hereditary steward of the Liberty of St Edmund (West Suffolk).[28]

In East Anglia, as elsewhere in England, Catholicism first emerged as an identity in Mary's reign; up to that point, what we call Catholicism had been the instinctive and complacent religion of Englishmen, but Edward's reign changed that and sharpened the distinctions between conservatives and reformers. Mary did not just restore Catholicism to England: she brought the Counter-Reformation. Duffy has argued, along with David Loades and others, that Mary was not so much reviving an old faith as establishing a new and militant form of Catholicism in England. Mary's reign was not a restoration of the old but the introduction of a new faith different from the new faith of Edward's reign. The English Reformation was about two competing faiths, both with their claims to modernity, rather than a narrative of Protestant progress triumphing over Catholic medievalism. The Catholics of Mary's reign were a new kind of self-conscious Counter-Reformation Catholics.

The East Anglian gentry went on to play their part in Mary's Catholic regime; Sir Henry Bedingfield of Oxburgh (1509–83) served as guardian (or 'gaoler') to the Queen's half-sister Princess Elizabeth, and Sir Henry Jerningham of Costessey (1509–72) was captain of Mary's guard; both were Privy Councillors. The Howard dukes of Norfolk, who owned vast tracts of land in East Anglia and maintained a palace in Norwich, became one of the mainstays of the Catholic regime. Loyalty to Queen Mary ran deep: these families, and many others like them in East Anglia, would remain loyal to the Catholic faith for the next three centuries.

This 'hard core' of devoted Catholics in Suffolk and Norfolk forms the background for the appearance of the phenomenon of recusancy in Elizabeth's reign, which is where Joy Rowe takes up the story in Chapter 1.

The historiography of Catholic East Anglia

Post-Reformation Catholics were very much aware of their lineage of faith, and consciously memorialised the martyrs and confessors as well as the pre-Reformation past. Examples include Roger Martin's lovingly detailed description of Long Melford church before the Reformation, probably written in the 1580s, and the pedigree of the Rookwood family begun in 1619 and continued into the eighteenth century.[29] Some local Catholics were themselves antiquaries with a particular interest in the past, such as Robert Hare of Bruisyard (d. 1611) and John Gage-Rokewode (1786–1842), who served as president of the Society of Antiquaries. Gage-Rokewode's monumental volumes on the Kitson and Gage families, *The History and Antiquities of Hengrave* (1822) and *The History and Antiquities of Suffolk: Thingoe Hundred* (1838) mean that they are amongst the best documented of East Anglia's recusant families.

In 1907, shortly after its foundation, the Catholic Record Society published some of the papers of the Bedingfield family in its records series, edited by J. H. Pollen,[30] and in 1912 the Benedictine monk Norbert Birt contributed an essay on the post-Reformation history of East Anglia to a volume on the region published by the Catholic Truth Society.[31] A year later a lavish book on Catholicism in Norwich and Norfolk, *A Great Gothic Fane* (possibly by J. W. Picton[32]), was published to celebrate the consecration of the new church of St

John the Baptist in the city. Although valuable in many
ways, these early forays into East Anglian Catholic
history, like much Catholic historical scholarship of
the early twentieth century, suffered from a mixture of
triumphalism and inadequate attention to the sources.
The first twentieth-century book-length study of an
East Anglian Catholic family was G. H. Ryan and Lyn
Redstone's *Timperley of Hintlesham*, which appeared
in 1931 (and is still an impressive piece of scholarship).[33] However, it was not until the late 1950s that
the modern study of East Anglian Catholicism began,
informed by the latest developments in the broader
historiography of the Catholic community rather than
just local antiquarianism.

In 1958 an important survey of Catholicism in Norfolk by Brigadier Thomas Byrnand Trappes-Lomax
appeared in *Norfolk Archaeology*,[34] and the following
year the first edition of Joy Rowe's *Story of Catholic
Bury St. Edmunds, Coldham and Surrounding District*
marked the beginnings of the study of Catholicism
in West Suffolk (a second edition appeared in 1981).
Rowe followed this with an article on the recusancy
of Sir Thomas Cornwallis in 1960.[35] The 1970s saw the
development of a new approach to the historiography
of English Catholicism, with the publication of J. C.
H. Aveling's *The Handle and the Axe* and John Bossy's
The English Catholic Community.[36] Aveling and Bossy
moved away from the 'hagiographical' model that had
hitherto prevailed and presented a new analysis of
English Catholicism as a variety of nonconformity.
They also jettisoned a providentialist narrative that
saw the restoration of the hierarchy in 1850 as the inevitable and natural culmination of a relentless process
of revival, and recognised that there were numerous
strands within English Catholicism and a diversity of

views, revealed for example by the Appellant Controversy at the start of the seventeenth century.

Many aspects of Aveling's and Bossy's analysis have
been challenged since, but the essentials of their argument are now widely accepted by scholars of early
modern Catholicism. Meanwhile, in the 1980s Joy
Rowe continued to produce a steady stream of articles
in collaboration with Patrick McGrath, and contributed valuable analyses of Catholicism in Suffolk and
Norfolk to the historical atlases of both counties published in 1988 and 1994 respectively.[37] Important contributions to East Anglia's religious history were also
made by Patrick Collinson and Diarmaid MacCulloch.
Drawing largely on examples from East Anglia in his
Stripping of the Altars (1992), Eamon Duffy revolutionised perceptions of late-medieval Catholicism. Also in
the 1990s, Alexandra Walsham and Michael Questier
radically reoriented views of the post-Reformation
Catholic community in the 1990s, emphasising the
importance of church papistry and occasional conformity in addition to recusancy.

Joy Rowe continued to produce important articles
at this time, contributing papers to conferences on religious dissent in East Anglia in 1991 and 1996.[38] In 1998
she also contributed a chapter on Suffolk Catholicism
to Nicholas Tyacke's *England's Long Reformation*, and
she authored a number of articles for the new *Oxford
Dictionary of National Biography* in 2004, thus ensuring that East Anglia's Catholic families received the
attention they deserved in this authoritative reference
work. Also deserving of mention are Geoffrey Holt
for his studies of East Anglian Jesuit missions and
Margaret Mason for her series of articles on East Anglian nuns.[39] Studies based on individual families have
always been central to East Anglian Catholic history,

such as Nesta Evans's 1980 article on the Tasburghs of
Flixton and Lyn Boothman and Richard Hyde Parker's
volume on the Savages of Long Melford.[40] In recent
years, my own studies of the Tasburghs of Flixton and
Bodney, the Shorts of Bury St Edmunds, the Gages
of Hengrave and the Rookwoods of Stanningfield
have considerably added to the literature on recusant
families.[41] These volumes have also made available
primary sources on the Catholic community such
as mission registers, constables' lists of Nonjurors,
and personal letters. Another recent contribution was
Frank Devany's *The Faithful Few* (2008, reprinted 2010),
an alphabetical survey of evidence for recusancy in
four hundred Norfolk parishes.[42]

Very little attention has been paid to East Anglian
Catholicism in the nineteenth and twentieth centuries,
although Fr Derek Lance's history of the Diocese of
Northampton, published in 2000, is a valuable introduction to the period after the restoration of the hierarchy. One notable exception to the dearth of scholarship
is the excellent collection on the history of Catholicism
in Cambridge edited by Nicholas Rogers in 2003, *Catholics in Cambridge*. Neither the Diocese of Northampton
before 1976 nor the Diocese of East Anglia thereafter
had a historical society, although history groups have
existed in individual parishes at various times and
produced parish histories. During the 1930s, 1940s
and 1950s, the Guild of St Felix and St Edmund, established in 1935 to promote East Anglian Catholic identity within the Diocese of Northampton,[43] published
the *East Anglian Guild Magazine*, which featured regular
articles on the history of different East Anglian parishes. Furthermore, the South Eastern Catholic History
Society, although dedicated primarily to the history of
the Diocese of Brentwood, has occasionally published

articles on East Anglian Catholicism in its journal *Essex Recusant* (now *South-Eastern Catholic History*). A steady stream of useful articles pertinent to Catholicism in East Anglia has also appeared in *Catholic Ancestor* (formerly *English Catholic Ancestor*), the journal of the Catholic Family History Society.[44] Michael Gandy's guide to the mission registers of the Midland District, including East Anglia, is also an invaluable resource for the researcher.[45]

East Anglia has many rich repositories of source material on Catholic families. In addition to the Diocesan Archives at St John's Cathedral, the Norfolk Record Office contains detailed returns of papists, especially from the eighteenth century. The Suffolk Record Office has three branches at Ipswich, Bury St Edmunds and Lowestoft; the papers of the Mannock family of Stoke-by-Nayland can be found in Ipswich, while documents relating to the Gages, Rookwoods and Martins of Long Melford can be found in Bury; Lowestoft has the papers of the Tasburgh family. In Cambridgeshire, Cambridge University Library is home to one of the most important collections of recusant family papers in the country, the Hengrave Manuscripts. These contain the papers of the Kitson, Gage and Rookwood families going back to the 1540s. Cambridgeshire Archives houses the extensive papers of the Huddlestone family of Sawston Hall. Further material can be found outside the region, such as the papers of the Jerningham family of Costessey at the Staffordshire Record Office and papers relating to the East Anglian mission in Birmingham Archdiocesan Archives, Northampton Diocesan Archives, the Archives of the English Province of the Society of Jesus in London. Downside Abbey holds material relating to the Benedictine mission at Flixton and Bungay.

The structure of the book

Chapter 1 surveys the position of Catholics in East Anglia after 1559, when the Mass was outlawed and recusancy became a crime for the first time. Recusancy was not all there was to being a Catholic in the reign of Elizabeth, and many Catholics were also church papists, people who were Catholic at heart but who attended church in order to avoid the crippling fines. Recusancy has often been seen as an elite phenomenon, but Joy Rowe argues that ordinary people appear as recusants in bishops' visitation records and elsewhere. Catholicism was socially diverse and widespread in Elizabethan East Anglia, and a powerful force that led Elizabeth's government to take severe action on a number of occasions.

In Chapter 2, John Morrill takes the story into the seventeenth century by examining the well-known martyrs of this period as well as some lesser-known historical figures. He pays particular attention to the period of the English Civil War, analysing Catholics who appear in records of the time such as the proceedings of the Committee of Sequestrations and the Committee of Compounding. The chapter goes on to consider the reliability of the Compton Census in 1676, the first national census of religious belief. John Morrill concludes that the census ought to be treated with caution. He also provides some demographic analysis of nuns and priests during the period.

Chapter 3 explores the lonely journey taken by the Catholic community from the Revolution of 1688 to Catholic Emancipation in 1829, when Catholics were granted civil and political rights. Catholics recovered remarkably quickly from the harsh backlash to James II's attempt to impose religious toleration, and the community experienced slow but steady growth up to the 1760s, when the 1767 Census of Papists gives a detailed insight into the composition of Catholic East Anglia. The Catholic population seems to have declined thereafter, but the arrival of refugee French priests in the 1790s gave a much-needed boost to the faith and led to much missionary activity in areas virtually untouched by Catholicism such as Ipswich and Huntingdonshire. By the time of Catholic emancipation in 1829 the Catholic community in East Anglia was small but growing and confident, with handsome public chapels that had long since managed to escape their dependence on the patronage of old recusant families.

Chapter 4, which covers the fairly short period between Catholic Emancipation in 1829 and the restoration of diocesan bishops in 1850, is divided into two parts by Timothy Fenwick and Francis Young respectively. The first part explores the meagre yet significant development of Catholic churches from the 1820s onwards, partly via an analysis of the 1851 Census of Religious Worship, and considers the continuing importance of Catholic families such as the Jerninghams, who inherited a noble title at this time. The second part of the chapter focuses more narrowly on the creation of the Eastern District in 1840, and on the attempts of the Vicar Apostolic (and later first Bishop of Northampton) William Wareing to establish a seminary at Giffords Hall in Suffolk.

In Chapter 5 John Charmley considers the period after 1850, when a series of bishops of Northampton were faced with the unenviable task of expanding Catholic mission (and the size of Catholic congregations) in Norfolk, Suffolk and Cambridgeshire. Uncharitably described by Cardinal Manning as 'the dead diocese', Northampton faced particular challenges, especially in its eastern section, but Charmley nevertheless argues that the efforts of Arthur George Riddell (Bishop 1880–1907) created the foundations of the future Diocese of East Anglia. He challenges the accepted narrative of stagnation and argues that Riddell prepared the East Anglian mission for the twentieth century.

In Chapter 6, Michael Edwards explains the factors that lay behind the creation of the Diocese of East Anglia in 1976, and analyses the struggles and challenges of East Anglian Catholics during the twentieth century as part of the Diocese of Northampton. He sets the creation of the diocese within the context of the pastoral aims of the Second Vatican Council and gives an insight into the processes, both in Rome and in England, which impelled the creation of a diocese which was the most sparsely populated by Catholics in the country. Edwards's chapter argues that the rapid post-War growth of the Catholic population was the main factor that made the creation of a new diocese both desirable and necessary; yet at the same time, the ancient identity of East Anglia and its distinct Catholic heritage were also contributing factors.

Finally, in Chapter 7 Tony Rogers offers an insight into the development of the diocese over the last forty years, under the leadership of its first four bishops: Alan Clark, Peter Smith, Michael Evans and Alan Hopes. As a priest whose ministry has spanned the period since 1970, when East Anglia was still part of the Diocese of Northampton, Fr Rogers provides an overview of the main events in the diocese's history since 1976 and a personal memoir of its chief pastors, taking this history right up to the present day, when the Catholics of East Anglia celebrate forty years since they received their own bishop.

Notes

[1] J. Rowe, '"The lopped tree": The Re-formation of the Suffolk Catholic Community', in N. Tyacke (ed.), *England's Long Reformation 1500–1800* (Abingdon: UCL Press, 1998), pp. 167–94.

[2] Mountford Scott's fellow martyr, Bd Brian Lacey, may have come from Hoxne in Suffolk (D. Lance, *The Returning Tide (1850–2000): A History of the Diocese of Northampton over the last 150 years* (Northampton: Diocese of Northampton, 2000), p. 12).

[3] R. Hoggett, *The Archaeology of the East Anglian Conversion* (Woodbridge: Boydell, 2010), p. 23.

[4] *Ibid.*, pp. 24–7.

[5] *Ibid.*, p. 28.

[6] *Ibid.*, p. 29.

[7] *Ibid.*, p. 31.

[8] For a discussion of the location of Dommoc see *ibid.* pp. 36–40.

[9] *Ibid.*, p. 31.

[10] On the life of St Felix, see S. Plunkett, *Suffolk in Anglo-Saxon Times* (Stroud: Tempus, 2005), pp. 100–3.

[11] *Ibid.*, p. 116.

[12] *Ibid.*, p. 121.

[13] *Ibid.*, pp. 123–4.

[14] Hoggett (2010), pp. 40–4.

[15] Plunkett (2005), pp. 162–8.

[16] On St Ethelbert see *ibid.*, pp. 171–4.

[17] *Ibid.*, p. 178.

[18] *Ibid.*, p. 194.

[19] Hoggett (2010), p. 35.

[20] A. Gransden, 'The Cult of St Mary at Beodericsworth and then in Bury St Edmunds Abbey to *c.* 1150', *The Journal of Ecclesiastical History* 55 (2004), pp. 627–53, at pp. 647–8. On the cult at Walsingham see G. Waller, *Walsingham and the English Imagination* (Farnham: Ashgate, 2011).

[21] E. Duffy, *Saints, Sacrilege and Sedition: Religion and Conflict in the Tudor Reformations* (London: Bloomsbury, 2011), pp. 83–130.

[22] S. A. Singer, 'Walsingham's Local Genius: Norfolk's "Newe Nazareth"', in D. Janes and G. Waller (eds), *Walsingham in Literature and Culture from the Middle Ages to Modernity* (Farnham: Ashgate, 2010), pp. 23–34, at pp. 32–3. On this

incident see also C. E. Moreton, 'The Walsingham Conspiracy of 1537', *Bulletin of the Institute of Historical Research* 63 (1990), pp. 29–43, at pp. 40–1.

23 P. Marshall, 'Crisis of Allegiance: George Throckmorton and Henry Tudor', in P. Marshall and G. Scott (eds), *Catholic Gentry in English Society: The Throckmortons of Coughton from Reformation to Emancipation* (Farnham: Ashgate, 2009), pp. 31–68, at pp. 54–5.

24 'Etheldreda', in D. Farmer (ed.), *The Oxford Dictionary of Saints*, 5th edn (Oxford: Oxford University Press, 2003), pp. 151–2.

25 F. Young, *Where is St Edmund? The Search for East Anglia's Martyr King* (Ely: East Anglian Catholic History Centre, 2014a), pp. 42–5.

26 On Mary's successful campaign in East Anglia see A. Whitelock and D. MacCulloch, 'Princess Mary's Household and the Succession Crisis, July 1553', *The Historical Journal* 50 (2007), pp. 265–87. For transcriptions of some of the original documents see J. Gage, *The History and Antiquities of Hengrave, in Suffolk* (London, 1822), pp. 142–5.

27 D. MacCulloch, *Suffolk and the Tudors: Politics and Religion in an English County 1500–1600* (Oxford: Clarendon Press, 1986), p. 234.

28 P. Wickins, *Victorian Protestantism and Bloody Mary: The Legacy of Religious Persecution in Tudor England* (Bury St Edmunds: Arena, 2012), pp. 281–2.

29 D. Dymond and C. Paine (eds), *The Spoil of Melford Church* (Ipswich: Salient, 1989); J. Gage (ed.), 'Pedigree and Charters of the Family of Rookwood', in *Collectanea Topographica et Genealogica* (London, 1835), vol. 2, pp. 120–47.

30 [J. H. Pollen (ed.)], *Bedingfield Papers, &c.* (London: Catholic Record Society, 1909).

31 H. N. Birt, 'Recusancy and Catholicity in East Anglia', in *The Catholic Faith in East Anglia: three papers read at the National Catholic Congress at Norwich, August 5, 1912* (London: Catholic Truth Society, 1912), pp. 3–25.

32 [J. W. Picton], *A Great Gothic Fane: The Catholic Church of St. John the Baptist, Norwich, with Historical Retrospect of Catholicity in Norwich* (Norwich: W. T. Pike, 1913). For the identification of Picton as the author see A. Rossi, *Norwich Roman Catholic Cathedral: A Building History* (London: The Chapels Society, 1998), p. 31. An article on an East Anglian Catholic family from this period is N. Goldie, 'The Last of the Norfolk Derehams of West Dereham', *Norfolk Archaeology* 18 (1914), pp. 1–22.

[33] G. H. Ryan and L. J. Redstone, *Timperley of Hintlesham: A Study of a Suffolk Family* (London: Methuen, 1931).

[34] T. B. Trappes-Lomax, 'Catholicism in Norfolk, 1559–1780', *Norfolk Archaeology* 32 (1958), pp. 27–46.

[35] P. McGrath and J. Rowe, 'The Recusancy of Sir Thomas Cornwallis', *Proceedings of the Suffolk Institute of Archaeology and History 28 (1960), pp. 226–71*.

[36] J. C. H. Aveling, *The Handle and the Axe* (London: Blond and Briggs, 1976); J. Bossy, *The English Catholic Community, 1570–1850* (Oxford: Oxford University Press, 1976).

[37] J. Rowe, 'Roman Catholic Recusancy', in D. Dymond and E. Martin (eds), *An Historical Atlas of Suffolk* (Ipswich: Suffolk County Council, 1988), pp. 88–9; J. Rowe, 'Roman Catholic Recusancy', in T. Ashwin and A. Davison (eds), *An Historical Atlas of Norfolk* (Norwich: Norfolk Museums Service, 1994), pp. 138–9.

[38] J. Rowe, 'Suffolk Sectaries and Papists, 1596–1616', in E. S. Leedham-Green (ed.), *Religious Dissent in East Anglia* (Cambridge: Cambridge Antiquarian Society, 1991), pp. 37–41; J. Rowe, 'The 1767 Census of Papists in the Diocese of Norwich: the Social Composition of the Roman Catholic Community', in D. Chadd (ed.), *Religious Dissent in East Anglia III* (Norwich: University of East Anglia, 1996), pp. 187–234.

[39] G. Holt, 'Some Letters from Suffolk, 1763–80: Selection and Commentary', *Recusant History* 16 (1983), pp. 304–15; G. Holt, 'An Eighteenth Century Chaplain: John Champion at Sawston Hall', *Recusant History* 17 (1984), pp. 181–7; G. Holt, *The English Jesuits in the Age of Reason* (London: Burns and Oates, 1993), pp. 88–102; M. J. Mason, 'Nuns and Vocations of the Unpublished Jerningham Letters', *Recusant History* 21 (1993), pp. 503–5; M. J. Mason, 'Nuns of the Jerningham Letters', *Recusant History* 22 (1995), pp. 350–69; M. J. Mason, 'Nuns of the Jerningham Letters … Benedictines at Bodney Hall', *Recusant History* 23 (1996), pp. 34–40; M. J. Mason, 'The Blue Nuns in Norwich 1800–05', *Recusant History* 24 (1998), pp. 89–120.

[40] N. Evans, 'The Tasburghs of South Elmham: the Rise and Fall of a Suffolk Gentry Family', *Proceedings of the Suffolk Institute of Archaeology and History 34* (1980), pp. 269–80; L. Boothman and R. Hyde Parker (eds), *Savage Fortune: An Aristocratic Family in the Early Seventeenth Century* (Woodbridge: Suffolk Records Society, 2006), pp. xiii–lxxxvi.

[41] F. Young, 'The Shorts of Bury St Edmunds: Medicine, Catholicism and Politics in the Seventeenth Century', in *The*

Journal of Medical Biography 16 (2008), pp. 188–94; F. Young, 'The Tasburghs of Bodney: Catholicism and Politics in South Norfolk', *Norfolk Archaeology* 46 (2011), pp. 190–8; F. Young, 'The Tasburghs of Flixton and Catholicism in North-east Suffolk, 1642–1767', *Proceedings of the Suffolk Institute of Archaeology and History* 42 (2012a), pp. 455–70; F. Young, *The Gages of Hengrave and Suffolk Catholicism, 1640–1767* (London: Catholic Record Society, 2015a); F. Young (ed.), *Rookwood Family Papers, 1606–1761* (Woodbridge: Suffolk Records Society, 2016).

42   F. J. Devany, *The Faithful Few: A History of Norfolk Roman Catholics, 1559–1778*, 2nd edn (Norwich, 2010).

43   See *The Tablet*, 6 July 1935, p. 28.

44   'Record of the Catholic Missions of Norfolk before 1837', *English Catholic Ancestor* 1 (1984); 'The Will of John Gooderiche of Bacton, Suffolk, Physician (1631)', *English Catholic Ancestor* 2 (1989); 'Memorial Inscription at Bury St Edmunds', *Catholic Ancestor* 3 (1990), p. 54; 'The Jailed Priests at Wisbech Castle', *Catholic Ancestor* 3 (1991), pp. 240–1; 'Assisted Catholic Emigrants from Cambridgeshire to Australia 1840–1879', *Catholic Ancestor* 4 (1993), pp. 198–9; 'Conformity in the Midlands and East Anglia 1590–1625', *Catholic Ancestor* 6 (1996) pp. 57–64; 'The Registers of the Catholic Chapel at Haughley Park, Suffolk, 1807–1809', *Catholic Ancestor* 6 (1996), pp. 114–16; C. R. Humphrey-Smith, 'The Walpoles and the Jesuits', *Catholic Ancestor* 6 (1997), pp. 230–1; A. Adolph, 'The Catholic Havers of Thelveton Hall, Norfolk', in *Catholic Ancestor* 7 (1999), pp. 144–60; 'Catholics in East Anglia, 1796', *Catholic Ancestor* 7 (1999), p. 250; A. Wilcox, 'The Seaman Family of Flixton, Suffolk', *Catholic Ancestor* 8 (2000), p. 12; 'The Catholic Registers of Bury St Edmunds, Suffolk', *Catholic Ancestor* 8 (2000), p. 118; A. Adolph, 'The Bonds of Bury St Edmunds and their Family Connections', *Catholic Ancestor* 9 (2002) pp. 61–4; 'Catholics in Cambridgeshire', *Catholic Ancestor* 9 (2003), pp. 177–8; F. Young, 'How did Catholic Families Survive and Flourish under the Penal Laws?', *Catholic Ancestor* 14 (2012b), pp. 105–19.

45   M. Gandy (ed.), *Catholic Missions and Registers 1700–1800 Volume 2: The Midlands and East Anglia* (London: Catholic Family History Society, 1993).

1

East Anglian Catholics in the Reign of Elizabeth, 1559–1603

Joy Rowe and Francis Young

O N 24 JUNE 1559, the feast of St John the Baptist, the Mass became illegal in England under the terms of Elizabeth I's Act of Uniformity. It was now a crime for a priest to say Mass, but it was also illegal not to attend the parish church and hear the English service. Those who refused to attend church on Sundays became a new category of criminal: recusants (literally 'refusers'). The first recusants were presented before the courts in the autumn of 1559, although the penalty was not particularly severe if someone had a modicum of wealth: a shilling for every Sunday or holy day on which a person was absent. In 1581 the penalties were stiffened, and recusants were obliged to pay £20 for every month of absence.[1] However, enforcement of the recusancy laws depended (at least in part) on local magistrates, whose attitude to gentry recusants was often ambivalent. Many were reluctant to present individuals who might be their patrons, landlords or neighbours, and social and regional ties often mattered more than religion, except to the most zealous of godly magistrates. Elizabethan bishops persistently complained about the patchy enforcement of the laws against recusancy.

Recusancy, however, is by no means the full story of post-Reformation Catholicism in England, and, as Alexandra Walsham and Michael Questier showed in the 1990s, Catholicism could take many forms along a spectrum ranging from out-and-out recusancy to occasional conformity (turning up at church when prosecution for recusancy seemed a threat) and church papistry (attending church but holding Catholic beliefs).[2] Indeed, it is now generally accepted by historians that church papists made up the majority of those English men and women who can reasonably be called Catholics in Elizabeth's reign, partly because only the wealthy were able to pay recusancy fines. The consciences of church papists might be salved by the fact that some ministers were former priests, ordained in the reign of Queen Mary or before, who might even share their conservative views and celebrate Mass in secret. However, the excommunication of Elizabeth by Pope Pius V in 1570 and the arrival of the first seminary priests in England in 1574 were to unsettle the status quo established in 1559 and plunge Catholics into a period of persecution that lasted for the remainder of Elizabeth's reign.

There were complex gradations within conformity itself. In Suffolk, 116 individuals were indicted as recusants in 1559,[3] but there were many more who went to church but declined to take communion or participate in the service in any way. Robert Rookwood of Stanningfield (d. 1566) made a show of conformity, attending Lawshall parish church, but did not take communion, while his wife Elizabeth Heigham did not come to church at all. Sir Thomas Kitson of Hengrave

(1540–1603) declared in 1569 that he 'did not receive the Communion these 4 or 5 years but sometimes came to sermons with the Lord Chief Justice'. However, he chose his words carefully, and referred to the Protestant faith as 'that truth, for which I dailie praye', suggesting that he did not actually believe in it at the time.[4] In 1578 Queen Elizabeth honoured him with a visit and knighted him; at Hengrave, he presented her with a 'riche jewell' during the course of 'a show representing the fayries'.[5] A further ambiguity was created by the fact that Hengrave contained a private chapel in which Kitson kept a Bible and an English service book.[6] In theory, he could claim that he worshipped privately there. Furthermore, when the parish of Hengrave was amalgamated with Flempton in 1589 its church (next to Hengrave Hall) became a private mortuary chapel, so when Kitson did not appear in his parish church, this did not prove that he was not worshipping elsewhere. A similar situation obtained for the Martin family of Long Melford, who owned their own proprietary chapel of St James across the road from Melford Place, and for the Mannocks of Giffords Hall, Stoke-by-Nayland, who owned the chapel of St Nicholas.[7]

Indications that many ministers and their congregations were still religious conservatives in the early 1560s can be found in the 1561 Visitation Articles of Bishop Parkhurst of Norwich:

> Item, that they (the clergy) neither suffer the Lord's Table to be hanged and decked like an altar, neither use any gestures of the Popish Mass in the time of ministration of the Communion, as shifting of the book, washing, breathing, crossing or such like … Item, that they see the places

filled up in walls or elsewhere, where images stood, so as if there had been none there. The stones, foundations, or other places, frames for tabernacles devised to advance imagery, holy water stoups also to be quite clean taken away, and the places where they were set, comely and decently to be made up with convenient expedition, or else to declare to the Ordinary the lets and stays thereof as soon as may be.[8]

Parkhurst's articles suggest that old habits died hard among the clergy, and the fact that in many East Anglian churches niches for statues and holy water stoups can still be seen is an indication that at least some incumbents and churchwardens disobeyed. One reason for this may have been the paucity of clergy, let alone clergy who shared the Elizabethan bishops' reformed ideals. In 1563, Parkhurst reported that 434 out of 1,200 parishes were without parsons; furthermore, twelve Justices of the Peace were 'not so well bent unto the advancement of the godly proceedings of this realm in causes ecclesiastical'.[9] Parkhurst enquired of the churchwardens 'Whether that any images, beads, books of service or vestments not allowed by law be reserved of any man or in any place, by whom and where they be reserved',[10] suggesting that people were holding on to church ornaments, perhaps in the belief that Catholicism might be restored, as it was in Mary's reign. At St Mary's church in Ely, the churchwardens were still in possession of vestments and banners in 1570, eleven years after such things had become illegal.[11]

Roger Martin (c. 1526–1615) went so far as to preserve the retable of Long Melford church in his house at Melford Place,[12] and he further proclaimed his recusancy by writing a detailed and nostalgic description of the pre-Reformation ornaments and ceremonies of Long Melford church.[13] A fifteenth-century book of hours which may have belonged to him has recently come to light, with its prayers for the feast of St Thomas Becket undefaced, in defiance of a royal edict of 1537.[14] Likewise, the physician John Caius, who re-founded Gonville and Caius College, Cambridge, during Mary's reign, concealed vestments and altar books in his college,[15] and Nicholas Rogers has speculated that a mid-sixteenth-century statue of the Virgin and Child, found in a building belonging to Emmanuel College in the nineteenth century and now in Our Lady and the English Martyrs, Cambridge, was the image set on the high altar of Great St Mary's church in 1558.[16] A later set of Norwich visitation articles, from 1569, suggest that 'rood-lofts, images, tabernacles, and all other monuments of idolatry' were still standing in some churches, and demanded that 'your church and chancel [be] decently reformed'. Indeed, the articles specifically address the issue of concealed Catholic items: '[Do] you know of any Popish and superstitious books, images, vestments or such like remaining within your parish, and in whose hands they be'.

The 1569 articles also give an insight into the small acts of resistance that may have taken place during the service itself: incumbents were asked 'whether there be any minister, priest, or other person or persons whatsoever within your parish ... that walk up and down jangling and talking in the time of Common Prayer, or administration of the Sacraments; any that use any other book of prayers than is set forth by common authority, and where such person or persons do remain and who they are that do maintain them'.[17] This suggests that some Catholics came to the Protestant service and behaved disrespectfully; the law obliged them to attend, but it could not compel them to respect what they considered a heretical service. The 'jangling' Parkhurst referred to may have been people saying the rosary, and it is clear that some people attended the service and read from Catholic prayer books.

In November 1569 the earls of Westmoreland and Northumberland rebelled in the north and restored the Mass in Durham Cathedral. Meanwhile, Thomas Howard, 4th Duke of Norfolk (1538–72), had been plotting for some months to marry Mary, Queen of Scots, who represented a serious threat to Elizabeth's claim to the throne. Norfolk's attitude to Catholicism was ambivalent, but in 1565 he had sheltered William Allen (1532–94), the future cardinal and founder of the English College at Douai, in his Norwich palace. During his stay there, Allen penned *Certain Brief Reasons concerning the Catholick Faith,* later printed at Douai.[18] On 22 September 1569 Norfolk heard that Elizabeth was about to confine him to the Tower and he fled to his manor of Kenninghall in Norfolk, although he later returned and was placed under arrest.[19] However, Norfolk's brief visit to East Anglia, where he had enormous influence, seems to have contributed to an attempted rebellion against Elizabeth initiated by some of the lesser gentry.

In May 1570 a Norfolk man, John Felton, nailed a copy of Pius V's bull *Regnans in Excelsis,* excommunicating and deposing Elizabeth, to the door of the Bishop of London's palace at Fulham. At the same time a former sheriff of Norfolk under Mary, Sir John Appleyard, began whipping up popular hostility in Norwich to 'strangers', Protestant refugees fleeing the religious war in the Low Countries, hoping that this anger would transfer itself to Elizabeth's government. Also involved in the abortive rebellion was the former prior of the Dominican Priory in Norwich, Edmund Harcocke. However, the rebellion was a complete failure, and thirty-two people were questioned and tried for treason at the Norwich assizes in July and August 1570.[20] Yet a rising of the East Anglian gentry who had proved so loyal to Mary in support of the Duke of Norfolk was a realistic possibility at this volatile time.

Some English regions retained a large body of religious conservatives at all levels of society unwilling to accept Elizabeth's religious changes (Yorkshire, Lancashire and County Durham, for example), but Catholics in East Anglia found a diversity of ways to circumvent the new regime. Michael Hare of Bruisyard, one of the Exchequer Tellers, built a chantry chapel against the south chancel wall of his parish church, in which he was able to be absent in spirit, though present in the flesh. Ralph Cantrell of Hemingstone, whose well-appointed chapel included a fireplace (designated 'Ralph's hole' by his neighbours) was similarly able to withdraw from any active participation in the Protestant service, while Sir Thomas Cornwallis used to sit in the squire's pew: 'This is notorious, all service tyme when others on their knees are at praiers, he will sett contemptuously reading on a book (most likely some Lady Psalter or portasse which have been found in his p[la]ce)'.[21] Some of the gentry of Norfolk, Suffolk and Cambridgeshire became recusants or church papists, but there were few popular acts of resistance to the Reformation. East Anglia's towns, on the whole, enthusiastically embraced reform and popular dissent soon took the form of Protestant agitation for a more thorough Reformation.

This traditional picture of the Reformation in East Anglia as a popular phenomenon has been accompanied by an assumption by historians that Catholicism was a gentry phenomenon.[22] However, this is only true if the evidence of the Recusant Rolls after 1592 is taken as normative; bishops' visitation articles and archdeaconry court records give the names of many recusants from the lower ranks of society, although care is needed in interpreting these because Protestant sectaries were also classed as recusants. Nevertheless, visitation articles record instances of recusancy by yeoman farmers, tradesmen, craftsmen and shopkeepers, suggesting a quite different pattern of recusancy from the traditional picture of elite Catholicism.

Close attention was paid to recusants after 1570, and in 1574 Bishop Freke reported that there were forty-nine in his diocese, including the Bedingfield, Lovell, Huddlestone, Downes and Jerningham families.[23] These were all names that would crop up frequently in presentments for recusancy throughout Elizabeth's reign. A list sent by Freke to the Privy Council in 1577 contained other familiar names: Drury of Hawstead, Timperley of Hintlesham, Dereham of West Dereham, Parris of Linton, and Rookwood of Euston and Stanningfield.[24] Recusancy flourished in the region throughout the 1560s and 1570s, but in 1578 Elizabeth made the decision to undertake a progress through East Anglia. Patrick Collinson argued that the progress of 1578 was 'a watershed in East Anglian history' when the balance of power definitively slipped away from the religious conservatives and towards Protestant gentry.[25] Publicly, the progress was a celebration of the Queen's rule and a chance for the landowners and corporations whose estates and towns she passed through to ingratiate themselves with the monarch and entertain her with elaborate masques and other performances. Behind the pageantry, however, the progress had a definite political purpose. The

Spanish ambassador Bernardino Mendoza described Elizabeth's entry into Norwich, a city that had nearly turned against her eight years earlier:

> During her progress in the north the Queen has met with more Catholics than she expected, and in one of the houses they found a great many images which were ordered to be dragged round and burnt. When she entered Norwich large crowds of people came out to receive her, and one company of children knelt as she passed and said, as usual, 'God save the Queen'. She turned to them and said, 'Speak up; I know you do not love me here'.[26]

However, the most striking incident of the progress occurred at Euston Hall in Suffolk. On leaving Bury St Edmunds on 9 August, Elizabeth stopped at Euston, where she was entertained by Edward Rookwood. Collinson proposed that Elizabeth's visit to Euston could have been planned in advance as a means of entrapping her host.[27] She was accompanied by Richard Topcliffe, an enforcer of religious conformity notorious for his cruelty towards Catholics. Rookwood was presented to the Queen, but as he was about to kiss her hand he was pulled away by the Lord Chamberlain, who asked him how he dared to approach his sovereign when he had been excommunicated for recusancy. The following evening a piece of silver plate belonging to the court disappeared; Rookwood's outbuildings were searched, and Topcliffe described what happened next:

> … in the hayrick such an image of Our Lady was there found, as for greatness, for gayness and workmanship, I did never see a match; and after a sort of country dances ended, in Her Majesty's sight the idol was set behind the people who

> avoided … Her Majesty commanded it to the
> fire, which, in her sight, by the country folks, was
> quickly done, to her content, and unspeakable
> joy of every one but some one or two who had
> sucked of the idol's poisoned milk.[28]

Edward Rookwood was subsequently summoned
to appear before the Bishop of Norwich (an unusual measure) and imprisoned in the gaol in Bury St
Edmunds.[29] By October 1588, when he made a protes-
tation of loyalty to the Queen before the Dean of Ely,
Andrew Perne, Rookwood was one of the Catholic
gentlemen imprisoned in the Bishop's Palace in Ely.[30]
In 1589 he was obliged to pay a hefty fine of £940.[31]

The humiliation of Edward Rookwood marked the
beginning of a more aggressive attack on East Anglian
recusants. On 13 September 1580 twenty-five leading
recusants were arrested and six were 'committed close
prisoners for their obstinacy': Edward Rookwood of
Euston, Robert Downes of Bodney, John Daniell of
Acton, Michael Hare of Bruisyard, Roger Martin of
Long Melford and Henry Drury of Lawshall. Fourteen
others were required to remain in specified towns so
that they might be 'conferred with': Sir Henry, Humphrey and Edmund Bedingfield, Edward and Thomas
Sulyard, Evan Fludd, Edmund Wyndham, Robert de
Grey, John Drury, John Downes, Ferdinand Parris,
Thomas and Robert Lovell and Henry Everard.[32]

The year 1580 saw another new development in the
government's policy towards recusants: internment of
prisoners in one place, Wisbech Castle in the far north
of Cambridgeshire. Wisbech was a property of the
Bishop of Ely, Richard Cox, who since 1577 had been
obliged to entertain the ex-Abbot of Westminster, John
Feckenham, at his palace in Ely. Hitherto prominent

Catholics had been subject to restraining orders but not always imprisoned; in 1561, for example, the former Gilbertine Prior of Sempringham, Roger Marshall, was confined to within six miles of Newmarket, and Henry Comberforde was obliged to live in Suffolk but allowed to visit Staffordshire twice a year. John Dale, an ejected Fellow of Cambridge, was to live within ten miles of Newmarket but banned from the city of Cambridge itself.[33] In 1580, however, Cox sent Feckenham to Wisbech along with Thomas Watson, the deprived Bishop of Lincoln, and John Young, who had been Regius Professor of Divinity at Cambridge in Mary's reign. Feckenham, Watson and Young were the first of many: after 1580 a total of seventy-two priests and thirty-nine laypeople were incarcerated at Wisbech, until they were moved to Framlingham Castle in 1600.[34] A further thirty-two laymen were imprisoned in the Bishop's Palace at Ely.[35]

In 1580 the first three Jesuits also set foot in England, a momentous event that would transform the face of the English mission. The secular priest Montford Scott, from Hawstead in Suffolk, was arrested in Cambridge in 1578, and then captured a second time in Hawstead. He was imprisoned and eventually executed in London's Fleet Street in 1591.[36] He was to be the first of many martyrs of the period, amongst whom were the Norfolk-born Jesuits Henry Walpole (*c.* 1558–93) and Robert Southwell (1561–95).[37] Walpole and Southwell had much in common apart from their origin in Norfolk; both were the sons of conformist yet possibly crypto-Catholic fathers, and both were of the minor gentry. However, whereas Southwell received most of his education on the Continent, Walpole was a product of Norwich School and Peterhouse, Cambridge, at a time when religious conservatism was still a power-

ful force in the university, and many Cambridge men
crossed the sea to train for the priesthood before or
after receiving a degree.[38]

The 1580s were a dark time for English Catholics, as
Spain increasingly menaced England and loyal Catholics suffered the consequences. The laws against recusancy were tightened in 1586 and a fine of 100 marks
(£66 13s 4d) was imposed for hearing Mass, in addition
to imprisonment.[39] In the same year a Catholic gentleman from Suffolk, Charles Tilney of Shelley, was
executed for his part in the Babington Plot.[40] In many
cases, the priests serving Catholic families were still
survivors of Mary's reign, such as the priest known
variously as Fox, Hale, Redman or Redshawe serving
the Audley family at Great Barton in 1586, and 'an
aged man made priest in Queen Mary's time' serving
Edward Sulyard, Ferdinand Parris, Lady Babthorpe,
Michael Hare, and Sir John Cotton of Cambridge. A
man called Jackson, 'priest in Queen Mary's time',
served Michael Hare at Bruisyard.[41] There was even a
priest called Moore, 'made priest in King Henry's time',
with Mrs Lovell at East Harling in Norfolk.

In 1585, Parliament had made it an act of treason
for an Englishman, having obtained orders under the
authority of the Bishop of Rome, to set foot in England. This meant that the old Marian priests were
safe from prosecution for treason, even though they
could be arrested for saying Mass. However, the new
seminary priests and Jesuits were fugitives from the
moment they arrived in England, often on the East
Anglian coast. Lowestoft, Reydon, Southwold, Orford,
Bawdsey and Felixstowe were all places where priests
were set ashore.[42] In January 1583 John Nutter and
John Conyers were captured on landing at Dunwich,[43]
while Thomas Simpson and John Godsalf were cap-

tured at Orford in May 1585.[44] In June John Robinson was captured at Lowestoft and imprisoned in London, although in recognition of the fact that he had first broken the law in Suffolk he was sent to Ipswich to be executed on 1 October 1588.[45] William Atkinson was more fortunate: he was taken at Harwich in 1595 but managed to escape.[46]

Catholic families constructed hiding places and escape routes for the fugitive priests: at Coldham Hall in Suffolk (built in 1574) a concealed staircase was built into a chimney stack,[47] while in 1593 the celebrated designer of hiding places Nicholas Owen constructed an ingenious space inside Sawston Hall, Cambridgeshire, which went undetected for centuries.[48] A network of carriers existed to pass information about the movements of priests. In 1598 a man called Darkyn of Chippenham, near Newmarket, was 'taken to be a carrier fo[r] letters from one papist to another'.[49] In the Cambridgeshire Fens a network of sympathisers facilitated the regular escape of priests from Wisbech Castle.[50]

In spite of the dangers, seminary priests were working throughout East Anglia by 1586, when an informant reported that John Maddock (made priest at Rheims) was to be found serving widow Bedingfield at Hale, and John Vivian, 'seminarist of Rheims', was with Roger Martin at Long Melford.[51] Some priests posed as tutors, like a certain Dallison at Wetherden Hall in 1578.[52] The Jesuits were also present, albeit in small numbers, and a priest called Dolman, serving Ferdinand Parris at Linton and Sir John Cotton at Landwade was described as 'a Provincial over the rest'.[53] In 1589 the Jesuit John Gerard began a major missionary campaign in Suffolk, basing himself until the winter of 1591 with Henry Drury at Lawshall

Hall and the Rookwoods at nearby Coldham Hall in Stanningfield.[54] Many East Anglian Catholics visited Gerard in order to make the spiritual exercises, including Thomas Everard (1560–1633) of Linstead Parva and Anthony Rous of Dennington. Both men were inspired by Gerard's teachings to seek ordination to the priesthood themselves, and Everard became a Jesuit and a noted translator of spiritual works into English.[55] The Rookwood family was profoundly affected by Gerard's visit, and continued to have close links with the Jesuits into the eighteenth century.

Table 1. East Anglian priests ordained before 1603[56]

NAME	ORDER	PLACE OF BIRTH	BORN	ORDAINED	DIED
Ballard, John	Sec.	West Wratting, Cambs	–	1581	1586
Bastard, Robert	SJ	Elm, Norf.	1571	1602	1633
Benstead, Thomas VEN.	Sec.	Norf.	1574	–	1600
Braddock, Edmund	Sec.	Norf.	–	1583	–
Braddock, Henry	Sec.	Norf.	–	1583	–
Broughton, Richard	Sec.	Gt Stukeley, Hunts	1561	1592	1635
Buck, Robert	SJ	Cambs	1573	1600	1648
Clark, Francis	Sec.	Norf.	1576	1600	–
Cornwallis, Richard	Sec.	Coxford Abbey, Norf.	1568	1599	–
Cornwallis, William	Sec.	Brome, Norf.	1527	1580	1600
English, Robert	Sec.	Ipswich, Suff.	–	1580	–
Everard, Thomas	SJ	Linstead Parva, Suff.	1560	1592	1633
Flack, William	SJ	Suff.	1561	1591	1637
Floyd, Henry	SJ	Cambs	1563	1592	1641
Floyd, John	SJ	Cambs	1572	–	1649

Gardiner, Bernard	Sec.	Coxford Abbey, Norf.	1563	1592	–
Jetter, George	Sec.	Lowestoft, Suff.	–	1581	1609
Lusher, Thomas	Sec.	Norf.	1575	1599	–
Montford, Francis	Sec.	Wereham, Norf.	1566	1591	–
Montford, Thomas	Sec.	Wereham, Norf.	1577	1600	–
Rous, Anthony	Sec.	Dennington, Suff.	–	1592	–
Ruffet, John	Sec.	Wood Dalling, Norf.	1567	1597	–
Sayer, Robert (Gregory)	OSB	Redgrave, Suff.	1560	1585	1602
Scott, Montford BD	Sec.	Hawstead, Suff.	–	1577	1591
Southwell, Robert ST	SJ	Horsham St Faith, Norf.	1561	1584	1595
Stephens, John	Sec.	Norf.	1578	1602	–
Swinburne, Robert	Sec.	Hunts	–	1583	–
Taylor, William (Maurus)	OSB	Ely, Cambs	1576	1602	–
Walpole, Christopher	SJ	Dersingham, Norf.	1568	–	1606
Walpole, Edward	SJ	Dersingham, Norf.	1560	1592	1637
Walpole, Henry ST	SJ	Dersingham, Norf.	1558	1588	1593
Walpole, Michael	SJ	Dersingham, Norf.	1570	–	1620
Walpole, Richard	SJ	Dersingham, Norf.	1564	1589	1607
Woodward, Lionel	Sec.	Suff.	–	1592	1609
Woodward, Phillip	Sec.	Suff.	1558	1583	1610

As Table 1 shows, the number of East Anglian men ordained to the priesthood before 1603 was small (thirty-five), and not all of these returned to the English mission. By far the most prolific provider of vocations was the Walpole family of Anmer and Dersingham in Norfolk, which produced five Jesuits, including the martyr Henry. Some East Anglian priests achieved fame in other ways, such as the Benedictine Gregory Sayer from Redgrave in Suffolk, who joined the Cassinese monastery of San Giorgio Maggiore and was the author of many celebrated works on moral theology. After Sayer's death his work was edited by his fellow monk and East Anglian Maurus Taylor, from Ely.[57] Another distinguished East Anglian exile was the translator John Fenn (1535–1615), Master of Bury St Edmunds Grammar School in Mary's reign, who fled to Louvain and was ordained by 1574. Fenn served as a military chaplain in the Dutch wars and translated the Catechism of the Council of Trent into English.[58]

In the summer of 1588, news of the approaching Spanish Armada prompted the Privy Council to arrest leading Catholic gentlemen and confine them to the Bishop's Palace at Ely and Banbury Castle. Ely's most prominent prisoner was Sir Thomas Tresham of Rushton, Northamptonshire. The East Anglian recusants who joined him were William ap Pryce of Washingley (Huntingdonshire), William Browne of Elsing (Norfolk), Thomas Crawley of Monewden (Suffolk), Michael Hare of Bruisyard (Suffolk), Ferdinando Parris of Linton (Cambridgeshire), Edward Rookwood of Euston (Suffolk), and Edward Sulyard of Wetherden (Suffolk).[59] However, other East Anglian gentlemen were sent to Banbury, as if deliberately to divide networks of neighbourliness and kinship. By December the last of the prisoners had been released on bond, but many of them found themselves repeatedly imprisoned at Ely until 1597.

Although the avowed intention of Elizabeth's government was the extirpation of Catholicism, recusants ironically provided the exchequer with a solid income to the Treasury from recusancy fines. In 1591 the exchequer began the practice of keeping recusant rolls, records of amounts due from individuals in each county for recusancy. In many cases, recusants fell into arrears and were forced to mortgage their estates; unpaid recusancy fines of deceased relatives were also a problem. The same names recur time and again in the recusant rolls, such as Townsend, Carvile, Yelverton, Yaxley, Willoughby, Cobbe, Mannock, Rookwood, Rous, Martin, Tostwood, Trott and Norton. By 1592 the unpaid recusancy fines of Robert Lovell and Robert Downes amounted to £1,480 each. As a consequence, two thirds of their estates were seized by the government and let out to tenants. By contrast, the Sulyard of Haughley, Rookwood of Stanningfield and Hare of Bruisyard families could afford to pay the punishing fines.[60]

Members of the artisan class and even humbler individuals also paid recusancy fines: in 1592, recusants in Norwich fined between £80 and £260 included a cordwainer, a woolcomber, a butcher, a blacksmith, a glazier, an innkeeper, a grocer, a tailor and a labourer.[61] Clearly, it would have been impossible for many of these individuals to pay such sums, and they faced prison as a result. Norbert Birt calculated that, between 1592 and 1610, 1,901 people were fined for recusancy: 116 in Cambridgeshire, 886 in Norfolk, and 899 in Suffolk.[62] However, it is necessary to treat these figures with some caution, since dissenting Protestants who declined to attend church were also classed as recusants; often the only way to determine if someone was a popish recusant is if their name can be recognised as that of a known Catholic family. According to a return of 12 July 1603, 153 men and 147 women in the Diocese of Norwich refused to attend church, and 77 men and 65 women refused to receive communion.[63]

Relations between Catholics and Protestants in East Anglia were not always strained. In Bury St Edmunds, Catholics continued to maintain their social position and were active as common councilmen and benefactors to the grammar school.[64] Throughout the 1570s and 1580s, the Bishop of Norwich, Edmund Freke, was at odds with Puritan-leaning elements in Bury in a battle to control the town's two parish churches, St James's and St Mary's. Thomas Badby, a kinsman of Sir Robert Jermyn of Rushbrooke, who was then living in the Abbot's Palace, supported a Puritan nominee as minister of St James's church, but Freke joined forces with Henry Drury of Lawshall and Sir Thomas Kitson, both recusants (or, at best, occasional conformists) who used their influence to instal Giles Wood, the Rector of Brome, as minister. Brome was the seat of another recusant (and Kitson's father-in-law), Sir Thomas Cornwallis, who was notorious for his patronage of non-preaching and 'popish' incumbents.[65] Diarmaid MacCulloch has observed that these 'Bury Stirs' 'reveal an interesting degree of co-operation between a new generation of anti-Puritan clergy and Catholic sympathizers among the Suffolk gentry'.[66] Clearly, Catholics could be relied upon to support the path of moderation in the established church.

By the end of the 1590s, the government's policy of imprisoning numbers of priests in Wisbech Castle was having unintended consequences. In 1586 the superior of the Jesuits in England, William Weston, was captured and interned at Wisbech. Weston was determined to transform the priests in the castle into a harmonious college of clergy under Jesuit spiritual control. At Christmas 1594 one of the secular priests,

Christopher Bagshawe, hired mummers and a hobby horse to perform in the great hall. The incident set Weston's vision of the priests as an apostolic college against Bagshawe's anti-Jesuit views. The priests were soon divided into two camps; although there were only ever nine Jesuit priests (and one laybrother) at Wisbech, their influence was disproportionate. The 'Wisbech Stirs' soon took the form of pamphlets for and against the Jesuit party, and in 1598 the dispute took on wider significance when Rome appointed the pro-Jesuit George Blackwell as archpriest with jurisdiction over the secular clergy in England. Bagshawe, who was encouraged by the government to oppose the Jesuits, launched a campaign amongst the secular clergy against the archpriest. By the end of Elizabeth's reign, thanks to events at Wisbech, the Catholic community was more divided than it had ever been.[67]

Catholicism was somewhat unevenly distributed in East Anglia; the greatest density of Catholics could be found in and around Norwich, in north-central Suffolk (High Suffolk) and in a band from Bury St Edmunds to Long Melford in the Stour Valley (the Liberty of St Edmund). In Cambridgeshire, there was a scattering of Catholics in the south of the county. In the early Elizabethan period Lothingland, in the far northeast of Suffolk, was a particular stronghold.[68] Recusancy was almost entirely absent from southeast Suffolk (the Liberty of St Etheldreda) and north Cambridgeshire (the Isle of Ely).[69] Collinson noted that 'the insubordination characteristic of the mixed economy of High Suffolk, with its weak manorial organisation and lack of gentry control' contributed to the rise of Puritanism.[70] The mixed economy consisted of woodland on the sandy Breckland and pasture on the chalk uplands, and freeholdings abounded.

'Stiff-necked independence and conservatism' were, of course, characteristics Catholics and Puritans shared equally.[71] J. C. H. Aveling argued that post-Reformation Catholicism was 'a haven for the nonconformist conscience',[72] and this was certainly as true of Catholicism in East Anglia as it was of Puritanism. Catholicism in Elizabethan East Anglia was socially diverse and not a purely gentry or elite phenomenon, although it was usually only the gentry who could afford the luxury of out-and-out recusancy. Yet recusancy was just one form of conservative dissent along a complex spectrum of behaviour. Furthermore, Catholicism in late-sixteenth-century East Anglia was sustained as much by the arrival of missionary priests on the east coast and the influx of priests destined for Wisbech Castle as it was by static landed Catholic families and their chaplains. A few East Anglian Catholics came close to open rebellion in 1570 and, although they remained loyal to Elizabeth for the remainder of her reign, Ambrose Rookwood's involvement in the Gunpowder Plot in 1605 showed that a few were still prepared to take up arms. With the benefit of hindsight, it is easy to see Elizabethan Catholics merely as the ancestors of the settled and passive recusants of the eighteenth century. In reality, they lived in a much less stable world in which the future was far from certain, and the prospect of a Catholic restoration may have glimmered on the horizon.

Notes

1   On the recusancy penalties see M. Questier, 'Catholicism, Conformity and the Law', in P. Lake and M. Questier (eds), *Conformity and Orthodoxy in the English Church, c. 1560–1660* (Woodbridge: Boydell, 2000), pp. 237–61, at p. 238.

2   See A. Walsham, *Church Papists: Catholicism, Conformity and Confessional Polemic in Early Modern England* (London: Royal Historical Society, 1993); M. Questier, *Conversion, Politics and Religion in England, 1580–1625* (Cambridge: Cambridge University Press, 1996), pp. 100–20.

3   C. Talbot (ed.), 'Recusants in the Archdeaconry of Suffolk', in *Miscellanea* (London: Catholic Record Society, 1961), pp. 108–11.

4   Gage (1822), p. 178.

5   J. Rowe, 'Kitson family (*per. c.* 1520–*c.* 1660)', in *ODNB*, vol. 31, pp. 843–6.

6   Gage (1822), p. 32. However, the chapel also contained an 'aulter' and a 'round cushion, w[i]th the picture of o[u]r ladye, wrought w[i]th gold'.

7   D. Spittle, 'Gifford's Hall, Stoke-by-Nayland', *Proceedings of the Suffolk Institute of Archaeology and History* 30 (1965), pp. 183–7, at p. 184.

8   Birt (1912), pp. 3–25, at pp. 4–5.

9   *Ibid.*, p. 6.

10   *Ibid.*, p. 5.

11   F. Young, 'Papists and Non-Jurors in the Isle of Ely, 1559–1745', *Proceedings of the Cambridge Antiquarian Society* 104 (2015c), pp. 161–70.

12   K. W. Woods, 'The Pre-Reformation Altarpiece of Long Melford church', *The Antiquaries Journal* 82 (2002), pp. 93–104.

13   Dymond and Paine (1989).

14   Cambridge University Library MS Additional 10079. See Young (2016), p. 63n.

15   C. Brooke, *A History of Gonville and Caius College* (Woodbridge: Boydell, 1985), pp. 72–3.

16   N. Rogers, 'A Catholic Interlude: Sidney Sussex College, 1687–1688', in N. Rogers (ed.), *Catholics in Cambridge* (Leominster: Gracewing, 2003), pp. 38–45, at p. 38. Another tradition links it to the Dominican friary on the site of the present Emmanuel College.

17   Birt (1912), p. 5.

18   *Great Gothic Fane* (1913), p. 69.

19   M. A. R. Graves, 'Howard, Thomas, Fourth Duke of Norfolk (1538–1572)', in *ODNB*, vol. 28, pp. 429–36.

20   M. Reynolds, *Godly Reformers and their Opponents in Early Modern England: Religion in Norwich, c. 1560–1643* (Woodbridge: Boydell, 2005), pp. 56–7.

21   The National Archives, Kew, State Papers 15/25 no. 19 (charge no. 36).

22   Gordon Blackwood, in *Tudor and Stuart Suffolk* (Lancaster: Carnegie, 2001), p. 113, thought that there were only three gentry recusants in 1568; J. J. Scarisbrick argued in *The Reformation and the English People* (Oxford: Blackwell, 1984), p. 149 that Catholicism could only survive in East Anglia under gentry patronage.

23   Birt (1912), p. 7.

24   *Ibid.*, p. 8.

25   P. Collinson, *From Cranmer to Sancroft* (London: Hambledon Continuum, 2006), p. 33. On Elizabeth's progress see Z. Dovey, *An Elizabethan Progress: The Queen's Journey into East Anglia, 1578* (Stroud: Sutton, 1996).

26   Bernardino Mendoza to Gabriel de Zayas, 8 September 1578, *Calendar of Letters and State Papers relating to English Affairs: preserved principally in the Archives of Simancas*, ed. M. A. S. Hume (London: HMSO, 1892–9), vol. 2, p. 524.

27   P. Collinson, 'Pulling the Strings: Religion and Politics in the Progress of 1578', in J. E. Archer, E. Goldring and S. Knight (eds), *The Progresses, Pageants and Entertainments of Queen Elizabeth I* (Oxford: Oxford University Press, 2007), pp. 122–41, at pp. 132–3.

28   Quoted in P. Lake, 'A Tale of Two Episcopal Surveys: The Strange Fates of Edmund Grindal and Cuthbert Mayne revisited', *Transactions of the Royal Historical Society* 18 (2008) pp. 129–63, at p. 149.

29   Dovey (1996), pp. 53–4.

30   F. Young, 'The Bishop's Palace at Ely as a Prison for Recusants, 1577–1597', *Recusant History* 32 (2014b), pp. 195–218, at p. 202.

31   Blackwood (2001), p. 115.

32   Birt (1912), p. 8.

33   *Calendar of State Papers, Domestic Series, of the Reign of Elizabeth I, 1601–1603 with Addenda 1547–1565* (London: HMSO, 1870), pp. 521–3.

[34] This figure can be arrived at by cross-referencing names from six sources: *The Calendar of State Papers, Domestic Series; Acts of the Privy Council of England*; G. Anstruther, *The Seminary Priests: A Dictionary of the Secular Clergy of England and Wales, 1558–1850* (Ware: St Edmund's College, 1969), vol. 1; H. Foley, *Records of the English Province of the Society of Jesus* (London: Burns and Oates, 1877–83); *ODNB*; A. Bellenger (ed.), *English and Welsh Priests, 1558–1800* (Bath: Downside Abbey, 1984).

[35] Young (2014b), pp. 216–17. On the imprisonment of recusants see P. McGrath and J. Rowe, 'The Imprisonment of Catholics for Religion under Elizabeth I', *Recusant History* 20 (1991), pp. 415–35.

[36] Rogers (2003), p. 39.

[37] See A. C. Ryan, 'Walpole, Henry [St Henry Walpole] (*bap.* 1558, *d.* 1595)', in *ODNB*, vol. 57, pp. 43–6; N. Pollard Brown, 'Southwell, Robert [St Robert Southwell] (1561–1595)', in *ODNB*, vol. 51, pp. 711–17.

[38] Rogers (2003), pp. 39–40.

[39] Birt (1912), p. 10.

[40] Blackwood (2001), p. 115.

[41] On Marian priests see P. McGrath and J. Rowe, 'The Marian Priests under Elizabeth I', *Recusant History* 17 (1984), pp. 103–20.

[42] Rowe (1988), pp. 88–9 features a map identifying these sites.

[43] Anstruther (1969), vol. 1, p. 258.

[44] *Ibid.*, vol. 1, pp. 133, 317.

[45] *Ibid.*, vol. 1, p. 294.

[46] *Ibid.*, vol. 1, p. 13.

[47] Rowe (1988), p. 88.

[48] C. Jackson, 'Glowing Embers: Catholic Life in Cambridgeshire in the Century before Emancipation', in N. Rogers (ed.), *Catholics in Cambridge* (Leominster: Gracewing, 2003), pp. 46–65, at p. 48. A possible hiding place was also described at Giffords Hall in 1886 ('General Meeting—Shelley, Polstead, Boxford, Kersey, and Hadleigh: August 23, 1883', in *Proceedings of the Suffolk Iinstitute of Archaeology* 6 (1886), pp. 321–5, at p. 323). The tradition identifying a room in the Ancient House, Ipswich as a secret Catholic chapel belonging to the Sparrowe family is dubious ([E. Neale], *Stray Leaves from a Freemason's Note-Book* (London: Richard Spencer, 1846), pp. 123–4; V. B. Redstone, *The Ancient House or Sparrowe House, Ipswich* (Ipswich: W. E. Harrison, 1912), p. 72).

49 Rowe (1988), n. p. 147.

50 Young (2015c).

51 Birt (1912), p. 16.

52 Rowe (1988), n. p. 147.

53 Birt (1912), p. 16.

54 J. Gerard (trans. P. Caraman), *The Autobiography of an Elizabethan* (London: Longmans, Green and Co., 1951), pp. 24–31.

55 J. Rowe, 'Everard, Thomas (1560–1633)', in *ODNB*, vol. 18, pp. 788.

56 Information is taken from Bellenger (1984) supplemented by Anstruther (1969), vol. 1.

57 E. J. Mahoney, 'Gregory Sayers O.S.B. (1560–1602): A Forgotten English Moral Theologian', *Catholic Historical Review* 11 (1925), pp. 29–37; F. Young, 'From Ely to Venice: the life of William Maurus Taylor OSB (b. 1576)', *Downside Review* 133 (2015b), pp. 152–75.

58 P. E. B. Harris, 'Fenn, John (1535–1615)', in *ODNB*, vol. 19, p. 295.

59 Young (2014b), pp. 216–17.

60 Birt (1912), p. 12.

61 *Ibid.*, p. 13.

62 *Ibid.*, p. 14.

63 *Ibid.*, p. 9.

64 Rowe (1991), p. 40.

65 MacCulloch (1986), p. 210. On the Bury Stirs see pp. 200–11. On Cornwallis see also McGrath and Rowe (1960), pp. 226–71.

66 MacCulloch (1986), p. 210.

67 On the Wisbech Stirs see P. Renold (ed.), *The Wisbech Stirs (1595–1598)* (London: Catholic Record Society, 1958).

68 MacCulloch (1986), 212–13; Blackwood (2001), p. 112.

69 For an analysis of the geographical distribution of Catholics in Suffolk see Rowe (1988), pp. 88–9.

70 Collinson (2006), p. 30.

71 Rowe (1998), pp. 167–94.

72 Aveling (1976), p. 21.

2

East Anglian Catholics in the Seventeenth Century, 1603–1688

John Morrill

IT REMAINED HARD TO BE A CATHOLIC in the seventeenth century. Far fewer died for the faith; financial penalties were intermittent, but when they hit they could be crippling; many had to witness to their faith from prison cells. Still, for much of the century, there was menace rather than a governmental drive to exterminate. Already, the words of Philip Yorke, 1st Earl of Hardwicke, Lord Chancellor of England and the proud owner of Wimpole Hall near Cambridge, uttered in 1745, rang true: 'The laws against papists as they stand in the statute book are so severe that they are the cause of their own non-execution'.[1] After 1610, priests were not hunted down on a regular basis, fines were only intermittently collected and much more frequently at the old rate of twelve pence per week rather than the revised twenty pounds per month, and searches for arms were less regular and less thorough. Still, Catholics were largely frozen out of public life (except, significantly, from the royal households of all Stuart monarchs down to 1688), some young men and women who converted from Protestantism were disinherited

by their parents or wider family, and there was intermittent persecution, especially, if unsurprisingly, in
the 1640s. On two occasions—in 1641 and 1688—mobs
descended on Catholic houses and ransacked them,
the greater violence being at Long Melford Hall in
August 1642.[2] There is no evidence of a decline in the
size of the Catholic community and some evidence of
an increase. Certainly, almost all the Catholic gentry
families of Elizabeth's reign who did not fail in the
male line stuck by their Faith. And strikingly, Norfolk
provided the fifth largest number of recruits to the
priesthood across the century amongst the fifty-two
counties of England and Wales (with Suffolk not far
behind).[3] It was a bit of a roller-coaster of a century.

Catholics continued to die for the faith. There are
four East Anglians amongst the forty martyrs of England and Wales and more than twenty men who died
on the gallows in the whole period 1570–1681, but
most of them had been butchered before 1603. Only
one priest was executed for his faith within the three
counties—Bd Thomas Tunstall (d. 1616). A Westmoreland man and descendant of Cuthbert Tunstal,
the trimming Bishop of Durham under Henry VIII,
Thomas was ordained in 1609, sent to England in
1610 and arrested in 1611. After five years in Wisbech
Castle, he escaped but was captured and arraigned at
Norwich assizes. Despite the fact that only one witness to his being a priest could be found (two were
required by the statute), he was convicted (so much
for the rule of law) and hanged, drawn and quartered
outside Norwich's Magdalen Gate on 13 July 1616. He
was beatified in 1929.[4]

After a lull in persecution in the period 1610–40,
there was an anti-Catholic panic in the 1640s, with
twenty priests being executed, almost all in London,

including four from East Anglia: a strongly contrasting group. Bd Henry Heath (1599–1643) was a Franciscan. He was born in Peterborough and studied in Cambridge (MA 1621). His study of patristics and encounter with George Fisher SJ led to his conversion in 1623. He spent nineteen years as a teacher in the Francisan House of St Bonaventure in Douai. But when a close friend on the mission was executed in December 1641, he offered himself as a replacement and became a mendicant friar in Kent. After less than twelve months, he was arrested, and writings sewn into his cap were used to convict him. He was martyred at Tyburn on 17 April 1643, and he was beatified in 1987. His *Documents of Christian Perfection* were published after his death (Latin 1651, English 1674).[5] His was a quiet, ascetic witness, in stark contrast to St Alban Roe OSB (1583–1642), a Suffolk man. He too was a convert in his early twenties and he was in Douai by 1609. He was an unruly student, expelled from the college for defiance of authority, but his campaign to be readmitted was finally successful. He became a founder member of the new English Benedictine community of St Edmund (appropriately enough) in Paris. He arrived on the English mission in 1615. He was three times imprisoned (1615–16, 1618–23, 1625–42), and twice banished on pain of death. Nothing deterred, he kept returning and, although formally in Newgate for his last seventeen years, was quietly allowed to go out by day so long as he returned at night. He had an unusual way of evangelising, playing cards and conversing in alehouses. He often persuaded the customers to play not for money, but for short prayers. As anti-Catholic hysteria mounted in 1641 he was transferred to close confinement in the Clink and then arraigned and sentenced to death. Notoriously he used his time on the scaffold as a final opportunity for evangelisation. He preached 'in a jovial fashion' according to one who heard him, and he then asked the sheriff if conversion to Protestantism would save him. The sheriff thought it would; allowing Roe to turn to the crowd and to tell them 'see then what the crime is for which I am to die and whether religion be not my only treason'. He is one of the Forty Martyrs of England and Wales canonised in 1970.[6] The third of the East Anglian Tyburn martyrs of the 1640s was Henry Morse of Tivetshall St Mary, Norfolk (1595–1645). He was brought up in a nicodemite family and conformed to the established church, attending Cambridge and an Inn of Chancery before being converted in 1614 and enrolling first at Douai and subsequently at the Venerable English College in Rome. He served on the missions in the 1630s, famously remaining in London to tend to those dying of the plague when most were fleeing. He was arrested in 1640, being released at the intercession of Queen Henrietta Maria. After serving as an army chaplain in the Spanish Netherlands, he returned in 1643 and served in the north-east, before being arrested when Newcastle surrendered to the Parliamentarians. He was sent south and executed on 22 January 1645, not coincidentally just a week after Archbishop William Laud, one of the charges against whom was the release of Morse in 1640.[7] Thus a priest from each of the three counties that make up the modern Diocese of East Anglia died for the faith in the 1640s.[8]

There was a final Catholic martyr during the Exclusion Crisis of 1678–81 and the moral panic induced by the false testimony of Titus Oates and others about a plot to assassinate Charles II and to put his Catholic brother, James, Duke of York, on the throne. Edward Coleman of Brent Eleigh, Suffolk (1636–78) was James's secretary and confidant, executed at Tyburn on 3 December 1678 for conspiring with Louis XIV's confessor to get money for the English mission—for evangelisation, he thought; for arms, his enemies thought. He was a convert in his late twenties who went on to convert many others, playing a part in his master's conversion. He was beatified in 1929, a shade fortunate perhaps, given his very political engagement.[9]

There were, of course, others who died for Catholic causes in the seventeenth century, most famously Ambrose Rookwood of Stanningfield (his mother was a Drury of Hawstead, as staunch a family as the Rookwoods), one of the Gunpowder Plotters in 1605. He was a late recruit to the conspiracy, providing gunpowder and horses and coming to London to take part in the aftermath. On the discovery of the plot, he fled to the Midlands but was brought back for trial and execution.[10] However, overwhelmingly the threat to Catholics was more to their property than to their lives. The *Responsa Scholarum*, short spiritual autobiographies dictated by every man arriving at a seminary in the late sixteenth or the seventeenth century, are full of stories of families in reduced and straitened circumstances.[11] Given that the Gunpowder Plot was the desperate final fling of Catholic political militancy, and given that successive monarchs—and even Oliver Cromwell as Lord Protector—started on the assumption that persecution was counter-productive and should be used only as a last resort, a kind of accommodation was reached between the Crown and the Catholic community not unlike that between the Church and Communist regimes in the 1960s and 1970s: a dour *de facto* toleration in return for political acquiescence. Catholics withdrew into fairly closed—indeed enclosed—family groups, with a high rate of intermarriage and an acceptance of the inevitability of intermittent harassment whenever there was a national security crisis or whenever the Crown was looking for a quick and unfair way of raising cash.

This makes it impossible to count the number of lay Catholics. Too much was left to the discretion of local magistrates, many of whom turned blind eyes or deaf ears to recusancy (well able to distinguish the faith, which they despised, and the ambitions of the papacy, which they feared, from their knowledge of their local Catholics, whom they might or might not like, but who they saw as little threat). It is very striking that so few Catholics took up arms in the Civil Wars, as we shall see. If the Crown saw persecution as counter-productive, Catholics saw political action as self-defeating.

The fullest modern analysis of recusancy rolls for the period is one for Suffolk in the half century before the Civil Wars. In 1592, there are 96 named heads of households (perhaps 500–600 Catholics altogether, including all household members (family and servants)). In 1606 there are 355 named heads of household (perhaps 2,000 Catholics). In 1641 it is back to 95 heads of household. The differences, of course, are a measure of the fluctuating levels of official anxiety, not of a rising and falling number of Catholics.[12] It is no surprise that 1606, in the immediate aftermath of Gunpowder Plot, was a peak year. It is true that some Catholic families in the 1606 list had died out by 1641 (e.g. the Hares of Bruisyard) and a few others like the Waldegraves of Bures had conformed to the Church of England, but what is striking is the continuity in the twenty most prominent and defiant Catholic families who kept the faith throughout the century. Among the families in all three lists are three branches of the Bedingfields, the Mannocks, Martins of Long Melford, the Kitsons and their

Darcy and Gage successors at Hengrave, the Rook-woods of Euston and Coldham Hall, the Sulyards of Haughley, the Tasburghs of Flixton, the Timperleys of Hintlesham, and two branches of the Yaxleys. Almost all these families provided men for the priesthood across the seventeenth century.[13] What we cannot know is how many of them were nicodemite, occasionally and without conviction attending Protestant worship while cherishing their Catholic faith. We do not have comparable figures for the other counties, although in the 1641 recusant rolls there were 68 heads of Norfolk families (perhaps 400 Catholics altogether).[14] For the 1640s we have a new source: the records of the Committees of Sequestration and Composition and later the Acts of Sale. As the costs of waging war against the king mounted, the Long Parliament decided to confiscate all the property of his supporters. Top of the list were all those who bore arms for the king, followed by all those who accepted any kind of civil commission from him. Also included were all those who voluntarily (not under duress) contributed men or supplies to his cause. But in the case of all Protestants, some overt act was needed: believing or even saying in public that the king (or more usually the established church) had the better cause was not sufficient for a sequestration order. But in the case of Catholics, the reverse was true. All Catholics were *assumed* to be culpable unless they could demonstrate overt acts of support for the Parliament (which none ever could). There was a lower limit to culpability. No-one with goods to a value of less than £200 was assumed to be a free agent, but rather under the control of others. So poor Catholics were as much exempt as poor Protestants. Only the top 30 per cent of adult males were liable. Since most of the money raised would be retained for local defence, there was a strong incentive on the commissioners to sequester the property of all those who fell within the terms of the ordinances.

If this was not tough enough on the Catholics, the process for regaining their estates was worse. Most of those sequestered appeared before the Committee for Compounding in Goldsmith's Hall in London and had to pay a fine fixed in relation to the extent of their culpability.[15] The basic fine on Protestant Royalists was one tenth of the total value of their land and property; those with a greater level of engagement were fined at a sixth or a third. Some 4,000 men were fined in that range. Simply being a Catholic led to a fine set at one third, and across the country Catholics represented a high proportion of those fined at one third. But even to get away with this crippling fine, all 'delinquents' had to take 'the Covenant', an oath to uphold and maintain a reformed Presbyterian system of Church government as the basis of a reformed Protestant state. This was even harder for Catholics than for Protestants. So many remained sequestered into the 1650s. At that point, the Commonwealth government, even more strapped for cash to pay for Cromwell's campaigns in Ireland, decided to sell the land of all those who had not compounded or had not been allowed to compound. The latter included all 'papists in arms'. Unfortunately, disentangling the records is the stuff of doctoral theses, and we only have two careful studies of the records, both relating to Suffolk, and even they reach rather different conclusions, which need to be combined to reach a provisional conclusion.[16] Keith Lindley's analysis of the papers of the Committee of Compounding found 70 Suffolk Catholics, 67 of whom were sequestered as 'mere Catholics', no overt act of Royalism being found against them. Lindley found only three 'active Royalists' in the records. Two-thirds of his group of 70 were from gentry families, one third tradesmen and yeomen. Only one of the 70 men he studied served in arms for the king, Sir Henry Torlingham.[17] Clear evidence of the neutralism of the leading Catholic families was found in the cases of the Timperleys, Sulyards, Martins and Mannocks.[18]

Gordon Blackwood found far fewer Suffolk Catholics in the records, but he found six *active* Royalists, adding three names to Lindley's three. In an appendix he lists them by surname and residence only and so we do not know whether they were heads of family or younger sons (common in other areas): Jettor of Oulton, Mounsey of Cotton, Rookwood of Coldham Hall and of Euston, Sulyard of Haughley Park and Tasburgh of Flixton.[19] The first two are names not otherwise found in recusant records. By definition these men cannot have borne arms or they would have been disqualified from compounding. An impressionistic survey by the present author using the indexes of the Calendar of the Committee for Compounding suggests a similar number of names for Norfolk and a much smaller number for Cambridgeshire, as well as that Catholics in these counties were adept at keeping their heads down and avoiding engagement in the Civil Wars. Although they had much to fear from the Puritans in Parliament, they owed Charles I few favours. He had stopped the execution of priests, but he had increased the efficiency of the collection of recusancy fines to help ease his fiscal deficit.

When we turn to the Acts of Sale of 1651–2,[20] only one East Anglian name appears: Sir Henry Bedingfield of Oxburgh. What is troubling about this case is that Sir Henry (who was over sixty when the Civil War broke out) seems to have been punished for the actions of his sons, three of whom had served in the Royalist army. A son-in-law was killed in cold blood as a papist at the end of the siege of Lincoln, and one of his sons was killed at the Battle of Worcester on 3 September 1651 and so was in arms at the time when his father was named in the first Act of Sale the previous July, by which time the others were in exile. Another son was a priest, and a daughter was the founder of the Bar Convent in York. All this seems to have been too much for the Commonwealth government, and despite his own lack of overt acts of Royalism,[21] Sir Henry carried the can. All his lands were put up for sale, and, like many others, he repurchased them, leaving him and his successors saddled with mortgage debt for decades to come. But the Bedingfields were unrepresentative of Catholic behaviour during the Civil Wars.[22]

Even less is known about Restoration Catholicism. Recusancy fines were collected with even less zeal — the two peaks of persecution, with the passage of the Conventicle Act in 1664 and the Popish Plot hysteria of 1679 led to only 115 (1664) and 130 (1679) Catholics being identified in Suffolk, only 21 of whom in 1664 and 59 in 1679 were gentry. What should have been more thorough was a survey ordered by the Bishop of London, Henry Compton, in 1676, with questionnaires about church attendance and recusancy addressed to the incumbent of every parish in England. In fact, many ministers made lazy or self-serving returns, not wanting to draw attention to dissenters in their parishes. So although we have the largest totals for any survey, there were no returns for many of the parishes where we know there were long-standing Catholic groups.[23]

The editors of the modern 800-page edition of the survey (having invested a great deal of their lives to the project) plead that the figures for Catholics 'are

probably reasonably reliable'.[24] This is wishful thinking. The one local historian to study the East Anglian
figures in depth is T. B. Trappes-Lomax. He concluded
that the Norfolk figures were completely unconvincing
and consisted only of those recusants who were radically disconnected from the Church of England.[25] He
probably had in mind those who would not acknowledge the existence of the established church, taking no
part in the life of the civil parish and perhaps not even
using the churchyard to bury their dead. Whiteman
and Clapinson think there is no ambiguity about the
questions asked in the questionnaire. While the other
questions ask about the number of persons over the
age of sixteen in each category, the second question is
quite specifically different: 'What number of Popish
recusants or persons suspected for such recusancy are
there?' Compare this with the next question: 'What
number of other Dissenters are resident ... which
either obstinately refuse or wholly absent themselves
from the Communion of the Church of England at
such times as by Law they are required?'[26] For Protestant Dissenters, it was all those over sixteen (men
and women, masters and servants) who refused to
come to the communion rail on those occasions (three
times a year in most parishes, monthly in others); for
Catholics it was all those who refused to attend on a
weekly basis and who were *recusants.* Now recusancy
was an offence only for heads of households. So while
it cast its net more broadly as far as Catholic dissent is
concerned, the Compton Census cast it more narrowly
in targeting heads of household only.

So how many Catholic recusants were returned by
the 9,324 parish priests in the Church of England? For
Cambridgeshire it was merely 14,[27] for Norfolk 233 and
for the western half of Suffolk it was 247 (the records

of the eastern archdeaconry are missing).[28] Given that
there were always more Catholics in the recusant rolls
for eastern Suffolk, we can say that the number of
Catholics returned was almost certainly in the region
of 500–600. How credible are these figures? What is
striking is the huge range. In Norfolk there are dean-
eries that return as many as 47 and others that return
fewer than 10. In Clare deanery in the archdeaconry of
Sudbury there were no returns for recusants at all, but
82 from the deanery of Thedwastre.[29] Catholics were
found in just over 200 parishes, but in 44 cases only
one person was returned, in 73 only two or three. This
is wildly improbable. Tokenism must be suspected.
In only 19 out of the 1,300 in Norfolk, Suffolk and
Cambridgeshire were 10 or more individuals said to
be Catholics. A significant number of the men in the
English College, Rome, in the later seventeenth century came from parishes where there were allegedly
no papists.[30] The document reeks of collusion between
clergy who either did not want extra work eliminating
popery, or wanted to spare their Catholic neighbours
further hassle. Far from being evidence of a miniscule
Catholic population (0.4 per cent of the population of
East Anglia), it suggests a stasis, a position where the
local authorities saw *their* Catholics as no threat and
as people who no longer deserved to be persecuted.

Closer scrutiny of the Compton Census shows
strong clusters of plebeian Catholics around some of
the major gentry houses (sixteen close to the Rookwoods in Stanningfield, eighteen at Wetherden under
the protection of the Sulyards, barely a mile away at
Haughley, thirty in Long Melford, where there were
three gentry Catholic families headed by the Martins,
and forty in Bury St Edmunds, a town surrounded by
longstanding Catholic families at Hengrave, Coldham,

Lawshall, Great Barton etc). But there were other clusters without any known seigneurial protection—the largest being a group of 17 in Eye, apparently led by the local surgeon, Thomas Hinchlow.[31] But seigneurial Catholicism remained dominant in one respect. A map of Mass Centres for the late seventeenth century compiled by Joy Rowe shows thirteen in all, every one associated with the estates of Catholic gentry.[32] How often Mass was said in these centres is far from clear. A very small number of noble households had their own priests, but most had to make do with itinerants. And they were not served by men born and brought up in the region. Nearly 150 priests emanated from the three counties across the seventeenth century: not one came back to serve in East Anglia. In fact we know far less about the priests who served in East Anglia than about almost any other aspect of the Catholic story. There was a permanent Benedictine presence in Suffolk from 1655, starting in Hintlesham, then Flixton and finally in Bungay, and we know that the Jesuits briefly established a college in a reconstructed 'palace' amidst the ruins of Bury Abbey in 1685, but they seem previously and subsequently to have been scattered and itinerant, meeting once a year together in one or other gentry house—indeed they called themselves a *collegium invisibilium.* As James II's regime crumbled, they withdrew about eight miles to the village of Beyton, where a minor gentleman from Yorkshire had moved, probably believing he would be less harried in East Anglia than he had been in the North. Thomas Burton had a son who was a Jesuit, and two daughters who became Carmelite nuns and a third an Augustinian canoness. The private spiritual diaries of his deeply pious daughter Catharine, before she was clothed, were converted into an autobiography by her spiritual director in the early eighteenth century.[33] Without it, we would have had no knowledge of this new Catholic 'cell' in Suffolk,[34] which makes one wonder how many more went under the Protestant radar.

Catharine Burton's autobiography gives us a rare glimpse into the way East Anglian Catholics worshipped in the seventeenth century. We know that she visited the medieval holy well at Woolpit, just two miles from Beyton, and we know that the family said morning and evening prayer and litanies together daily, almost certainly from one of the many copies of the manuals of prayers available by this time.[35] Catharine was especially devoted to the Little Office of the Immaculate Conception of the Blessed Virgin Mary and the Litanies of St Joseph. After a bout of illness, she determined penitentially to say her prayers in public places, willing to accept Protestant scorn, but unafraid of more active persecution. Thomas Burton promised his children money if they could memorise a Catholic catechism and the results were that he produced a priest, a nun and a deeply pious daughter. Mass was said monthly by a visiting Jesuit, who also heard confessions, and from the late 1670s on, it was perfectly safe for the Mass to be said in an ordinary room in full view.[36]

Just as suggestive are two manuscripts in the Bedingfield papers. The first is a volume that begins with a series of sixteen meditations on the Passion written (or perhaps copied out) by Sir Henry Bedingfield and sent from his prison in the Tower to his wife Elizabeth (Houghton), together with a series of prayers, apparently ancient (one headed 'St Austin's prayer unto the Holy Spirit'), concluding with 'Ten aspirations and effections of a devout soul'.[37] All the material is conventionally pious, with a dualistic loathing of the body and love of the soul, and with an exaggerated account of the tortures to which Jesus was subjected (e.g. he repeats the late medieval trope that when the Cross, with Christ attached to it, was raised up, it was allowed to fall forward again to the earth—they 'threw ower sweete Jesus hedlong into a pit, which they had diged for the purpose, to teare his blessed flesh and vaines, to torture him the more').[38] This obviously became a treasured and much-consulted work in the library at Oxburgh, as did a prayer book, almost certainly assembled in the 1590s, which provided a wide range of hymns, poems and prayers very clearly supplementary to the printed manuals of prayers. This volume, probably not written within or for the Bedingfield household, nonetheless became a prized family possession, with many genealogical notes added by members of the family across the early decades of the seventeenth century.[39] Another example of East Anglian practical devotion is the volume of *Miscellanea: Meditations, Memoratives* drawn up by Elizabeth Grymstone, born in Gunton, Norfolk, the wife of a nicodemite Cambridge don and published after her death by Richard Verstegan, no less. She had much to meditate on: she lost eight of her nine children and was disowned by her birth family. This series of meditations was drawn up for her only surviving son, and it touched the spot of many oppressed Catholics facing the arbitrary ravages of disease and death.[40]

Beyond this, the day-to-day details of Catholic life are lost to us. The impression must be one of fortitude and persistence; of a community deeply self-conscious about its struggle to hold on to the faith and willing to endure periodically nasty but not ruinous persecution and a culture of neighbourly disdain from the Protestant majority, especially the Protestant clergy; and of a community needing to keep itself to itself. Scattered sources suggest that the vast majority of Catholics sought out Catholics to marry, with perhaps 80 per cent of all male and female members of Catholic households marrying within the faith. Thus Catholics might have to look further afield for husbands or wives than Protestants had to look: the proportion of marriages between two Catholics was over 80 per cent, but proportion finding a spouse in the same or contiguous counties may have been barely 50 per cent.[41]

Yet, in order to keep their neighbours at bay, to make those neighbours less likely to wreck Catholic houses in searches for arms, to make it less likely that their horses would be seized whenever there was a security alert, and certainly in order to reduce the risks of prosecution for recusancy for non-attendance at their local parish church, many Catholics certainly became nicodemite to some extent. The legal obligation to attend divine worship (morning or evening prayer) in their local church was only ever placed on heads of households, and never on their families or servants, so it was the head of household who had to consider whether to attend church and to minimise the hazard to his soul by reading quietly but aloud, by humming or otherwise by distracting himself (activities which were never actually proscribed). Many Catholics allowed their children to be baptised once by a Catholic priest, and once by a schismatic priest (or bribe a vicar to make an entry in his registers of a baptism he did not perform); they might have a double wedding so that records could be made which removed all danger of the legal protections of spouses or children coming into question.[42] This issue of church popery had been very contentious at the height of the persecution, with most priests counselling against any contamination with heresy. But there were always priests, though not Jesuit priests, who were willing to take a more lenient view. Given the risk of whole families finding the demands of rigid separation too much to bear and defecting, many priests counselled that some minimal conformity could be permitted so long as it was confessed and kept always under review.

Of course, as the priests well knew, contamination from Protestantism could not only lead to the avoidance of penalties but to increasing collusion and ultimately to surrender to the convenience of conformity and abandonment of the Catholic Faith. An interesting example is a man whom we have already met as the most defiant East Anglian Catholic of the Civil War period — Sir Henry Bedingfield of Oxburgh — who seems in the 1620s to have 'temporised' or 'wavered'. Certainly his pricking as sheriff of Norfolk in 1620 and appointment as a Justice of the Peace in 1626 are inconsistent with the view that he was a committed recusant — they were precisely the rewards offered to those who had just tipped over into conformity.[43] At about that time, however, he seems also to have gained the patronage of the Queen Mother, and this may have been enough to pull him back;[44] and indeed in July 1639 he was granted a *non-obstante* under the Great Seal: 'His Majesty's letters of grace in bar of the laws against Recusants'.[45]

Beyond this, our best glimpses of Catholic life are to found in Anthony Kenny's edition of the brief spiritual autobiographies provided by men as they entered seminary, the biographical information provided by Dom Aidan Bellenger in his 'working list' of priests, Tom McCoog's dictionary of Jesuit priests, and the information garnered by those who in recent years have created the 'Who were the nuns?' database.[46] Let us take the nuns first. Between 1600 and 1700 153 nuns born and raised in East Anglia were clothed in 23 English convents in continental Europe, two-thirds (96) of them from Suffolk, most of the rest (40) from Norfolk and just 7 from Cambridgeshire.[47] What is striking is what a very high proportion came from the leading gentry families. Very few were converts, or even the children of converts—the clearest example being Elizabeth Warner of Parham, Suffolk, whose father was a convert (her mother was brought up as a Protestant and it is not clear if she was also a convert). Elizabeth entered the Sepulchrine Convent in Liège in 1664, at the age of 23; but Catherine Holland, daughter of the Puritan MP Sir John Holland of Quidenham is surely another (although it is possible that her mother was a Catholic). She was professed as a choir nun in the Augustinian house in Bruges in 1663.

The family that provided by far the largest number was the Bedingfields, more than thirty nuns if we include those with mothers as well as fathers in the extended Bedingfield clan. Thus Philippa Bedingfield (1609–34) of Redlingfield, professed as a Benedictine nun at Ghent, had eighteen sisters, cousins, nieces and great-nieces who were clothed and bore their father's name of Bedingfield, and eleven who bore other names but who had Bedingfield mothers. The Bedingfields were far ahead of the next family, the Rookwoods of Coldham, who produced ten nuns by 1700, three or four in each of three generations. Other prominent families with four or more vocations to take the veil before 1700 included the Huddlestones of Sawston, the Cornwallises of Beeston, the Jerninghams of Costessey, the Cobbes of Sandringham, the Timperleys of Hintlesham, the Warners of Parham and the Yaxleys of Yaxley. Over 140 of the nuns came from prominent and long-established Catholic families. Of course, the dowries demanded by the convents made plebeian nuns scarce, but there are about ten who appear to have come from families about which we know little and who do not appear in the recusancy rolls. For example, Helena Bolens, professed as a lay sister at the Benedictine convent in Ghent in 1641, was the daughter of a Robert Bolens and Maria Lowe/Lauwe of Norwich, the latter almost certainly from the Low Countries; or Sara Chenery of Barton Mills in Suffolk, professed as a choir nun in the Franciscan House in Brussels at the unusually early age of seventeen in August 1625 — Barton Mills does not feature in any lists of recusants and is not close to a recusant gentry manor house or known Mass centre.

There is a great contrast between the backgrounds of the women who left England for convents abroad and the men who left for the seminaries. Aidan Bellenger's working list of English and Welsh priests covers the years 1558–1800.[48] Extrapolating the seventeenth-century data from it yields totals of those ordained to the priesthood and in active ministry between 1600 and 1700 as 147, of whom 68 were born and raised in Norfolk, 59 born and raised in Suffolk and 20 born and raised in Cambridgeshire.[49] Three counties (5.8 per cent of the 52 counties) produced 147 of the 2,558 priests ordained in the century, also 5.8 per cent, an identical proportion. This is something of a surprise for three counties presumed to be amongst the least Catholic parts of England and Wales. Of these 147 priests, four were executed under the penal laws and one died in prison.[50] It is likely that more than a third of the priests working in England in the period 1603–41 spent significant periods in prison and most of those (unless they escaped) were then deported, only to return, at greater risk to their lives, after a year or two. Nationally a simple majority of all priests were seculars, a third were Jesuits and less than a sixth were members of other religious orders. But the largest number of priests from East Anglia were Jesuits (65), followed by the seculars (57), with a larger proportion than nationally being in other religious orders—29 in total (about 20 per cent), of whom 22 were Benedictines.

For more detailed information we need to turn to _Responsa Scholarum_ of the English College in Rome for the period 1600–85, supplemented by the biographical dictionaries of English Jesuits 1600–1700.[51] The men who studied at Rome may or may not have been representative of the whole, but between them they cover more than half the priests ordained in the seventeenth century and born and educated in East Anglia. There are 56 entries relating to priestly lives in the _Responsa_ and an overlapping group of 65 Jesuit lives contained in McCoog's biographical dictionaries.

The first striking thing about these more detailed studies is that not one of the future priests born and brought up in East Anglia died there. The entries give details of these men's priestly activities and their places of death. None returned to East Anglia. Indeed, the total number of priests who did serve in East Anglia was almost certainly much lower. The second striking thing is that, in comparison with the nuns, far fewer priests were of gentry extraction, and far more men were converts, or men one or both of whose parents were converts. As we shall see, some cases are very complicated but those self-identifying as converts were more than 40 per cent, and most of those had clearly been baptised and schooled as Protestants. In the _Responsa_ they were encouraged to tell their faith journeys. So although many just say that they were

Catholics from birth, many others had complicated tales to tell. At least ten were the sons of East Anglian Protestant ministers, and an overlapping group of twelve men were converted while at university in Cambridge. A few had been fellows of Cambridge colleges, including Thomas Normanton, son of Bury clothworkers and a Fellow of Pembroke until his conversion as a result of reading the works of St Thomas More and St Robert Bellarmine,[52] or Richard Cornwallis, Fellow of Gonville and Caius and an alumnus of Norwich School who was converted by his half-brother who was a priest on the mission to England.[53] They also include Charles, the son of John Cosin, master of Peterhouse and chaplain to the king. He was converted by 'reading and conversation' and was admitted to the seminary in October 1652.[54]

Reading and conversation were indeed the keys to conversion. John Gogley, also a Cambridge student from Norfolk, and nephew of an Anglican clergyman who was supporting him financially, was converted by reading *The Imitation of Christ* and the works of Robert Persons; William Alabaster from Hadleigh was converted by the polemical works of William Rainolds, one of the translators of the Douai Bible;[55] and Alabaster in turn converted Henry Copinger, the son of a tailor from Bury St Edmunds, just after he had completed his BCL and was set fair for a career as a canon lawyer in the established church.[56] The most fully described case is that of Charles Yelverton of Bawsey near King's Lynn. He was the product of a mixed marriage: his father, a minor gentleman on fifty pounds a year, was a Catholic, his mother a schismatic. His siblings were also divided, one sister being a Catholic who had lapsed because of the 'violence of her husband', Sir Philip Woodhouse. Charles himself spent eight years in Cambridge, but doubts about Protestantism mounted. He read Calvin 'without satisfaction'. He read Bernard of Cluny's *De Contempu Mundi* and 'grew dissatisfied with heretical opposition to the evangelical counsel'. He visited his uncle Edward, who lent him 'books of controversy and meditation'. On his return to Cambridge he bought an enchiridion of controversies and, 'he was overcome with shame in church one day realising that he was simulating heresy while a Catholic at heart; on his way home he was tortured by fear of death'. He left Cambridge, was pursued by the Bishop of Norwich and went into hiding for some months, before crossing to the Continent and hence to Rome.[57]

He was just one of the men from families warring over religion where the Catholic side won out in the end. Robert Drury was the son of a Suffolk man and a canon lawyer who, with his wife, converted not long before his death, but several of whose children remained in schism until persuaded by their sister to be reconciled to the Church.[58] An even more complicated case is that of William Forster of Haverhill, whose father fell on hard times (recusancy fines?) and was forced to become an estate steward in Sussex. William was brought up by his schismatic mother (who had separated from her husband over religion) and her father. When he was thirteen years old his father summoned William to London, and introduced him to Fr Pigott, an imprisoned priest who converted him.[59]

Others were converted from working in Catholic households. Henry Lanman from Westhorpe in Suffolk was educated by a Puritan minister in Northamptonshire, where he lived with his uncle. His father placed him in the household of the crypto-Catholic Christopher Hatton, Elizabeth's Lord Chancellor, who in time passed him on to Viscount Montagu, a high-profile Catholic. The Catholic influence in his household was too great to be resisted. Lanman was converted when twenty-two (in 1595) 'through discussion with William Coningsby whom he met in the family of Lord Montagu; read many books lent to him by this man, especially those written by Rastell and Harding against Jewel;[60] when convinced, was introduced by Coningsby to Mr Winkfield, a priest, who reconciled him'. In 1600 he entered the English College in Rome.[61] The Havers of Thelveton served as steward of the estates of the dukes of Norfolk over several generations and wavered between church popery and recusancy in much the same way.[62]

William Forster was not the only man to go through agonies of doubt before surrendering. Edward Carey, born in Long Melford, was from a Catholic family, but was wracked by doubts even as he presented himself in Rome for formation for the priesthood: *nonnullis scrupulis et animi angoribus saepius deditus sum, qui subito advenient[es] subito evanescunt* ('I am very often given to scruples and agonies of soul which suddenly arrive and suddenly vanish').[63] So these are not especially serene stories.

Finally, there are those converted as a result of living too close to death. Robert Cowper of Rushall, Norfolk, Bury St Edmunds and Cambridge University 'has entirely heretical kinsfolk' and 'suffered disquiet of mind about the choice of a state of life' and was converted from heresy 'by a doctor friend',[64] and John Nixon, another Cambridge student and son of a parson, 'converted from heresy two years ago by Fr Thomas Percy SJ on the occasion of a dangerous disease'.[65]

Many of the above seminarians come from non-noble backgrounds. In comparison with the nuns, more than

90 per cent of whom came from gentry families, more than a third of the priests self-identify as being of non-gentry stock—e.g. describing themselves as *media sors* ('the middling sort')[66] or as *honestae conditionis* ('of honest condition') or pursuing a particular trade (merchant, tailor, clothworker).[67] No-one self-identified as a yeoman or husbandman. And many of these plebeian Catholics came from places where we have no evidence from the recusancy rolls of a strong Catholic presence. There may have been far more Catholics under the radar of the state than has been realised.

One dynasty of non-noble Catholics who may have played a vital part in the dissemination of Catholic ideas are the Shorts of Bury St Edmunds, who produced eight doctors and two priests (a Benedictine and a Dominican) in the period 1660–1750.[68] Two members of the family were amongst those thrust into power in Bury during the reign of James II. Notoriously, James took on the whole Protestant establishment, removing three quarters of the Lords Lieutenant and replacing them by Catholics and removing three quarters of all Justices of the Peace, replacing them by a mixture of Protestant Dissenters and Catholics, and purging the corporations of towns, again removing the vast majority of conformist Protestants. All this was prelude to an audacious and doomed attempt to pack the House of Commons with men who would agree to revoke the Test Acts and the Penal Laws, thus removing all legal discrimination against Catholics. Boroughs where MPs were elected just by the corporation (aldermen and common council) were especially vulnerable, and Bury St Edmunds proved an extreme case. The Compton Census had identified only forty Catholics in a population of 3,693 in Bury, but in successive purges of the corporation, several of them were given prominent places in the government of the town. The appointed mayor, John Stafford, was a Catholic silk merchant and the aldermanic bench was strengthened not only by two members of the Short family but also by local gentry with town houses in Bury, including Ambrose Rookwood. The fanatical convert Henry Jermyn, Lord Dover, now a privy counsellor and Lord Lieutenant, oversaw the transformation from his brother's house at nearby Rushbrooke Hall.[69] By mid-1688, all was set for Bury to send two MPs willing to do James's bidding at Westminster.

There followed a day of reckoning. After James's attempts to have seven Church of England bishops convicted of criminal libel for opposing his policy of full religious liberty and equality, and in consequence of the birth of a Catholic son and heir to James, leading Protestants invited William of Orange, married to the hitherto Protestant heir to the throne, James's daughter Mary, to invade England to save 'Protestantism and liberty'. William landed on 5 November 1688 and James fled the country in the middle of December as his power melted away. This is normally portrayed as a peaceful or bloodless Revolution (although it was far from bloodless in Ireland or Scotland). And indeed little blood was shed in East Anglia. But there was a popular uprising against the men who had implemented James's catholicising policies. In late November, a mob including many from Bury sacked Lord Dover's own home at Cheveley across the county boundary in Cambridgeshire, then returned to Bury intent on looting and pillaging the homes of James's collaborators. Most of the violence was prevented by the quick intervention of local Protestant gentry, but some damage was done to Catholic homes and to the Jesuit College in the old abbey ruins. Smaller groups also targeted gentry homes in the surrounding district. Catharine Burton's autobiography records that 'in the Revolution in which King James was cast out of the kingdom, the storm which threatened all Catholics fell very heavy upon us, and our house was pillaged to that degree they left us not so much as a chair or a bed, excepting one which escaped their knowledge'. The Jesuits withdrew for a few years and never re-established themselves as openly in the region, returning to their invisible college. But, as Francis Young has demonstrated, the aggressive Catholicism of the late 1680s was soon replaced by the live-and-let-live philosophy which had become more real as the seventeenth century progressed. The Shorts kept on tending to the medical needs of the town, all public memory of the Catholic putsch was erased, Catharine Burton's father was allowed a discreet burial in the hallowed ground of a medieval parish church under Protestant occupation. [70]

East Anglian Catholicism was fervent but furtive, persistent, unflinching and slowly growing. It was no longer being hunted to destruction, but still vulnerable to deep popular prejudice as well as some indulgence. It still had a long way to go before Catholics would achieve full liberty, let alone equality in public life.

Notes

1 Cited in Jackson (2003), pp. 38–65, p. 46.

2 Boothman and Hyde Parker (2006), pp. lx–lxi and 124–5; J. Walter, *Understanding Popular Violence in the English Revolution: The Colchester Plunderers* (Cambridge: Cambridge University Press, 1999). For the riots in 1688, see Chapter 3 below.

3 Calculated from the county tables in Bellenger (1984), p. 247.

4 A. C. Ryan, 'Tunstall, Thomas (*d.* 1616)', in *ODNB*, vol. 55, p. 557. See Appendix 1 below.

5 T. Cooper (rev. M. E. Williams), 'Heath, Henry [*name in religion* Paul of St Magdalen] (*bap.* 1599, *d.* 1643)', in *ODNB*, vol. 26, pp. 173–4. See Appendix 1 below.

6 G. Scott, 'Three Seventeenth-Century Benedictine Martyrs', in D. H. Farmer (ed.), *Benedict's Disciples* (Leominster: Fowler Wright Books, 1980), pp. 266–82. See Appendix 1 below.

7 P. Caraman, *Henry Morse: Priest of the Plague* (London: Catholic Book Club [1957]); P. Holmes, 'Morse, Henry (1595–1645)', in *ODNB*, vol. 39, pp. 363–4. See Appendix 1 below.

8 To these we can add Bd Arthur Bell OFM, martyred on 11 December 1643 after being captured in Stevenage. He had been Franciscan Provincial for Scotland before coming to England in 1634. He was in the Household of Viscountess Rivers, certainly in Colchester, and quite possibly at Melford Hall in Suffolk. Although born in Worcestershire, he was educated by his mother's family at Acton Place, Suffolk. See T. Cooper (rev. M. E. Williams), 'Bell, Arthur [*name in religion* Francis] (1591–1643)', in *ODNB*, vol. 4, p. 906. See Appendix 1 below.

9 A. Barclay, 'The Rise of Edward Coleman', *The Historical Journal* 42 (1999), pp. 109–31. This article is well summarised in A. Barclay, 'Colman [Coleman], Edward (1636–1678)', in *ODNB*, vol. 12, pp. 760–1. Another victim of the Popish Plot was Ven. Thomas Downes, who died in prison on trumped up charges in 1678. His mother was a Bedingfield and he had served as a domestic chaplain to James, Duke of York. See Appendix 1 below.

10 M. Nicholls, 'Rookwood, Ambrose (*c.* 1578–1606)', in *ODNB*, vol. 47, pp. 699–700. His great-grandson and namesake was executed as a principal in the foiled Jacobite plot to assassinate William III in 1696 (P. Hopkins, 'Rookwood, Ambrose (1664–1696)', in *ODNB* vol. 47, pp. 700–1).

11   For some examples, see A. Kenny (ed.), *The Responsa Scholarum of the English College, Rome* (London: Catholic Record Society, 1962–3), vol. 1, pp. 259, 338. Kenny prints the lives in their original Latin with English summaries.

12   Calculated from the recusancy rolls in The National Archives, Kew, Exchequer E377 by Blackwood (2001), pp. 117–18.

13   Blackwood (2001), p. 118 and map.

14   R. W. Ketton-Cremer, *Norfolk in the Civil Wars* (London: Faber and Faber, 1969), p. 49.

15   For an admirably clear example of the process at work for an East Anglia Catholic family, see Young (2012a), pp. 456–9.

16   One of these scholars systematically went through the Calendars looking for specific cases, the other used a number of lists drawn up at different stages of the process. The key record used by both is M. A. Everett Green (ed.), *The Calendar of the Committee for Compounding with Delinquents* (London: The Public Record Office, 1889), 5 vols.

17   I can find no trace of this man in any other records, and in any case as a papist in arms he was excluded from composition, so I fear this is probably an error on Lindley's part.

18   K. Lindley, 'The Part played by Catholics', in B. Manning (ed.), *Politics, Religion and the English Civil War* (London: Edward Arnold, 1973), pp. 127–76, at pp. 135, 147–52.

19   And we can be sure that none of these served in arms: no one with those surnames appears in the comprehensive dictionary of Royalist officers: P. R. Newman, *Royalist Officers in England and Wales 1642–1660* (New York: Garland, 1981).

20   C. Firth and R. S. Rait (eds), *Acts and Ordinances of the Civil Wars and under the Interrregnum* (London: HMSO, 1911), vol. 2, pp. 520–45, 591–8, 623–52.

21   It is possible that he was in King's Lynn when Cromwell captured it in late 1643, although we are only told this third-hand; and it is true that he was imprisoned in the Tower of London for almost all of 1646 and 1647 for reasons that are not known. But he does appear to have been released at the end of 1647 and allowed to sue (unsuccessfully) to compound in June 1648 (J. H. Pollen (ed.), 'Bedingfield Papers', in *Miscellanea VI* (London: Catholic Record Society, 1906), pp. 2–4).

22   W. J. Sheils, 'Bedingfield [Bedingfeld] family (*per.* 1476–1760)', in *ODNB*, vol. 4, pp. 782–5; Newman (1981), p. 21.

23   The results were resorted parish by parish in three columns giving the number of conformists, of popish recusants and of Protestant dissenters. It includes numbers but not names.

24 A. Whiteman and M. Clapinson (eds), *The Compton Census of 1676: A Critical Edition* (Oxford: Oxford University Press, 1986), p. lxxviii.

25 Trappes-Lomax (1958), pp. 27–46.

26 Whiteman and Clapinson (1986), p. xxix.

27 This very much reinforces the historian of early modern Cambridgeshire: M. Spufford, *Contrasting Communities: English villagers in the sixteenth and seventeenth century* (Cambridge: Cambridge University Press, 1974), p. 270: 'Cambridgeshire was one of the least papistically-inclined counties in the country.'

28 *Ibid.*, pp., 155–69 (Cambridgeshire and Isle of Ely), pp. 201–30 (Norfolk), 231–41 (half of Suffolk).

29 *Ibid.*

30 This has to be impressionistic; but I would think about 30.

31 Whiteman and Clapinson (1986), pp. 195, 238.

32 Dymond and Martin (1988), pp. 88–9. Her map gives locations but does not identify each one as a place or by a family.

33 For Catharine Burton, see Appendix 1 below.

34 F. Young, '"An Horrid Popish Plot": The Failure of Catholic Aspirations in Bury St. Edmunds, 1685–88', *Proceedings of the Suffolk Institute of Archaeology and History* 41 (2006), pp. 209–25, at pp. 214–16.

35 For extracts from four *Manuals of Prayer* across the seventeenth century, see J. Saward, J. Morrill and M. Tomko (eds), *Firmly I Believe and Truly: The Spiritual Tradition of Catholic England from 1483–1999* (Oxford: Oxford University Press, 2011), pp. 134–7, 182–6, 223–8, 241–5.

36 Young (2006), pp. 215–17; T. Hunter, *An English Carmelite: The Life of Catherine Burton, Mother Mary Xaveria of the Angels* (London, 1876), pp. 29–66.

37 Pollen (1906), pp. 4–13.

38 *Ibid.*, p. 9 and referencing H. Thurston, *Stations of the Cross* (London: Burns and Oates, 1906), p. 75.

39 *Ibid.*, pp. 22–34.

40 There are extracts from her *Memorials* in Saward, Morrill and Tomko (2011), pp. 158–60. See also Appendix 1 below.

41 These are impressionistic and provisional findings, based on such family papers as are in print and more particularly on the autobiographical material to be found in the *Responsa* of men entering the Venerable English College in Rome and on material in the modern collective biography of English nuns

(http://wwtn.history.qmul.ac.uk/). For further discussion, see below.

[42] The classic study is by Walsham (1993).

[43] *Ibid.*, p.1

[44] *Ibid.*, pp.1–2.

[45] *Ibid.* Pollen (1906) cites the *Calendar of State Papers Domestic* for July 1639 but I have been unable to locate this document.

[46] This is the result of a major AHRC-funded project and the results are freely available on the project's website (http://wwtn.history.qmul.ac.uk/). To find any of the people or families mentioned in what follows, simply visit the site and enter the names of the people concerned into the search engine. To achieve these totals, I simply in turn entered the names of the three counties into the 'place association' pane. As I sorted out those born and educated in each of the counties, I noticed that there were a significant number whose mother came from Norfolk or Suffolk but who was married to a Catholic living elsewhere in England.

[47] For some short biographies of the otherwise under-represented Isle of Ely (fenland) part of Cambridgeshire, see Young (2015c).

[48] Bellenger (1984).

[49] This is working from the county lists collected at *ibid.*, pp. 131, 177–9, 183–4 and the table on p. 247

[50] This is confirmed from material in Bellenger (1984), pp. 131, 177–9, 183–4.

[51] T. M. McCoog (ed.), *English and Welsh Jesuits 1555–1650* (London: Catholic Record Society, 1994), 2 vols; G. Holt (ed.), *English and Welsh Jesuits 1650–1829* (London: Catholic Record Society, 1984).

[52] Kenny (1962–3) vol. 2, pp. 464–5.

[53] *Ibid.*, vol. 1, pp. 4–5.

[54] *Ibid.*, vol. 2, pp. 536–7.

[55] *Ibid.*, vol. 1, pp. 3–4.

[56] *Ibid.*, vol. 1, pp. 183–4.

[57] *Ibid.*, vol. 1, pp. 99–103.

[58] *Ibid.*, vol. 1, pp. 152, 153.

[59] *Ibid.*, vol. 1, pp. 162–3.

[60] The books referred to here are J. Jewel, *Apologia ecclesiae Anglicanae* (London, 1562); J. Rastell, *A briefe shew of the false wares packt together in the named, Apology of the Churche of England* (Louvain, 1567); T. Harding, *A confutation of a booke intituled An apologie of the Church of England* (Antwerp, 1565).

61   Kenny (1962–3), vol. 1, pp. 84–7. See also M. Questier, *Catholicism and Community in Early Modern England: Politics, Aristocratic Patronage and Religion, c. 1550–1640* (Cambridge: Cambridge University Press, 2006), pp. 202 and n., 238, 315–16, 320n., 321.

62   Adolph (1999), pp. 144–60.

63   Kenny (1962–3), vol. 2, pp. 500–1.

64   *Ibid.*, vol. 2, pp. 548–9

65   *Ibid.*, vol. 2, pp. 658–9

66   For example Thomas Cowper, *ibid.*, vol. 2, p. 549; William Draper, *ibid.*, vol. 2, p. 642.

67   *Ibid.*, vol. 2, pp. 129, 133; 183–4, 464–5.

68   Young (2008), pp. 188–94.

69   For Dover, see J. Miller, 'Jermyn, Henry, third Baron Jermyn and Jacobite earl of Dover (*bap.* 1636, *d.* 1708)', in *ODNB*, vol. 30, pp. 46–7, and Appendix 1 below.

70   P. Murrell, 'Bury St Edmunds and the Campaign to pack Parliament, 1687–8'; *Bulletin of the Institute of Historical Research* 54 (1981), pp. 188–206; Young (2006), pp. 209–26.

East Anglian Catholics in the Eighteenth Century, 1688–1829

Francis Young

I T IS POSSIBLE that the years between 1688 and 1829 saw a greater transformation in East Anglian Catholic life than any other period chronicled in this volume. The last decade of the seventeenth century began with many Catholics in hiding or in exile, while Catholic chapels in Bury St Edmunds and Norwich were smouldering ruins. By the early nineteenth century, public attitudes to Catholicism had changed so much that several religious orders fleeing from the French Revolution were able to take refuge in the region, and many French priests were ministering openly and founding missions in towns where no Catholic life of any kind had existed before. Where once gentry families had been the mainstay of the Catholic faith, priests ran their own self-funded chapels, and by 1829 handsome Catholic churches had sprung up at Norwich, Bungay, Thetford, Withermarsh Green and elsewhere. This chapter will explore the ways in which the East Anglian Catholic community survived the so-called 'long eighteenth century'. It was a period in which Catholics weathered stricter penal laws, the dynastic politics of Jacobitism and the threat of genealogical extinction, before the French Revolution at the end of the century heralded a gradual transformation in both popular attitudes and the legal position of Catholics.

The 'long eighteenth century' considered in this chapter is a construct of historians who see the period from the 'Glorious' Revolution of 1688 to the Reform Act of 1832 as a single period in Britain's political development. This is true insofar as it was the era in which Britain moved towards constitutional monarchy, although the significant support that Jacobite risings could still command in 1715 and 1745 demonstrated that the fledgling constitutional monarchy was by no means as stable as it seemed at the end of the century. Furthermore, Great Britain itself did not exist until the Act of Union of 1707, and Ireland's incorporation into the Union did not take place until 1801. However, there is a certain logic to treating the period 1688–1829 as a single era in the history of English Catholicism, framed by the repeal of James II's Declarations of Indulgence and the final award of civil and political rights to Catholics in 1829. In the intervening years, Catholics endured a long and weary pilgrimage through the wilderness and, until the 1750s, were liable to be accused of disloyalty not only because they refused to conform to the established church, but also because they were presumed to be supporters of the Jacobite claimant.

The history of Catholic emancipation is long and complex, but its roots lay in the British government's need to accommodate the religious beliefs and practices of two Catholic colonies: Quebec, which was captured from the French in 1763, and Ireland, where a Protestant religious settlement had failed to make inroads into the country's majority religion and a burgeoning Catholic middle class was making its voice heard. A significant motivation for the First Catholic Relief Act of 1778 was the need to grant commissions in the British army to Irish Catholics. Even the very limited provisions of this act, however, met with strong resistance and provoked the 'Gordon Riots' in London and elsewhere in 1780. However, the outbreak of the French Revolution and persecution of Catholics by the revolutionary government had a transformative effect on English attitudes to Catholicism, at least among the aristocracy and gentry — the more radical citizens of the city of Norwich did not share such a negative view of the Revolution.

The Second Catholic Relief Act of 1791 permitted Catholics to worship at licensed chapels for the first time, and Great Britain's union with Ireland in 1801 increased the pressure on the government to extend the franchise to Catholics. Tory resistance held back Liberal emancipation bills throughout the 1820s, and the eventual passage of the Roman Catholic Relief Act of 1829 heralded the resignation of the Duke of Wellington and the election of the Liberal government that brought in the Reform Act of 1832, which extended the franchise and put an end to 'rotten boroughs'. Catholics moved from their position in the 1690s as a marginalised minority whose existence the government was determined to stamp out to a confident Nonconformist minority in the 1820s, with their own chapels, societies and openly acknowledged ecclesiastical organisation. However, toleration of Catholics in East Anglia was nothing new, and the East Anglian gentry proved time and again that ties of sociability mattered more than differences in religion. Slowly but surely, after a rocky start in the years 1688–1715, life got better for East Anglian Catholics in the eighteenth century, as confessional differences receded in importance and

Protestants came to realise that Catholics in their communities presented no threat to the *status quo*.

Few in 1688 would have anticipated that mutual toleration between Catholics and Protestants would ever become the norm. The days preceding William of Orange's invasion of England on 5 November saw the worst outbreaks of religious violence in East Anglia since the Civil Wars. In Bury St Edmunds, a Catholic called Mr Prettyman was killed trying to defend the 'Mass house' attached to the Jesuit College in the abbey ruins, which was pulled down by an angry mob. Another mob attacked the home of Henry Jermyn, Lord Dover, at Cheveley in Cambridgeshire, and private houses of Catholics in Bury and Norwich were ransacked and pulled down.[1] In response, Catholics went to ground. The Jesuits of the College of the Holy Apostles took refuge at the home of Thomas Burton at Beyton, a few miles outside Bury, while other Catholics who had been prominent in local government escaped abroad. Events in Norwich followed a similar course, and the Jesuit chapel located in one of the old monastic granaries between St Andrew's and the River Wensum was burnt down on 7 and 8 December 1688.[2]

In response to Catholic support for the regime of James II, the new government of William and Mary brought in draconian new laws aimed at squeezing the Catholic community out of existence. The Double Land Tax of 1692 meant that any taxes had to be paid twice on land owned by a Catholic. This penalised Catholics but also discouraged non-Catholics from tenanting Catholic-owned land, since they might end up paying the tax. The Popery Act of 1698 disqualified anyone who refused to take the Oath of Allegiance (which included an explicit renunciation of transubstantiation, so as to exclude Catholics) from inheriting or purchasing land, making provision for their existing lands to pass to their Protestant next of kin. Given the extreme pressure exerted by the law, it is remarkable that none of East Anglia's prominent Catholic families conformed to the established church at this time.

Popular distrust of Catholics was exacerbated by the behaviour of a minority determined to unseat the new government. In 1696, Ambrose Rookwood, the younger brother of Thomas Rookwood of Coldham Hall, was executed for high treason for his participation in the Barclay Conspiracy, a plot by soldiers in the service of the exiled James II to assassinate William of Orange while his coach was driving through Hyde Park. As a result of his brother's actions, Thomas Rookwood was forced to spend the next nine years in exile while his estates were mismanaged by another younger brother. However, the local gentry evidently did not feel that Thomas should be judged by his brother's behaviour, and in 1703 they even petitioned Queen Anne for him to be restored to his lands.[3]

For some, exile was a permanent option, such as Henry Timperley of Hintlesham, who sold up in 1721 and apparently moved to France.[4] One member of the Tasburgh family likewise moved to Champagne as a naturalised French subject, changing his name to 'Tasbourg'.[5] Most, however, were determined to survive, and they adopted the usual cunning devices to do so. Wealthy Catholics vested their lands in trusts in order to avoid fines and confiscation, and as in previous generations, poorer Catholics survived with the protection and support of the wealthy. However, the patrons of Catholic missions were not always members of the landed gentry. In Bury St Edmunds a dynasty of medical doctors, the Short family, patronised a mission that may have been founded as early as

1691, when the secular priest Hugh (or Henry) Owen arrived in the town. Originally from the Isle of Man, Owen ministered in inns and coffee houses until his death in 1741, braving regular epidemics of smallpox and measles.[6]

In 1687, East Anglia had become part of the new Midland District, whose Vicars Apostolic were usually based as far away as Staffordshire. At such a great distance from episcopal authority, East Anglia was a patchwork of scattered missions, and apart from the chapels in Norwich and Bury St Edmunds they were virtually all supported by gentry patrons. Priests often rode out from Catholic houses to serve a circuit of Mass centres on a so-called 'riding mission'. Major centres included Costessey Hall and Oxburgh Hall in Norfolk, Sawston Hall in Cambridgeshire and Hengrave Hall, Coldham Hall, Melford Place and Flixton Hall in Suffolk. By the 1740s, a Vicar Forane appointed by the Vicar Apostolic of the Midland District had authority over the secular priests in East Anglia and administered four separate mission funds: one for Bury St Edmunds (West Suffolk), one for King's Lynn (West Norfolk), one for the rest of Norfolk and an 'itinerant fund' for everywhere else, presumably the areas most sparsely populated by Catholics (Cambridgeshire and East Suffolk).[7]

However, the secular clergy were by no means the only players in the East Anglian mission. By the early years of the eighteenth century, the main Jesuit mission in the region was at Stoke-by-Nayland, where the Mannock family owned Giffords Hall. In 1717 the Benedictines, whose earliest mission was at Flixton Hall, arrived at Coldham Hall, and by the 1730s they had taken over the mission at Hengrave Hall. The monks subsequently took over the town mission in

Bury St Edmunds on Hugh Owen's death in 1741.[8] Two monks remained in charge of the Bury mission until 1755, when it was taken over by the Jesuit John Gage.[9] Gage built a new chapel and inaugurated a long period of Jesuit mission in Bury that only ended in 1929, when the church of St Edmund, King and Martyr, was handed over to the secular clergy of the Diocese of Northampton.

In the early eighteenth century the Catholic community in East Anglia was troubled by the continental controversy between the Jesuits and Jansenists concerning the theology of grace. The leading lay supporter of the Jansenist position in England was the physician Richard Short of Bury St Edmunds (1641–1708), who had served briefly on the Bury Corporation in James II's reign and believed that most of the misfortunes that had befallen Catholics in England could be traced back to the extremism of the Jesuits.[10] Jansenists adopted a severe interpretation of the Council of Trent's theology of grace, rejecting many popular devotions promoted by the Jesuits, and opposed the Jesuit emphasis on papal authority. Short translated the works of the prominent Jansenist Pasquier Quesnel and, in the year of his death, even invited Quesnel to move to England (the invitation was not taken up). Short did not live to see Quesnel and Jansenism condemned by Pope Clement XI's bull *Unigenitus* in 1713.

In spite of the condemnation of the Jansenists, the Jesuit Francis Mannock (1670–1748), a younger son of Sir Francis Mannock, 2nd Baronet of Giffords Hall, remained concerned about heresy amongst English Catholics. Mannock served in Cheshire, Yorkshire and Staffordshire before returning to Giffords Hall on the outbreak of the Jacobite rising of 1715. He was a fanatical anti-Jansenist who denounced seventy-seven sup-

posedly heretical propositions and tried to persuade
the Vicar Apostolic of the Midland District, John Talbot
Stonor, to forward them to Rome. Stonor concluded
that they 'were nowhere to be met with in print, and
were unworthy of notice, and ... the accusations were
too vague and general—indeed, no one knew when
or by whom they were advanced, as they were not
fathered on anyone'. Eventually, in 1738, Mannock
was able to persuade Thomas Dominic Williams, Vicar
Apostolic of the Northern District, to send his propositions to the Papal Internuncio at Brussels. However,
Williams declined to condemn Mannock's proposi-
tion that 'The most useful way of hearing Mass for the
unschooled who cannot read is to recite the rosary of
the Blessed Virgin Mary'.[11] It is no accident that Williams was a Dominican.

Another member of the Mannock family advocated
a theology with greater popular appeal. John Anselm
Mannock (1681–1749), a younger son of Sir William
Mannock, 3rd Baronet, was educated at St Gregory's,
Douai, where, some time after 1694, he accidentally
killed his brother by dropping a cannon ball from an
upper window. John decided to join St Gregory's as
a Benedictine monk and devoted his life to spiritual
writing, most of which was published posthumously.
Nevertheless, in Joseph Gillow's view 'The "Poor Man's
Catechism" alone stamps his name with immortality',
and this work was indeed reprinted many times, well
into the nineteenth century (in 1752, 1762, 1770, 1797,
1827, 1843, 1848 and 1855). Mannock's *Poor Man's Catechism* was credited with many conversions in the days
before the sophisticated apologetic of the Tractarians,
and appealed to the educated and uneducated alike,
ensuring that Catholicism remained a religion of the
common people.[12]

The prospect of a Jacobite restoration supported by a French invasion was an ever-present reality between 1688 and the final defeat of Prince Charles Edward Stuart at Culloden in 1746, and in 1715 and 1744 special instructions were issued to magistrates to make lists of 'popish Nonjurors' (i.e. Catholics) and confiscate horses and firearms from the Catholic population. The Jacobite army reached Derby in December 1745, and it was thought that the Jacobites' next move might be to march towards Cambridge and rendezvous with a sea-borne French invasion on the Suffolk coast. The First Regiment of Guards was despatched to defend Huntingdon.[13] Nevertheless, although rumours circulated of a priest inciting Catholics to join the Jacobite cause at Bungay and Wymondham in 1745,[14] most Catholics seem to have taken little or no notice of events in the north. Sir William Gage of Hengrave, a conspicuous loyalist, rode to Euston Hall to pledge his support for George II to the Duke of Grafton. When he realised his guns and horses were about to be confiscated, Gage reached a gentleman's agreement to deposit them for safekeeping with one of his Protestant tenants, and the constables subsequently filed an implausible report that none of his horses was worth more than five shillings.[15] When it came to the landed gentry, social deference prevailed, whatever their religion.

Some East Anglian Catholics, especially those with strong Jacobite sympathies, made the decision to leave England entirely and enter the service of foreign governments. Thomas Rookwood received a French knighthood at some point during his long exile between 1688 and 1705,[16] and Sir Thomas Dereham (d. 1739), the nephew of the English ambassador to the Grand Duchy of Tuscany, established himself in Florence in 1718 as a mediator between the courts of the Grand Duke, the Pope and King James III (the 'Old Pretender'). However, as an Italianised Englishman, Dereham also mediated between the Royal Society in London and scientists in Florence, playing a key but still largely unrecognised role in the European Enlightenment in the 1720s.[17] Dereham's splendid memorial, by the sculptor Fillippo della Valle, can still be seen in the chapel of the English College, Rome, commemorating the last of the Derehams of West Dereham.[18]

The Jesuits and Benedictines in England were organised independently of the secular clergy, and although in theory the Pope expected them to recognise the authority of the Vicar Apostolic, there was little incentive for them to do so, since the financial wherewithal for their mission came from their gentry patrons. Gentry control of the clergy meant that priests felt obliged to side with their patrons in ecclesiastical disputes, as happened in 1753 when Alban Butler, then chaplain at the Duke's Palace in Norwich, was tasked by the Vicar Apostolic with promulgating a bull of Benedict XIV that required regular clergy to return regularly to their mother house. Thomas Rookwood Gage of Coldham Hall was outraged that 'his' priests would be absent for part of the year, and his Jesuit chaplain accordingly declined to sign the document—notwithstanding a special vow of obedience to the Pope.[19]

Chaplains to the gentry did much more than just minister to the spiritual needs of the household: John Champion at Sawston Hall communicated with his fellow Jesuit in London, Edward Galloway, asking him to send anchovies, oysters and herrings down to Cambridgeshire and helped to arrange the marriage of Richard Huddlestone to Jane Belchier in the 1730s.[20] The Benedictine chaplain at Hengrave Hall, Francis Howard, was asked to draw up a pedigree of the Gage family,[21] and both Howard and his confrere Alexius Jones, the Bond family's chaplain, were obliged to accompany their patrons on a fishing trip to Thetford to escape smallpox in Bury St Edmunds in 1733.[22] In 1769 James Dennett, the Jesuit chaplain at Coldham Hall, accompanied the son of Sir Thomas Rookwood Gage, 5th Baronet, on the Grand Tour as his tutor.[23] In addition to these domestic responsibilities, many of the regular clergy also served in official capacities within their orders as Superior of the College of the Holy Apostles (Jesuits), or definitor or procurator of the province (Benedictines). Versatility was a requisite quality in the eighteenth-century missionary priest.

By the 1760s the Jacobite threat was long gone, and Catholics became more confident in their public expressions of faith. In 1761, assisted by donations from the Jesuit Provincial, James Dennett, his uncle Sir William Gage and his brother Sir Thomas Rookwood-Gage, as well as legacies left by his mother Elizabeth Rookwood, the Jesuit John Gage opened the first semi-public chapel in East Anglia in Westgate Street, Bury St Edmunds. The Chapel of the Immaculate Conception was invisible from the street but was attached to the back of a handsome red-brick house; unlike previous chapels, it was on the ground floor and a purpose-built structure of ecclesiastical appearance, with modest Gothic plasterwork and permanent fittings.[24] The chapel was replaced in 1836 by the huge church of St Edmund, King and Martyr, next door, but survived as a drawing room for the presbytery. In 1979, the wall between the chapel and the church was knocked through and the chapel re-consecrated as the Blessed Sacrament Chapel, as it remains to this day.

A few years after the opening of Gage's chapel, in 1764, the 10th Duke of Norfolk built a new chapel

attached to the Palace in Norwich for the secular
priest Edward Beaumont, with public access from St
Andrew's Street.[25] This later became a waiting room for
the Poor Law guardians' offices, but was demolished
in 1974, along with the rest of the remaining buildings
of the Duke's Palace, to make way for a multi-storey
car park. However, like Gage's chapel in Bury it was a
semi-public space that was invisible from the outside
but made no attempt to hide its purpose from within:
gone were the days of attic chapels that could be dis-
mantled in minutes at the first sign of an informant.

We are fortunate to have an extremely detailed snap-
shot of East Anglia's Catholic community in the year
1767, when the government ordered a census of all
papists to be made by incumbents of parishes in every
diocese. The records kept in most dioceses gave the
ages and professions of Catholics yet omitted names,
but a surviving copy of the census for the Diocese of
Norwich (which covered all of Norfolk and Suffolk)
features names as well. This was edited by Joy Rowe
in 1996, and reveals that the highest concentration of
Catholics in the diocese was in Norwich, followed by
Bury St Edmunds. The analysis of the 'top ten' parishes with high concentrations of Catholics in the table
below reveals that six out of ten were urban, which
casts doubt on the idea that Catholicism was a rural
gentry phenomenon in East Anglia in the second half
of the eighteenth century.

However, the four rural parishes that do make the
top ten, Costessey, Stoke-by-Nayland, Stanningfield
and Oxburgh, were indeed communities sustained by
gentry patronage (the Jerninghams, Mannocks, Rookwood Gages and Bedingfields respectively). Furthermore, Catholics were spread fairly evenly between
Norfolk and Suffolk. However, the observation that

Catholicism was an urban phenomenon needs to be qualified by the fact that Catholics were almost entirely absent from Ipswich (a single 'Surgeon and reputed priest' in the parish of St Matthew) and Cambridge (whose only Catholic was a gardener's wife living in the parish of St Benedict).[26] The city of Peterborough recorded no Catholics at all. The 1,286 Catholics in the Dioceses of Norwich and Ely made up just 1.89 per cent of the total Catholic population of England recorded in 1767 (although it is to be noted that E. S. Worrall's analysis excluded Chester, the diocese with the highest Catholic population since it included Lancashire).[27]

Table 2. Parishes with high concentrations of Catholics in 1767[28]

PARISH	COUNTY	NUMBER OF CATHOLICS
Bury St Edmunds St Mary	Suffolk	80
Costessey	Norfolk	80
Bury St Edmunds St James	Suffolk	72
Stoke-by-Nayland	Suffolk	38
Norwich St Peter Mountergate	Norfolk	34
Norwich St Stephen	Norfolk	32
Stanningfield	Suffolk	32
Norwich St Swithin	Norfolk	30
Oxburgh	Norfolk	27
Norwich St Laurence	Norfolk	25

The earliest surviving complete record of confirmations administered by a Vicar Apostolic in East Anglia dates from the summer of 1768, when Bishop Joseph Hornyold undertook what must have been a punishing journey across the region.[29] The confirmations testify to the vitality of Catholicism, especially in Norwich, which had by far the largest number of confirmands in the whole Midland District that year. The confirmations began at Great Staughton in Huntingdonshire on 19 June, where Hornyold confirmed 9 people. He then travelled into Norfolk, confirming another 9 at Buckenham on 24 June, 7 at Bodney two days later and 13 people at Oxburgh (including 4 who had come from King's Lynn) on 29 June. At the Jesuit chapel in Norwich on 3 July he confirmed no less than 80, and 101 at the Duke's Palace chapel on the same day. On 6 July he administered the sacrament to 58 people at Costessey, and then to 21 (including 3 from Flixton) at Coulsey Wood on 12 July.

Carrying on into Suffolk, the Bishop confirmed 31 people at Bury St Edmunds on 17 July and 18 at Coldham two days later. They included the fifteen-year-old Elizabeth Simpson (the future Elizabeth Inchbald), who took the confirmation name Anna. Finally, Hornyold travelled south-east to Stoke-by-Nayland and confirmed 11 people in St Nicholas' chapel at Giffords Hall on 24 July.[30] The confirmation registers demonstrate that, in this pre-industrial period before major Irish immigration, Norwich could reasonably be considered one of the principal Catholic centres of the Midland District. However, they also show that Catholicism in East Anglia was far from just an urban phenomenon. Geographically dispersed riding missions were a major feature of East Anglian Catholic life and sustained small communities in surprising places, such as Coulsey Wood House, in the parish of Stoke Ash between Needham Market and Scole. Founded by the Bedingfields of Redlingfield, by the middle of the eighteenth century the house was rented by the Catholic Farrill family, but by the 1760s a shortage of priests meant that the mission was increasingly difficult to staff and it fell to John Gage in far-away Bury St Edmunds to resolve the problem.[31]

Riding missions were partly driven by the missionary zeal of priests who chose to spend hours in the saddle, but they were also created by the laity's desire to have Mass said in a convenient place and reflected the wider problem of lay control of the missionary agenda; Gage found himself in dispute with the Catholic gentry over Coulsey Wood for this very reason. In the late eighteenth century, the only priest to the south of Bury St Edmunds was the Jesuit chaplain at Coldham Hall, who was obliged to take responsibility for the Catholics of Long Melford and the Stour Valley. In 1786 John Baptist Newton complained bitterly of 'ignorance, stupidity and sometimes a total neglect of religion, attended with such indifference as one would not expect to meet with even in a Canadian who had once learned the truth taught in the Gospel'. He went on to complain that 'I carry the blessed sacrament twenty or thirty miles to people as full of health as I am myself, and only because they do not think it worth their while to wait upon Almighty God at Coldham'.[32]

Newton may have been appalled by the ignorance he encountered, but the sporadic nature of contact with priests in rural areas probably made this inevitable. When priests did make contact, the impact was often long-lasting; in 1826, a Woolpit woman in her nineties recalled that a 'Pilgrimage of Holy Nuns from Ireland' came to visit the holy well of Our Lady of Woolpit; Clive Paine suggested that these might have been the Augustinian canonesses who stayed at Hengrave between 1794 and 1802,[33] but the woman was recalling a story she had heard in her youth rather than the recent past. It is possible to interpret the nuns from Ireland as a garbled memory of much older missionary activity. In the 1690s Catharine Burton of Beyton, a future Carmelite nun and her brother, a future Jesuit, regularly visited the well at Woolpit, and Catharine's confessor was the Jesuit Francis Rockley, known to Catharine as Fr Ireland.[34] Local people still resorted to the well at Woolpit for its healing properties in the early nineteenth century, and there are good reasons to believe that Woolpit, rather than Walsingham, was the East Anglian shrine of Our Lady that survived the Reformation and remained a place of pilgrimage. As late as the 1890s, one man found elderly people in remote Norfolk cottages with little or no knowledge of the Catholic faith preserving rosaries, medals and holy pictures that had been given to their forebears by Catholic priests.[35]

In 1773 Pope Clement XIV dealt what was apparently a considerable blow to the Catholic mission in East Anglia by suppressing the Society of Jesus. However, in reality the suppression had little effect on Jesuits in the region, who stopped using the title 'Jesuit' but retained their provincial and collegiate organisation as a society of secular priests. In practice, the suppression was unenforceable in England in any real way. Nevertheless, whether connected to the suppression of the Jesuits or not, from a probable peak in the 1760s East Anglian Catholicism seems to have gone into a slow decline. If the figures collected by Anglican clergy in the next Census of Papists are to be believed, by 1780 East Anglia's Catholic population had shrunk by 9 per cent to 1,170.[36] On 29 June 1778 Bishop Talbot came to Norwich and delivered a sermon 'On doing good, and doing it well' before confirming 86 people from the Jesuit mission and 25 from the Duke's Palace,[37] a total of 111, compared to 181 in 1768.

In 1784, the French aristocrat François de la Rochefoucauld visited Suffolk and recorded his impressions of the Catholic community in Bury St Edmunds: 'The

Justice of the Peace always evades the rigour of the law', he reported, and 'never is it put into force'. De la Rochefoucauld observed that 'Catholics feel completely at ease: despite the severity of the laws against them, they practise their religion without concealment, and everyone knows without demurring'. Furthermore, Catholics worshipped 'on Sundays and Feast Days without the least trouble'. At the same time, however, it was clear to de la Rochefoucauld that Catholics were 'absolutely separated from the body politic of the English'. Yet he reflected wittily that the piety of East Anglian Catholics contrasted favourably with French attitudes: 'I find the Catholics much more zealous in England than in France: they are more scrupulous in their religious observance: it is because they are discriminated against. It is the disposition of all men in all countries to like doing what is forbidden'.[38]

The First Catholic Relief Act of 1778 had little effect on the everyday life of English Catholics, and the violence of the anti-Catholic Gordon Riots in London in 1780 did not spread to East Anglia. However, the popular backlash at this time did cause Charles Howard, Earl of Surrey, to conform to the Church of England.[39] Howard became Duke of Norfolk in 1786 and, although the Howards had not lived at their Norwich Palace since 1710, the Duke remained a significant landowner in East Anglia and a protector of Catholic interests. The accession of a Protestant Duke led to the closure of the chapel in the Duke's Palace,[40] causing Edward Beaumont to move his congregation to three garret rooms in a house in Willow Lane.[41]

In 1791 the Second Catholic Relief Act allowed Catholic chapels to receive a licence for the first time as authorised places of worship, provided they did not advertise their purpose from the outside or summon the faithful by bells. In Bury St Edmunds, John Gage's chapel became one of the first in the country to receive such a licence, while in Norwich the new climate of freedom allowed Beaumont to purchase a plot of land on 'the Dancing Master's Estate' in St John's Alley, behind Strangers' Hall and across the lane from the church of St John the Baptist, Maddermarket.[42] The 'Maddermarket Chapel' opened in 1794 and is still standing to this day, although it is now the Maddermarket Theatre. Most significantly, however, the dedication of this chapel to St John the Baptist, borrowed from the medieval church next door, would eventually become the dedication of the cathedral of the Diocese of East Anglia. Meanwhile, the Jesuit Edward Galloway maintained a chapel in Ten Bell Lane in the parish of St Swithin from around 1750, when the mission was moved from Chapel Field (close to the site of the present St John's Cathedral).[43] The move was funded by a donation of £280 and the sale of property owned by the College of the Holy Apostles in Ringland.[44]

The execution of Louis XVI of France and his Queen Marie Antoinette in 1793 marked the beginning of a severe persecution of Catholics in revolutionary France, as well as heralding Britain's entry into the French revolutionary wars. Hostility to the Revolution amongst England's elite was matched by a corresponding decline in anti-Catholicism, as the aristocracy from George III downwards welcomed persecuted Catholic aristocrats, priests and nuns into exile in England. François de la Rochefoucauld, who had visited Bury during the *ancien régime*, returned to England as an exile, and a number of French priests took up residence in East Anglia, some supported by local Catholics and some self-supporting. Not only did the overstretched Catholic clergy suddenly acquire additional help, but they also benefited from the sympathy extended to the French priests by the population at large.

Table 3. French exiled priests in East Anglia[45]

NAME	LIVED	CONNECTION WITH EAST ANGLIA
Anglade, François	1762–1838	May have stayed with the Huddlestone family at Sawston in 1792
Bedel, Mathieu Jacques ('John Bidell')	–	Lived at Palgrave, Suffolk and said Mass at George Gardiner's house in Botesdale from 1814; chaplain at Thelveton Hall 1824–33
La Bissachere, Jean de le Mounier	–	Performed two baptisms at King's Lynn in January 1816; chaplain at Bodney 1809–11
Chatellier, Charles Louis de Salmon du	d. 1804	Chaplain to prisoner of war camp at Norman Cross, Peterborough in 1807
De Couffon, Émile Claude Marie	–	Living at Dedham in 1799; signed Bury St Edmunds register in 1829 and Stoke-by-Nayland register in 1831–4; Easter communicant at Stoke-by-Nayland 1830–3
La Cour, Joseph Pierre	1758–1846	Died at Sawston
Dacheux, Pierre Louis	1760–1843	At King's Lynn in 1811; signed register there in September 1813; built chapel in Coronation Square in 1828
Desgalois de la Tour, Étienne Jean Baptiste	1754–1820	Chaplain to the prisoner of war camp at Norman Cross, Peterborough 1807–14; lived at the Bell Inn, Stilton
Deterville, Thomas Denis	1768–1843	Teacher of French, Italian and Spanish in Norwich
Le Febvre, Antoine Charles	d. 1828	At Bury St Edmunds in 1794

Fleury, Jean	d. 1828	Chaplain at Sawston, *c.* 1803–28
La Fontaine, Jean Baptiste Fouet de	1739–1821	At Thelveton 1768–74; at Bodney in 1792 and 1795–6; at Bury St Edmunds 1800; at Haughley 1807
Girard, Jean	–	At Bodney 1794–1802
Lavenant, François Mathurin	–	At Bodney 1797–1802
Louvel, Christophe	–	Chaplain at Sawston in 1803
Marie, François	1739–1823	At Coldham Hall in 1801
Martinet	–	At Sawston 1793–8
Le Roux, Louis	1757–1843	At Bodney 1802–11, possibly at Sawston in 1820
Saingevin, Nicolas Jean	1748–1813	At Bodney 1806–9
Simon, Louis Pierre	1768–1839	Naturalised after 1815; began mission register in Ipswich in 1811; opened church in Woodbridge Road in August 1827
Trotier, Louis	–	Chaplain at Bodney

As the above table shows, the number of French priests who sought refuge in East Anglia was quite small (21), but their influence on the life of the Catholic community was disproportionate to their numbers. The French priests did not minister solely to the émigré community and enthusiastically embraced the idea of mission to the English. Some settled in rural areas and began new missions, like Mathieu Jacques Bedel, a priest of the Diocese of Chartres, who was living at Palgrave in Suffolk in 1814 and saying Mass at George Gardiner's house in Botesdale. By 1824, now known by the Anglicised epithet 'John Bidell', he was the chaplain to the Havers family at Thelveton Hall, where he remained until 1833.[46] Other priests supported themselves in other ways, such as Thomas Deterville (or

D'Etreville) who taught French, Italian and Spanish to the young George Borrow in Norwich.

However, the three French priests who bequeathed the most important legacies to East Anglia were perhaps Pierre Louis Dacheux (1760–1843), Étienne Desgalois de la Tour and Louis Pierre Simon (1768–1839), who re-established Catholicism in three important towns that had hitherto been without a permanent Catholic mission. Dacheux established a mission in King's Lynn in 1811 and eventually built a church there in 1828, and Desgalois de la Tour began a prison chaplaincy to the huge prisoner of war camp at Norman Cross near Peterborough. The Masses he celebrated at the Bell Inn in Stilton could be considered the first beginnings of mission in Huntingdonshire and the Peterborough area.

Louis Pierre Simon, the 'Apostle of Ipswich', arrived in the town in February 1793 as a French teacher at John Carter's boarding school in Upper Brook Street. Before 1794, when a state pension was introduced for French priests, the refugees were forced to support themselves in other professions. Simon learnt that a Catholic lady, Margaret Wood, was living with her sister-in-law in Silent Street and began to say Mass in her house.[47] Wood moved several times and Simon followed her to addresses in Carr Street, Pottery Street and St Helen's Street. However, in the early years of the nineteenth century he was appointed chaplain to a garrison of German and Irish troops stationed in Suffolk, which gave him a salary and allowed him to travel to Woodbridge and Harwich to say Mass. The baptismal register at Ipswich commences in 1802, suggesting that a stable core of Catholics had been established by this time.[48]

Following the defeat of Napoleon in 1815, Simon returned to his home town of Rouen, but soon felt called to return to Ipswich and continue his mission there; he purchased a house in Woodbridge Road and intended to build a chapel, although opposition to this plan meant that he had to confine the celebration of Mass to a room of the house at first. Eventually, however, he was able to construct a chapel next to the house: 'This stood east to west and was about 60 feet long and 20 feet wide, with seating for nearly two hundred people. The entrance was by a small door hidden from the road by a cluster of trees'.[49] The chapel was consecrated by the Vicar Apostolic of the Midland District, Thomas Walsh, on 1 August 1827 and was dedicated to St Anthony of Padua. The prospect of seeing 'The Catholic Bishop … in his pontifical robes with the mitre and crozier' attracted many non-Catholics to the consecration Mass.[50]

In addition to the priests, religious communities also sought refuge in East Anglia and monastic life flourished in the region for the first time since 1539. In 1794 the nuns of the ancient Benedictine abbey of Montargis found a home at Bodney Hall in Norfolk; they eventually moved to a new purpose-built monastery at Princethorpe in Warwickshire in 1833.[51] In 1800 the 'Blue Nuns' (Order of the Immaculate Conception of Our Lady), an English community founded in Paris in 1658, settled in Norwich under the protection of the Jerningham family.[52] The Canonesses Regular of St Augustine from Bruges, an exclusively English community whose Convent of Nazareth was known simply as 'the English Convent', settled at Hengrave Hall under the protection of the Rookwood Gage family in 1794; within a month they were able to re-open their school, even though they had just two pupils.[53]

The English Convent had long been a home from home for exiled East Anglian Catholics: both Thomas

Rookwood and his parents took refuge there at times of persecution, his mother was buried in the convent church and his daughter Elizabeth was educated by the canonesses. However, it was a family connection with the Gages through Sr Penelope Stanislaus Gage (1687–1772) that led Sir Thomas Rookwood Gage, 6th Baronet, to offer Hengrave Hall to the community.[54] However, the prioress, Mary More (one of the last descendants of St Thomas More) was determined to return to Bruges and reclaim the Convent of Nazareth after the Peace of Amiens in 1802; the canonesses were one of very few communities to choose to return to the Continent. On their departure the local newspaper praised 'the courtesy shown to their visitors by the sequestered females and their amiable patroness, Mrs. More', but Sir Thomas's steward resented the fact that Mother More insisted on taking with her a tabernacle made for the chapel at Hengrave, which he considered belonged to the house.[55]

Without the contribution of these French priests and nuns, it seems likely that East Anglian Catholicism would have remained confined to the traditional centres of Norwich and Bury St Edmunds and the villages where it was supported by a gentry family. As it was, the establishment of Catholic missions in other towns meant that in later decades, when a large influx of Irish immigrants came to build the railways, there were already Catholic churches for them in many areas. The French priests were free from the burden of gentry patronage, but the native clergy were also beginning to move beyond the traditional role of chaplain. In many cases this was necessitated by the extinction of recusant families; throughout the eighteenth century, a pattern of late marriages ensured that the greatest threat to the old Catholic families was a genealogical one. As Joy Rowe explained, 'The loss to a celibate priesthood of a high proportion of men, the numbers of girls entering convents abroad, both established houses and new foundations for English women, and the attrition of the penal statutes all led to the ruin of a number of gentry families'.[56]

In 1767 the main line of the Gages of Hengrave died out as the 4th Baronet died childless; the estates passed to the Rookwood Gage family, uniting two of Suffolk's great Catholic dynasties. Before the end of the century there were already self-sustaining chapels in Bury St Edmunds and Stanningfield. Anticipating the extinction of the Tasburghs of Flixton (which occurred in 1736), the Benedictine monk Felix Tasburgh made sure that the Benedictine mission in the village had its own source of funding independent of family patronage.[57] The death of George Tasburgh of Bodney in 1783 likewise brought an end to that branch of the family, although the Catholic Crathorne-Tasburghs, relatives by marriage, continued to own Bodney Hall, which originally belonged to the recusant Downes family before the Tasburghs acquired it in the seventeenth century.[58]

Other families that went extinct in this period included the Timperleys of Hintlesham, the Martins of Long Melford and the Mannocks of Giffords Hall, whose last representative, Sir George Mannock, died in an overturned coach at Bures in 1787, just after setting out for Rome to seek dispensation from his Jesuit vows.[59] Other families moved away, such as the Eyres of Bury's Hall near Swaffham, who sold the house in 1746, leaving behind trunks containing 'an apparatus for a chapel'.[60] The sale of a house or the extinction of a family was often disastrous to the local Catholic community, since it meant the end of a Mass centre (or several), and a major setback to the mission of the secular clergy or a particular religious order. Another problem which affected many missions, but which did not prove a major one in East Anglia, occurred when a Protestant branch of a family inherited an estate on the extinction of the Catholic branch, putting an immediate end to mission.

Increasingly, the Catholic community in late eighteenth-century East Anglia was becoming a cosmopolitan one, even apart from the priests and other émigrés from France. The Gage family's ownership of a plantation on the Caribbean island of Montserrat led the Farrill family to migrate from Montserrat to Suffolk, bringing with them a black servant girl who was baptised by John Gage in 1759.[61] Gage's successor at the chapel in Bury St Edmunds was an American Jesuit from Maryland, Charles Thompson, and one of the nuns at Hengrave in the period 1794–1802, Frances Henrietta Jerningham (b. 1745), was also from Maryland, the daughter of a younger son of the Jerninghams who emigrated to America.[62] John Reilly, an Irish-born member of the new gentry, was a key figure in the Suffolk mission, as was the half-Portuguese illegitimate son of Sir William Gage, William Olivarez.[63] The Gages and Jerninghams maintained town houses in London, and the Jerninghams in particular were at the heart of English high society, patronising the Catholic author John Polidori as well as producing their own poet and playwright, Edward Jerningham, an 'exquisitely affected poet' who conformed to the Church of England but nevertheless conveyed messages between the Prince Regent and his Catholic mistress, Mrs Fitzherbert.[64]

However, the most famous East Anglian Catholic of the early nineteenth century was Elizabeth Inchbald (1753–1821), born Elizabeth Simpson at Stanningfield, who was educated by the Jesuit Superior

at Coldham Hall, James Dennett. She later immortal-
ised Dennett as the austere Jesuit 'Mr Sandford' in her
novel *A Simple Story* (1791), which has many signs of
being based on personalities and families she knew
in Suffolk. Although Inchbald left for London in 1772
she frequently returned to East Anglia throughout
her life and was close to the Rookwood Gage family.
A Simple Story was a novel of manners, profoundly
influential on Jane Austen, whose significance lay in
the fact that the main characters were Catholics. Inchbald subverted literary stereotypes of Catholicism in
this and other works, such as her play *The Massacre*
(1792), which was set during the St Bartholomew's Day
Massacre of 1572 (a trope of anti-Catholicism) but was
intended, ironically, to draw attention to contemporary
persecution of Catholics in France.[65]

The early nineteenth century saw a significant
expansion of chapels and churches. If the first generation of Catholic churches consisted of those constructed before and after the Second Catholic Relief Act
of 1791, the second generation in the 1820s displayed
greater confidence in their architecture. One of the first
was St Edmund's, Bungay, which was opened in 1823
after the Benedictine mission at Flixton moved to the
nearby town, but was later replaced by the present
church. Two churches that do survive from the period
are St Mary's, Thetford, and Our Lady Immaculate and
St Edmund, Withermarsh Green. St Mary's, Thetford,
opened in 1824 as a central focus for the old Bacton
mission, which covered south Norfolk and north Suffolk, and is the oldest Catholic church in continuous
use anywhere in East Anglia. Withermarsh Green
replaced the private chapel of the Mannock family in
nearby Giffords Hall in 1827, and was one of the first
Catholic churches in the region to have its own burial

ground. On a visit in March 2014, the oldest tombstone I could discover was that of Mary Paine, who died on 10 November 1828. The interior of the church at Withermarsh Green has been preserved in its original form, and gives a flavour of what Catholic chapels looked like before the vogue for Gothic architecture took hold in the 1840s.

In spite of the significant setbacks it faced during the period, East Anglian Catholicism survived the eighteenth century and even experienced modest growth, especially in the 1760s in Norwich and Bury St Edmunds. However, East Anglia did not see the kind of exponential growth in the Catholic population that took place in the great industrial cities of the North, and although congregations no longer depended entirely on the gentry, the role of the old Catholic gentry in sustaining the Catholic community remained crucial. Even if the gentry did not offer financial support, their social ties with magistrates and other local notables cushioned the impact of the penal laws on Catholics in East Anglia. The antiquity and loyalty of the recusant families commanded a degree of respect from the gentry at large that largely transferred itself to ordinary people, although as late as 1745 locals searched a cart in Suffolk on its way to a Catholic house to check for weapons,[66] and John Stevenson has suggested that anti-Methodist riots in Norwich in 1751–52 had anti-Jacobite and anti-Catholic overtones.[67] Yet by the end of the eighteenth century, partly owing to the French Revolution and partly because they were a small and unthreatening minority in the region, Catholics were accepted and tolerated in East Anglia, at least in those areas where they maintained an established presence.

Notes

[1] Young (2006), pp. 217–19.

[2] *Great Gothic Fane* (1913), p. 71.

[3] On the Rookwood family see Young (2016), pp. xiii–xl.

[4] Ryan and Redstone (1931), pp. 89–91.

[5] Young (2012a), p. 462.

[6] Young (2015a), pp. 117–23. On the Short family see also Young (2008) pp. 188–94.

[7] Young (2015a), p. 138.

[8] *Ibid.*, pp. 109–23.

[9] *Ibid.*, pp. 137–53.

[10] *Ibid.*, pp. 63–5.

[11] J. Gillow, *A Literary and Biographical History, or Biographical Dictionary of the English Catholics* (London: Burns and Oates, 1885–1902), vol. 4, pp. 457–8.

[12] *Ibid.*, vol. 4, pp. 458–61.

[13] F. MacLynn, *The Jacobite Army in England 1745: The Final Campaign* (Edinburgh: John Donald, 1988), pp. 137–8.

[14] N. Rogers, 'Popular Jacobitism in a Provincial Context: 18th Century Bristol and Norwich', in E. Cruickshanks and J. Black (eds), *The Jacobite Challenge* (Edinburgh: J. Donald, 1988), pp. 123–41, at 133.

[15] Young (2015a), pp. 134–5.

[16] Gaol delivery of Thomas Rookwood, 28 August 1696, Cambridge University Library MS Hengrave 76/2/20.

[17] P. Findlen, 'Founding a Scientific Academy: Gender, Patronage and Knowledge in Early Eighteenth-Century Milan', *Republics of Letters: A Journal for the Study of Knowledge, Politics, and the Arts* 1 (2009), pp. 1–43.

[18] V. H. Minor, *Passive Tranquility: The Sculpture of Filippo della Valle* (Philadelphia, PA: American Philosophical Society, 1997), pp. 171–6.

[19] Young (2015a), pp. 138–40.

[20] Holt (1993), pp. 90–1.

[21] Young (2015a), p. 106.

[22] *Ibid.*, pp. 120–1.

[23] Holt (1993), pp. 114–26.

[24] On the building of John Gage's chapel see Holt (1983), pp. 304–15. For Gage's mission register see Young (2015a), pp. 201–11.

25 *Great Gothic Fane* (1913), pp. 74–5.

26 E. S. Worrall (ed.), *Returns of Papists, 1767: Dioceses of England and Wales except Chester* (London: Catholic Record Society, 1989), p. 121.

27 *Ibid.*, pp. viii–ix.

28 Information taken from Rowe (1996), pp. 202–34.

29 M. Gandy (ed.), *The Bishops' Register of Confirmations in the Midland District of the Catholic Church in England, 1768–1811 and 1816* (London: Catholic Family History Society, 1999), pp. 1–8.

30 It is unclear whether this was the thirteenth-century chapel of St Nicholas to the south of Giffords Hall, which was in ruins in the nineteenth century, or a chapel in the house that shared its dedication.

31 Young (2015a), pp. 144–5.

32 Quoted in Rowe (1998), pp. 167–94.

33 C. Paine, 'The Chapel and Well of Our Lady of Woolpit', *Proceedings of the Suffolk Institute of Archaeology and History* 38 (1993), pp. 8–12, at p. 10.

34 Young (2006), pp. 215–16.

35 *Great Gothic Fane* (1913), p. 87.

36 Worrall (1989), p. ix.

37 *Great Gothic Fane* (1913), p. 89.

38 F. de Rochefoucauld (ed. N. Scarfe), *A Frenchman's Year in Suffolk* (Woodbridge: Suffolk Records Society, 1988), pp. 67–8.

39 G. Goodwin (rev. S. J. Skedd), 'Howard, Charles, Eleventh Duke of Norfolk (1746–1815)', in *ODNB*, vol. 28, p. 327.

40 Rossi (1998), p. 1.

41 Rowe (1994), p. 138.

42 *Great Gothic Fane* (1913), p. 75; Rowe (1994), p. 138.

43 *Ibid.*, p. 90.

44 Rowe (1994), p. 138.

45 Information taken from A. Bellenger, *The French Exiled Clergy in the British Isles after 1789* (Bath: Downside Abbey, 1986).

46 *Ibid.*, p. 260.

47 S. Smith, *The Apostle to Ipswich: l'abbé Louis Pierre Simon* (Ipswich: Wolsey Papers, 1977), pp. 6–7.

48 *Ibid.*, p. 9.

49 *Ibid.*, pp. 12–13.

50 *Ibid.*, pp. 13–14.

51 Mason (1996), pp. 34–40.

52 Mason (1998), pp. 89–120.

53 F. Young, 'Mother Mary More and the Exile of the Augustinian Canonesses of Bruges in England: 1794–1802', *Recusant History* 27 (2004) pp. 86–102.

54 Young (2015a), p. 83.

55 Young (2004), p. 95.

56 Rowe (1994), p. 138.

57 Young (2012), pp. 463–4.

58 Young (2011), p. 196.

59 Gillow (1885–1902), vol. 4, p. 461.

60 Holt (1993), pp. 101–2.

61 Young (2015a), pp. 148–9, 202.

62 W. Betham, *The Baronetage of England* (Ipswich, 1801), vol. 1, p. 230.

63 Young (2015a), p. 149.

64 J. Smith, 'Jerningham, Edward (1737–1812)', in *ODNB*, vol. 30, pp. 51–3.

65 See Saward, Morrill and Tomko (2011), pp. 373–5; F. Young, 'Elizabeth Inchbald's "Catholic Novel" and its Local Background', *Recusant History* 31 (2013a) pp. 573–92.

66 Young (2015a), p. 136.

67 J. Stevenson, *Popular Disturbances in England, 1700–1832*, 2nd edn (Abingdon: Routledge, 1992), p. 39.

4

From Royal Assent to the Flaminian Gate: East Anglia between Emancipation and the Restoration of the Hierarchy, 1829–1850

Timothy Fenwick and Francis Young

Part 1: A *progrès tumultueux*

T HE PERIOD 1829–50 was one of transition that has been called a *progrès tumultueux*.[1] It was certainly characterised by some very real progress for the Catholics of East Anglia, as well as a number of paradoxes and even confusion. Emancipation should have removed the division of loyalties that the Catholics had endured since the Elizabethan religious settlement and the condemnation of Elizabeth by Pius V in the bull *Regnans in Excelsis* of 1570. In fact there remained a number of issues and ambiguities, some of which subsist to this day. In 1829 the papacy was still a very real, if increasingly fragile, temporal power, and the Church of England was, by law, the established religion of England. The older generation of both Catholic clergy and leading laity had been educated at Douai or elsewhere in Europe. This gave them a wider international view missed by most of their contemporaries in England. They had seen that Catholicism was not just a religion for an eccentric minority, but 'catholic' in a very real sense. It also meant that they had had a much more direct experience of the French Revolution and its consequences.

Before the French Revolution there had been a tradition of English Catholics serving in the armies of Catholic Europe: now they were free to take commissions in the British army, and many did so, while a few still served with the Habsburgs. Henry Stuart, Cardinal Duke of York, last of the Jacobite line of succession, had only died in 1807. Queen Victoria, by keeping largely out of politics and leading a respectable private life (unlike her immediate predecessors) won the respect, and in the long term, love, of all her English subjects, including the Catholics. But the Irish were not won over by British misrule in Ireland, carried out at the same time as many in the English establishment were encouraging the Italian patriots to unite Italy and bring to an end the Papal States.

The years 1830 and then 1848 saw very violent changes in Europe, with the Pope's flight to Gaeta in 1848, while in England the First Reform Act of 1832 passed relatively peacefully into law. Catholic peers were able to take their seats in the House of Lords, and these included the Duke of Norfolk and Lord Stafford, Sir George William Jerningham, who had obtained the reversal of the attainder of the Staffords to become the 8th Baron in 1824. In 1830 the first Catholics since the Elizabethan Settlement were elected to the House of Commons. The Earl of Surrey, son and heir of the Duke of Norfolk, and the Hon. Henry Valentine Stafford-Jerningham, son and heir of Baron Stafford, were among those elected. Both of these families had close ties to East Anglia. The English Catholics were rejoining the main stream of English political life. But what was the position in East Anglia? This chapter will look in turn at the numbers of Catholics in the future diocese, who and where they were, their clergy and their churches.

Counting Catholics has always been a hazardous exercise, but at least in the nineteenth century we have the 1851 religious census to help us. This had obliged all ministers of religion to return the number of people attending church services on 30 March 1851.[2] The report listed results by county, as well as reporting for certain boroughs. However, reporting was not universal and, in a number of instances, certainly incomplete or approximate. The results may be summarised as in Table 4.

Table 4. East Anglian Catholics in the 1851 religious census

COUNTY	PLACES OF WORSHIP	TOTAL ATTENDANCE	MORNING
Cambridgeshire	3	770	360
Norfolk	6	2,168	1,321
Suffolk	4	651	371
Cambridge Borough	1	640	260
Gt Yarmouth	No return	No return	No return
Ipswich	1	400	200
King's Lynn	1	–	200
Norwich	1	–	250

It is clear from these figures that the census is far from complete, and includes some very obvious rounding of the results. By assuming that 50 per cent of the Catholic population was able to attend Mass that Sunday, and that this is the number returned for attendance at morning service, adding 30 per cent to compensate for under-reporting, the Catholic population of East Anglia may have been in the order of 5,200 by 1851.

This is the only systematic source available. If, however, we look at other sources this estimate may be too low. The 1841 census gives nearly 900 as Irish-born in Cambridgeshire alone, most of whom can be assumed to have been Catholics. The 1840 *Catholic Directory* estimates the Catholic population of Norwich to have been 5,000, where we know that there were actually two chapels, but the total population was only some 65,000, so even if the under-reporting in 1851 may have been even higher than assumed above, Catholics were unlikely to be more than 2 or 3 per cent of the population of this notoriously Protestant city.

These results may be compared with Bishop John Hornyold's report to Propaganda as Vicar Apostolic of the Midland District in 1773:[3]

Table 5. East Anglian Catholics in 1773

COUNTY	NUMBER OF ORATORIES	NUMBER OF CATHOLICS
Cambridgeshire	1	70
Norfolk	7	980
Suffolk	4	360

Lesourd offers the following table of the number of churches:[4]

Table 6. East Anglian Catholic places of worship
between 1815 and 1850

COUNTY	1815	1825	1840	1850
Cambridgeshire	1	1	1	4
Norfolk	3	8	8	8
Suffolk	1	6	5	6

The clear conclusion that may be drawn is that, however unreliable the statistics, while the number of Catholic places of worship and the number of priests did not greatly change, the Catholic population of East Anglia did grow significantly over the first half of the nineteenth century.

At the time of emancipation Catholics of East Anglia seem to have been either in three of the main towns, Norwich, Ipswich and Bury St Edmunds, of which Norwich was by far the largest, or else grouped around a decreasing number of gentry clusters. Norwich had been the centre of the Jesuits' College of the Holy Apostles, which included Essex as well as the three East Anglian counties. Bury St Edmunds and Great Yarmouth had also been traditionally served by the Society. On 29 September 1829, just six months after the royal assent had been given to the Act of Emancipation, the Jesuits opened a new public chapel in Willow Lane designed in the classical style by James Patience and dedicated to the Holy Apostles, while the seculars continued to man an unassuming chapel in Maddermarket that had been opened in 1793. Although the Jerninghams and other Catholic gentry seem to have maintained town houses in Norwich, there seems to have been quite an active town congregation here. William Eusebius Andrews was born here,[5] of convert parents, in 1773, only moving to London in 1813 to lobby for Catholic emancipation and promote some very progressive, even radical, political ideas with his various publishing ventures, as well as being a pioneer of Catholic charities in the capital.[6] We also learn that there were Catholic shawl-makers in Norwich at the beginning of the century,[7] so the Catholic population of Norwich does not seem to have depended on the gentry to the same extent as we find in most other places.

In the 1820s new chapels were also opened in Ipswich, Thetford and at Withermarsh Green, Stoke-by-Nayland.[8] In Bury St Edmunds the town's Catholic life was dominated by the Rookwood Gages (or Gage Rokewodes) of Hengrave and Coldham Hall. The small chapel opened in 1761 by the Jesuits now serves as the Blessed Sacrament Chapel to the 1836–7 Grecian church of St Edmund, built by the Jesuits, who had been restored by Pius VII in 1814, at the end of the 1794–1839 tenure of the Abbé Thomas Aungier, a French émigré. When the present writer was a child the 1761 chapel served as a drawing room housing Fr Bryan Houghton's fine collection of eighteenth-century furniture.

Cambridgeshire for a long time had only the Huddlestone family-sponsored Sawston Hall mission. In Cambridge itself Pugin built St Andrew's in Union Street as late as 1843, to be replaced at the end of the century by Mrs Lyne Stephens's Our Lady and the English Martyrs on Hills Road. This is perhaps surprising, as the first decades of the century saw a number of Cambridge converts, the most prominent of whom were Kenelm Digby and Ambrose Phillipps de Lisle, who used to ride to St Edmund's Old Hall Green at Ware for Mass. After their conversion, unlike at contemporary Oxford where Catholics were simply banned, they were allowed to attend the university, but not to proceed to their degrees. In 1837 Digby was involved, with Bishop Walsh and Richard Huddlestone of Sawston, in an unsuccessful 'plot' to establish the Jesuits in Cambridge.[9]

King's Lynn developed from the Pastons' chaplaincy at Appleton and received a Pugin chapel in 1845, replaced by a larger church in 1896 to accommodate the Prince of Wales's Catholic guests at Sandringham. Wisbech got its own chapel in 1840. Great Yarmouth, first served rather irregularly, later became a Jesuit mission, where the very fine St Mary's church was built to plans by J. J. Scoles at a cost of £10,000 in 1848–50.[10] The Bedingfelds had a house here in the 1820s but whether there was a priest stationed here then is unclear.

Perhaps the best documented of the town missions is Bungay, which had its roots in the Tasburghs' house chaplaincy at Flixton, and moved to the town in 1823 towards the end of Dom Dunstan Scott's fifty-four-year (1772–1826) tenure of the mission.[11] But Flixton had already become an 'independent' mission, albeit supported by a moderate endowment established by the Tasburghs, by the middle of the eighteenth century. The Duke of Norfolk gave the land for the new church, and later more land for a school. The 1823 church was largely financed by two local families, the Cuddons and the Smiths, who at this juncture were respectively timber and hemp merchants. Its 1823 opening was quite an elaborate and very public affair, considering this was still six years before emancipation. There was High Mass in the morning, and Vespers and Benediction in the afternoon, with a sermon at each, with preachers from Norwich and London. The hand-bill published by Fr Crouzet advertises the event with seats at two shillings and three shillings, about a week's wages for many labourers.[12] It seems very strange to us today that not only were people ready to listen to sermons that often lasted over an hour, but that they were happy to pay for the privilege. Indeed paying to listen to sermons was quite a common way of raising funds for good causes. Providing good music in churches was also considered to be a good way of attracting Protestants to Catholic churches, introducing them to Catholicism.[13] Successive generations of Cuddons and especially the Smiths would continue their generosity, and were largely responsible not only for building the present magnificent church of St Edmund in Bungay, but also for making large contributions to the building of the churches in Beccles and Southwold.

The other 'gentry' missions largely followed the fate of their respective patrons. Some, such as Bodney in Norfolk and Haughley in Suffolk, had been abandoned by 1829, even if Bodney had for a number of years (1792–1813) harboured the Montargis Benedictines and their school, who later moved, eventually to Princethorpe Priory (unlike most Benedictine convents the Montargis Benedictines were ruled by a prioress because they claimed Our Blessed Lady as their abbess).[14] Haughley was inherited from the Sulyards by the Jerninghams, but they had sold the property to Protestants by 1820. Giffords Hall and Coldham Hall gave birth to the chapels known as Withermarsh Green and Coldham Cottage, and were served by secular priests.

The manor of Sawston, with its hall, was ruled throughout nearly all our period by Richard Huddlestone (1768–1847), who was succeeded by his brother Edward (1774–1852). Both had been educated by the Dominicans at Bornhem in the Austrian Netherlands. Richard had considered a Dominican vocation, but instead took his place as lord of the manor, with an active part in local life, including enclosing the parish's common lands, and was to be Cambridgeshire's first Catholic high sheriff. He did not, however, take a direct part in the paper and tanning industries that sprang up in Sawston at this time. He remained unmarried and is said to have been extremely pious: he certainly kept a chaplain at the hall to officiate in the early-eighteenth-century chapel.[15]

Oxburgh Hall has belonged to the Bedingfelds since the fifteenth century. Henry Richard Bedingfield (1800–

29) was the son of Sir Richard (1767–1829) and Lady (née Jerningham) Bedingfield, and succeeded his father as 6th Baronet in the year of Catholic emancipation. In 1826 Henry married Margaret Paston, the last of the ancient Norfolk recusant family that produced the famous 'Paston Letters' in the fifteenth century. Henry changed his name and arms to Paston-Bedingfield and made use of Margaret's fortune of £50,000 to repair the crumbling Oxburgh Hall.[16] He commissioned J. C. Buckler (1793–1894) to 'modernise' the house and to design the present neo-Gothic chapel, which was sited in the park and no longer in the house itself. Buckler was also the architect for Sir Henry's Jerningham cousins at Costessey. He also worked at Hengrave. Elsewhere in England Catholics had undertaken some major building projects during the eighteenth century and into the nineteenth, and this despite the rigours of the recusancy laws. Thorndon, Buckland and Wardour are perhaps the grandest, but by no means the only, examples. East Anglian Catholics contented themselves with the older charms of Giffords Hall, Sawston, Hengrave, Coldham and Oxburgh.

The only exception was the Jerninghams at Costessey. Sir George William Stafford Jerningham (1771–1851) succeeded to the Jerningham baronetcy as 7th Baronet in 1809, and in 1824 succeeded in having reversed the attainder of his ancestor Bd William Howard, 1st Baron Stafford (1614–1680), executed for treason at the time of the Popish Plot. A series of other inheritances meant that he was also extremely rich. He commissioned Buckler to design a greatly extended Costessey Hall to become a Gothic pile to rival Lord Shrewsbury's Alton Towers, as extended by Augustus W. N. Pugin. The first stage of the building works was a new Gothic chapel to seat up to 200 people, built alongside the hall and opened in

1809 just in time to receive the earthly remains of the 6th Baronet. Surviving illustrations show a very elaborate chapel, but how much of this was original to the 1809 construction and how much may have been added later by Buckler is not clear. Buckler's major building works were carried out between 1826 and 1836. As well as tripling the size of the house itself Lord Stafford, as he had now become, built a new parish church and presbytery on the edge of the village. This was the present church of Our Lady and St Walstan opened in 1841. The Jerninghams were the recipients of royal patronage as well. On the accession of William IV in 1830, Queen Adelaide made Charlotte Bedingfield a woman of the bedchamber and installed her in Brighton Pavilion. In 1836 Lord Stafford further strengthened his family's position by marrying a wealthy American, Elizabeth Caton, who was descended from the Carrolls, the leading Catholic family of Maryland.[17] One of the motivations of Lord Stafford in securing the reversal of the attainder in 1824 is said to have been to obtain a seat in the House of Lords to be able to vote in favour of the Emancipation Bill, but this would seem to be some *post factum* justification as he could not actually have taken his seat before the passage of the Act. However, as soon as the Act had passed he was one of the first Catholic peers to sit in the House of Lords. Almost simultaneously, his eldest son and heir, the Hon. Henry Stafford-Jerningham (1802–84), was elected MP for Pontefract, Yorkshire, a pocket borough controlled by Lord Harewood. His career in the Commons was cut short by the Great Reform Act of 1832 and he did not stand in the 1834 election. Mark Bence-Jones has observed that the Jerninghams' inheritance of the barony of Stafford was not automatic, and therefore the appearance of a batch of Catholic peers at the start of

Queen Victoria's reign (such as baronies of Camoys, Vaux and Beaumont) can be seen as a conscious attempt on the part of the sovereign to recognise that Catholics were an integral part of the British aristocracy.[18]

We know a great deal about the life of the Jerninghams and Bedingfelds thanks to the extensive correspondence between the Dowager Lady Jerningham (née Dillon) and her daughter Lady Bedingfield.[19] The family counted a large number of nuns among their relations, but far fewer priests. Among the nuns special mention should be made of Mother Anastasia Stafford (1722–1807), sometime abbess of the Blue Nuns in Paris, and *de jure* Baroness Stafford, who died in Paris while of unsound mind, having remained there when her *con-sœurs* left for England. Another remarkable religious leader was Sr Mary of St Francis (née Laura Stafford-Jerningham, 1811–86), sœur de Notre Dame de Namur, daughter of Sir George William and Lady Jerningham and widow of the Hon. R. E. Petre.[20] She was largely instrumental in bringing this teaching order to England, including to Norwich, but this was later in the century. In addition to those members of the Jerningham family who played an active part in the religious and political life of Victorian England, other family members were prominent lawyers, soldiers and even colonial administrators.

If the Jerninghams were clearly the leading East Anglian Catholic family, their long-term resident priest, Frederick Charles Husenbeth (1796–1872), was the outstanding local Catholic churchman of the period.[21] Ordained at Oscott in 1820 he spent almost the whole of his priestly life in Costessey, where he became a prolific author. His best-known work is a life of Bishop John Milner (1752–1826). More curiously, in 1834 he published *A Guide for the Wine Cellar; or a practical treatise on the cultivation of the vine, and the management of the different wines consumed in this country.* This is curious because he was a teetotaller and supporter of Fr Mathew's temperance movement. Fr Mathew preached and administered the pledge at Costessey in September 1843.[22] Husenbeth was also the Vicar Apostolic's Grand Vicar, and later provost of the Northampton Diocesan Chapter. It is also said that he had been picked by the Vicars Apostolic to go to Rome in 1848 for the discussions regarding the re-establishment of the hierarchy, but that he declined and Bishop Ullathorne went instead. It is sometimes pointed out that Lord Stafford built Husenbeth a new presbytery in the village as an example of a missioner not getting on with his patron. If there had actually been friction between them, it is certain that Husenbeth would have been moved to another mission, not left in the same place for half a century. It is much more likely that the move was prompted by the ongoing building works at the hall. The Staffords were often absent in London and elsewhere, but the missioner had to stay put.

The number of priests who stayed at the same locations is a good indication of the stability of Catholicism at this time. Although numbers increased steadily over the first half of the nineteenth century and many new chapels were built, these were almost all in the same places as had been served by gentry missions, or in some of the bigger towns, especially where the Jesuits had been long established. The increase in new parishes and the increase in the number of priests came largely over the next hundred and ten years, 1850–1960. It is also noteworthy that after the refugee nuns from France had moved on, there do not seem to have been any female religious in East Anglia, until the Brussels

Benedictines came from Winchester to East Bergholt in the 1850s, followed by the convents of the teaching orders in a number of the towns. If there were no nuns, nor were there many Irish, owing no doubt to the lack of modern industries that were to be found elsewhere and that attracted the flood of Irish workers fleeing the hardships of the famine and English misrule.

Part 2: Bishop William Wareing and the Eastern District, 1840–1850

In 1840 Rome took the decision to divide the Midland District by creating the Eastern District, which included the counties of Lincolnshire, Rutland, Northampton-shire, Bedfordshire and Buckinghamshire in addition to East Anglia. The creation of the Eastern District was a prelude to the creation of the Diocese of Northampton a decade later, but for a brief period, between 1842 and 1844, the Vicar Apostolic of the Eastern District, William Wareing, took up residence in East Anglia, at Giffords Hall in Stoke-by-Nayland. However, the failure of the seminary project and Wareing's subsequent return to Northampton left East Anglia once more a marginalised poor relation within both the Eastern District and the English Church as a whole.

In the early Victorian period England's transport infrastructure was revolutionised by the advent of the railways, which drastically shortened travel times and linked towns in East Anglia. In 1836 the Grand Eastern Counties Railway came into being, with the avowed intention of linking Great Yarmouth and Colchester. As it happened, construction of the line stopped at Colchester and a separate company was obliged to construct a line between Norwich and Yarmouth in

1844. By 1845 Cambridge, Ely, Thetford and Norwich were all linked by rail. The Eastern Union Railway extended the line from Colchester to Ipswich in June 1846, reaching Bury St Edmunds by December. By 1850 Ipswich was also linked to Norwich and a line connected Sudbury to London.[23] The railways allowed priests in towns with well-established missions to travel with comparative ease and speed to other areas to celebrate Mass and build up the Church where there had previously been nothing.

In 1824 there were only thirteen priests serving Norfolk and Suffolk, six of whom were French priests in exile, such as the Abbé Thomas Deterville (or D'Etreville) who served as deacon to Fr Frederick Charles Husenbeth at the requiem Mass for the repose of the soul of Lady Jerningham at Costessey in 1832.[24] The number of clergy that East Anglia contributed between emancipation and the restoration of the hierarchy was very small. Fr Henry Thrower (1824–91) ministered in the Eastern District (and later Diocese of Northampton) until his transfer to the Diocese of Liverpool in 1858. Thrower was born in Suffolk and ordained in 1849.[25] Likewise, Fr William Harris, who was born in Suffolk in 1813 and ordained in 1837, was transferred to the Diocese of Nottingham from Northampton in 1864, three years before his death.[26] Fr Francis Edward Martyn (1782–1838), from Norfolk, was the first seminarian educated as Oscott, where he was ordained in 1805.[27]

A few East Anglian men joined the religious orders. The Norfolk-born Fr Joseph Bunn (1823–78), who took the name of the Norfolk saint Walstan as a Capuchin friar, and was ordained in 1847, left the Capuchins to join the secular clergy in the Diocese of Plymouth.[28] Another Norfolk man, Fr Charles Havers (b. 1817), was ordained as a Jesuit priest in 1842 but left the Society of

Jesus in 1847.[29] Fr Robert Havers (1813–60), who was ordained in 1840 and was probably Charles's brother (since both men came from Norfolk) remained in the Society.[30] Both Robert and Charles were members of the Havers family of Thelveton, the mainstay of the Catholic mission in the Diss area of south-central Norfolk. Two East Anglians also became Benedictines: Dom Charles Ambrose Feraud (1786–47) from Suffolk joined St Gregory's at Acton Burnell and was ordained in 1810,[31] and Dom John Athanasius Clarkson (1819–64), also from Suffolk, joined St Edmund's, Douai, and was ordained in 1840.[32]

The journalist and publisher William Eusebius Andrews (1773–1837), the son of two converts, was a leading member of the Catholic community in Norwich in the early nineteenth century, editing the *Norfolk Chronicle* between 1799 and 1813, before moving to London and founding the *Orthodox Journal* and other periodicals which advanced the cause of the Ultramontane party, led by Bishop John Milner.[33] In July 1824 John Shadalow Wells, John Rose and William Scott, on behalf of the 'Catholic Club of Norwich', presented £5 and an address to Andrews 'in recognition of his championship of the "good cause" in London', suggesting that Norwich Catholics remained interested in his work. Like another East Anglian Catholic, Elizabeth Inchbald, Andrews made common cause with radical liberal politics in order to advance the cause of emancipation and his 'combination of traditional theology with populist politics' appealed to a disenfranchised and often poor urban Catholic community both in London and Norwich.[34]

In 1826 a Catholic Tract Society was formed, with a secretary appointed from the secular mission at St John's, Maddermarket, and the Jesuit chapel at St

Swithin's. The Society resolved that the tracts should be purchased from 'our worthy fellow-citizen, W. E. Andrews'.[35] Norwich was a major centre of printing in the early nineteenth century, an industry that sustained the city's radical tradition. The mission of the secular clergy at the Maddermarket Chapel remained one of the most important in the region, as evidenced by the appointment of the learned controversialist Fr Ignatius Collingridge, nephew of a Vicar Apostolic of the Western District, to lead the mission between 1835 and 1839.[36]

Anti-Catholicism remained a real obstacle to the development of churches and congregations, especially in areas such as Cambridgeshire and east Suffolk where people knew little of Catholicism. Increasingly, the press was adopting a more relaxed attitude to Catholicism, however. In October 1840 *The Tablet* reported *The Express*'s reaction to an anti-Catholic meeting in Woodbridge which opposed the establishment of a Catholic institute in Woodbridge: 'The wheat will grow — the turnips flourish — ... the sun and moon will continue to rise and set — and, in short, ... every thing will go on much the same as before, even if there should be established a Roman Catholic Institute in Ipswich'.[37]

Any fears that Protestant East Anglians had of a Catholic takeover were certainly unfounded. The size of the Church in the region was tiny: in 1838, there was one chapel in Cambridgeshire (at Sawston Hall) and none at all in Huntingdonshire. Norfolk had eight chapels and Suffolk five.[38] The Norfolk chapels were at Costessey (served by Husenbeth), King's Lynn (served by the Abbé Pierre Dacheux), the secular and Jesuit chapels in Norwich, the chapel at Oxburgh serving Stoke Ferry, a chapel at Thelveton which 'supplied every Indulgence from Bungay', and the chapels at

Thetford and Great Yarmouth.³⁹ The Suffolk chapels were at Bungay, Bury St Edmunds, Stanningfield (Coldham Hall), Ipswich and Stoke-by-Nayland (Withermarsh Green).⁴⁰ Worryingly, no new missions had been founded in the nearly ten years since emancipation. By 1843 only two more missions had been added, both in Cambridgeshire: Cambridge itself and Wisbech, served on the first Sunday of the month by John Dalton, a priest from King's Lynn.

Bury St Edmunds remained a flourishing centre of East Anglian Catholicism, and in 1836 what was then by far the largest church in East Anglia was built in Westgate Street, next to the house built by the Jesuit Fr John Gage, the founder of the mission, in 1761. The building cost £9400, partly funded by a loan secured by the rent from the manor of Fresels in Westley, originally a gift from Elizabeth Rookwood to her son John Gage in 1735 and passed by him to the English Province of the Society of Jesus on his death in 1790. On 6 April 1836 *The Bury and Norwich Post and Suffolk Herald* reported that 'A number of immense blocks of Ketton stone (some of them weighing 3–4 tons each) have been put on barges at Wansford to be used in building a large Catholic church at Bury St Edmunds. We believe that the expense of this edifice is defrayed from the general fund for the creation of Catholic chapels upon which every town has a claim in its turn'.⁴¹ In reality, of course, there was no such 'general fund'; Bury, as a Jesuit mission, did not have to depend on the meagre funds of the Midland District alone, and was also in the very fortunate position of owning a valuable piece of land. The church was complete by the end of 1837 and was consecrated on 14 December. Typically, in a town where tolerant co-existence had long been the norm, the Bury Musical Society agreed to sing the Mass. Fr

Henry Brigham, who became parish priest of Bury in 1838, was appointed Superior of the College of the Holy Apostles in 1842, another indication of Bury's importance as a key Jesuit centre.[42]

Bury's Catholic educational tradition also continued in the nineteenth century. By 1838 a Mr Chapman had established a Catholic 'academy' or boarding school at 6 Risbygate Street, offering 'a liberal, commercial and useful education', which included English grammar, French and Latin. For five shillings a year a boy could secure a seat at Mass in St Edmund's church, and for six shillings he could be trained in drilling.[43] In 1843 the school was described as a 'Classical and Commercial Academy'.[44] Meanwhile, at 22 Westgate Street (next to St Edmund's church) 'Mrs White's establishment for young ladies' catered for Catholic girls, offering 'reading, writing, arithmetic, English grammar, geography, history sacred and profane' as well as 'The useful branches of useful and ornamental needlework, and the French language'. Not only the Jesuits at Bury but also the clergy of Willow Lane in Norwich and the Great Yarmouth mission recommended the school, suggesting that it was the only source of Catholic education for girls in the whole of East Anglia.[45]

On 11 May 1840 Propaganda Fide in Rome split the vast Midland District into three, creating the District of Wales and the Eastern District, which included East Anglia. The Eastern District was still huge, and was even larger than the subsequent Diocese of Northampton because it contained the counties of Lincolnshire and Rutland, later absorbed into the Diocese of Nottingham.[46] The man chosen as Vicar Apostolic of the new Eastern District was William Wareing (1791–1865), vice-president of St Mary's College, Oscott, who was consecrated titular Bishop of Aristopolis. Pamela

Gilbert has suggested that Wareing's appointment served primarily to make room for Nicholas Wiseman as president of Oscott. Many bishops were sceptical of the division of the districts, and Dr Griffiths, Vicar Apostolic of the London District, doubted that there would be a restoration of the hierarchy within ten years. There were also serious financial concerns about the new vicariates, as they were not entitled to any part of the income of the previous jurisdictions.[47]

On 6 October 1840 Wareing informed readers of *The Tablet* that he had established himself at Northampton and announced the appointment of Frs James Semkiss and Ignatius Collingridge, then in charge of the Ipswich mission, as Grand Vicars in the Eastern District. 'I find an immense and desolate tract of country before me', Wareing reflected, 'where the "harvest indeed is great, but the labourers few". I must trust, however, to the blessing of God, and the assistance of the influential among my flock, to enable me to bring things about gradually.'[48] This was something of an understatement: the task facing Wareing was Herculean. Although Catholicism had experienced modest growth in East Anglia in the 1790s, and the contribution of exiled French priests had been especially helpful in this regard, the faith had stagnated in the region compared with the explosion of the Catholic population in London and the North. As one East Anglian correspondent to *The Tablet* put it in March 1842, calling himself 'Orientalis':

> An extensive tract of country, reaching from the Humber to the Orwell, and from Banbury to Yarmouth, lately detached from the midland district, is left in a state of unsurpassed destitution. To state the case as I have heard it stated on incontrovertible authority: the Vicar Apostolic

of the Eastern District not only has absolutely
nothing at his disposal for the extension of our
holy religion, but does not command any fund
whatever, either for increasing the efficiency, or
for supplying the occasional necessities of the
missions already existing. Many of these are
partially, not a few are entirely, dependent upon
the bounty of individuals; while hardly any are
provided with a stipend sure and adequate.

'Orientalis' was describing a district behind the times,
in which many missions still did not enjoy proper
financial independence from the patronage of local
gentry, with all the genealogical and political pitfalls
associated with such associations. The dependence
of the Church on the laity was out of fashion by the
1840s, as the Vicars Apostolic pressed for a properly
organised and self-governing national Church. 'Orientalis' predicted that many missions would simply close
down, citing the example of chapels like Ipswich which
could not get a priest: 'To hear Mass, its inhabitants
must walk six-and-twenty miles; while many, who live
to the north of the town, cannot get an infant baptized,
without carrying it twice as far'. 'Orientalis' continued,

If the urgent wants of the Eastern District
continue unrelieved, ignorance of its real state
can no longer be pleaded as the reason. The
Vicar Apostolic is the more to be pitied, and
I may say his claims to help are the stronger,
because, before his appointment, he was
cheered with hopes, which many, to this day,
probably mistake for realities, but which have
led only to disappointment.[49]

The gap that 'Orientalis' perceived between hope and
reality is well illustrated by the case of St Felix's Sem-

inary at Stoke-by-Nayland. One of Wareing's first priorities was to train priests for the new district, and he announced the seminary project in a pastoral letter of 8 June 1842:

> We have obtained, by the kindness of P. Mannock, Esq., a short but beneficial lease of his venerable mansion of Gifford Hall, in the parish of Stoke-by-Nayland, in the county of Suffolk, a mansion dear to religion from many pious and ancient memorials. We propose to commence our undertaking forthwith by opening Gifford Hall for the reception of youths of pious disposition and good abilities, who must be recommended by their pastors, and paid for by their parents and patrons to the amount of twenty-five pounds per annum, we ourselves supplying the deficiency by such means as the piety of the faithful may furnish to us. We place this our seminary under the patronage of St. Felix, the Apostle of the Eastern Angles, who, in the seventh century, by his labours and preaching, diffused the light of the gospel chiefly in the counties of Norfolk, Suffolk, and Cambridge.

Wareing's letter made clear that the seminary was to be established initially in Giffords Hall itself, but that the district had purchased the freehold of an adjoining piece of land on which he hoped a seminary could be built, which the seminarians would then move into:

> We count this our undertaking, however arduous, most necessary and important, and we commence it without loss of time at Gifford Hall, in the full hope and expectation of being enabled, by the pious contributions of the faithful, to erect a suitable building on our own freehold land adjoining, before the expiration of our present

short lease of three years. To our beloved clergy
we need make no appeal on this head, but rely
most confidently on their zealous co-operation in
this important work. They will encourage their
flocks to increase the proceeds of the Eastern
District Fund, which will be chiefly employed
in supporting the seminary of St. Felix.[50]

Wareing's lease of Giffords Hall commenced in June
1842 but the first students did not arrive until August.
So committed was Wareing to this project that he
himself took up residence at Giffords Hall alongside
the Rector, Fr Joseph North. An advertisement that
appeared in the *Catholic Directory* for 1843 explained
the aims of the seminary:

The Seminary of St. Felix is a strictly Clerical
Establishment, founded by the Vicar Apostolic
of the Eastern District, as a nursery for a body
of virtuous and zealous ecclesiastics, who may
labour with him for the salvation of souls in the
widely extended tract of country committed to
his spiritual charge. He confidently trusts, that
his beloved flock, both Clergy and Laity, will aid
and support him in this important undertaking;
that the Clergy will discreetly select such subjects
as they may judge eligible for virtue and talents;
and that those of the Laity whom heaven has
blessed with opulence will assist the good work,
by willingly contributing a portion of their
earthly means.

Wareing went on to explain why he had decided to
live in Suffolk himself:

He has taken up his residence in the Seminary,
with a view to encourage, to superintend, and
direct the studies and discipline of the students,

and to prove the deep interest he takes in the welfare and success of this undertaking;— an undertaking which he considers of vital importance to the interests of religion in the Eastern District; and which affords the faithful an opportunity of doing much for the glory of God, and the good of souls.[51]

One contemporary account of the seminary was provided by seventeen-year-old Frances Lescher, who was born at Stoke-by-Nayland in 1825 and, in September 1842, was staying with her grandmother in one wing of Giffords Hall. On 5 September she wrote to a friend from the 'College of St. Felix', reporting that 'here folk do as our ancestors did in the thirteenth century'. She described the hall as 'Such a delightful place, where one can easily transport oneself into the beautiful days of chivalry. I am never tired of contemplating the old baronial hall, with its magnificent carved oaken ceiling'. Lescher noted that 'The seminary was opened only three weeks ago and at present there are but three students here, so we have the whole house almost entirely to ourselves'.[52]

The emptiness of Giffords Hall, delightful to a teenage girl, presented a major problem for Bishop Wareing. It seems unlikely that many more students than the three Lescher encountered that autumn ever trained at Giffords Hall. A year later, in September 1843, Wareing announced that he would be moving the seminary to Northampton when the lease expired in June 1844:

> I was induced by many urgent motives last June ... to take a short lease of Giffords Hall, Suffolk, for the purpose of establishing there an ecclesiastical seminary for the eastern district.

I did expect, in this rather spirited step to have been supported and encouraged so far as to be enabled to erect in Suffolk something of a regular building, suitable to our seminary purposes. I am sorry to have to state (absit verbo invidia) that my expectations have been disappointed, and that I must be content with less than I had wished and expected. I have not, however, in the least relaxed in my most anxious wish to provide a seminary for my extensive district: on the contrary, every day's experience shows me more clearly the imperative necessity of procuring this most necessary and effectual means of extending religion. I have, therefore, after mature deliberation and consultation with confidential friends and advisers, resolved upon building at Northampton a collegiate chapel, and incorporating the present chapel with my house, so as to provide the necessary accommodation for a certain number of students. Instead, therefore, of changing my residence, I propose to remodel and enlarge my present premises, and transfer the seminary of St. Felix hither, when our lease of Giffords Hall expires in June, 1844.[53]

If Wareing is to be believed, the main cause for the failure of the Suffolk seminary was the lack of funds to build a chapel, but it seems very likely that another problem was the impracticality of the Vicar Apostolic taking up residence in southeast Suffolk, on the outermost fringe of the Eastern District, when he had responsibilities that took him as far north as the Humber and as far west as Daventry. Furthermore, it is unlikely that Wareing's decision to direct the entirety of the mission funds of the Eastern District to the building of a seminary met with unqualified support from the clergy. Could pressure from Wareing's own clergy have been partly to blame for the failure of the seminary? Husenbeth attributed it purely to financial factors, bemoaning the lack of wealthy sponsors in 'this desolate portion of the vineyard':

> We have no Lord Shrewsbury to assist us by munificent donations; no noble Duke to relieve us in our necessities. In several large and respectable towns there are as yet no missions formed, because priest and means are wanting: Wisbech, Peterborough, Ely, Sleaford, &c., are in this destitute state … And yet there is not, perhaps, any other part of England which, before the Reformation, was so rich in ecclesiastical buildings as that portion which now forms the "eastern district". But its glory has long since departed, and the old Catholic benefactors are nowhere to be found. Still we must not despair. Other benefactors we trust are amongst us, to assist our zealous bishop in his endeavours to establish his new seminary.[54]

Husenbeth was referring to the magnanimity of the dukes of Norfolk and earls of Shrewsbury, who had funded the building of churches in Derbyshire, where the Howards had vast estates, and in Staffordshire, where the Talbots still wielded much influence. Indeed, in spite of the fact that the Duke of Norfolk still occasionally visited his estate at Fornham All Saints, just north of Bury St Edmunds, there was little sign at this period that England's foremost Catholic family had much interest in advancing the faith in East Anglia. Yet in spite of the failure of the Seminary of St Felix, the years leading up to the restoration of the hierarchy did see the Catholic faith make inroads into the three largely untouched towns of East Anglia: Cambridge, Ipswich and Peterborough.

The idea of a Cambridge mission was first mooted in 1827, when Fr Edward Huddlestone was appointed as chaplain at Sawston Hall. By 1828 Huddlestone had raised £900, part of which he may have used to buy two cottages in Union Road, in the parish of St Andrew-the-Less. However, Huddlestone was replaced in 1831 by the young and inexperienced Fr John Scott, and the project foundered. The Jesuits approached Bishop Walsh about founding a Cambridge mission in 1835, but two years later Walsh decided to pull out of negotiations with the Jesuits for fear of causing a 'storm' with his own secular clergy. However, Christopher Jackson has argued that the creation of the Eastern District in 1840 gave a new geographical significance to Cambridge, since it was roughly in the middle of the new territory and a town of obvious significance. Bishop Wareing appointed an outsider, Fr Bernard Shanley from the Irish College in Paris, to take charge of founding the Cambridge mission. Shanley began by celebrating Mass in a house in Newmarket Road, where the floor nearly collapsed, before relocating to a small hut and then the cottages on Union Road. His congregation was largely made up of two hundred Irish Catholics in the town.

In May 1841 Bishop Walsh sent £500 raised for the Cambridge mission, and work began on Union Road. However, on the night of 5 November 1841 a group of Cambridge University undergraduates descended on the site with the avowed intention of destroying the foundations; Shanley, supported by a strong contingent of Irishmen, prepared for a siege, but in the event he was supported by the mayor, town clerk and clerk of the peace who, between them, drove off the students. The church of St Andrew was opened on 4 December 1842, by which time the mission was led by Fr Norbert Woolfrey, a Cistercian monk. Charles Perry, the vicar of the new St Paul's church, a few hundred yards away from the new Catholic church, did all he could to try to 'put down Popery' in his parish, but without success, and St Andrew's endured until its replacement, after the restoration of the hierarchy, with the splendid Gothic church of Our Lady and the English Martyrs.[55]

The mission at Ipswich founded by Abbé Pierre Simon in 1793 continued to grow in the 1830s, and in 1837 he began to extend the original chapel of St Anthony, which was proving too small, to the north and south. The old chapel now formed a transept of a new church with a nave 76 feet long. The new church was consecrated by Bishop Walsh on 10 October 1838, rededicated to St Mary. The Bishop confirmed seventeen people (including five converts) during the Mass and struck a conciliatory tone in his sermon to 'our dearly beloved Protestant brethren', in a town where anti-Catholic attitudes were still entrenched. However, in spite of its splendid reconsecration St Mary's church remained the personal property of Mary Wood, the niece of Margaret Wood who first supported Abbé Simon in his mission, and was only passed to the Diocese of Northampton in 1854.[56]

Progress in Peterborough was a great deal slower. The town experienced extremely rapid growth after the arrival of the railway in 1845, when Peterborough became—as it remains today—the 'gateway to East Anglia' from the Midlands. However, in the 1830s the population was around 6000, and the town had no Catholic tradition. It was not until 1832 that a young Scottish draper named John Copeland arrived in the town and made contact with two Catholic families, the Birds and the Buckles. Both families, however, had ceased to practise and they advised him not to make his Catholicism public. Undeterred, Copeland contacted a group of Irish travellers and arranged transport for him and them to attend Mass at King's Cliffe in Northamptonshire or Stamford in Lincolnshire.[57]

In 1845, Copeland was joined by his sister Fanny, who discovered two German Catholics and an Irish recruiting sergeant resident in the town. The priest at Stamford, Fr O'Connor, began making occasional visits to Peterborough to celebrate Mass. On the opening of the Peterborough and Northampton Railway in 1845, Bishop Wareing paid a visit to Copeland and discussed the opening of a mission. Ironically, Peterborough was only a short distance away from the seat of the Vicar Apostolic in Northampton, yet virtually a desert as far as the faith was concerned. Wareing met with Copeland and an Italian gentleman named Montaganni at Wisbech, which had been a Mass centre since 1840, and it was agreed that Copeland would contribute £25 and Montaganni £15 per year for the maintenance of a priest to serve both towns.

The man chosen for the job was the Norfolk-born Jesuit Fr Charles Havers, who arrived in 1847 and lodged near the Copelands, who provided him with meals. However, the Copelands did not have the room to provide a permanent chapel, and a tailor, Mr Connolly, agreed to convert a back room in his house in Westgate for the purpose. Sir Henry Bedingfield of Oxburgh donated a tabernacle, but the poverty of the mission was evident in the fact that the first collection reportedly raised only 27 shillings. Havers said Mass on alternate Sundays in Peterborough and Wisbech, and when he left in autumn 1847 Bishop Wareing himself took the train to Peterborough and said Mass in the Copelands' home. At around this time the town's

Catholics tried to purchase an old theatre at the west end of St John's church, but the vicar, Dr James, deliberately bought it to prevent the Catholics acquiring it, even though he was obliged to sell it on at a loss. The local paper was scathing of the tactic.[58]

In January 1848 Fr Thomas Seed arrived in Peterborough to find a community of about twenty Catholics, with no proper chapel. However, the railway once more came to the rescue in the form of Mr Kelly, an employee of the London and North Western Railway, who offered two rooms to be used as a chapel at his house in Priestgate. However, the gathering of seasonal Irish labourers in the street at harvest time, waiting for Mass, caused Kelly's landlord to force him out. By 1849 the Peterborough congregation was meeting at a house in Cumbergate, where Seed had the lease and knocked together two rooms. By the time of the restoration of the hierarchy in 1850, the congregation had increased to around eighty, but Peterborough was still decades behind the development of other East Anglian towns in its Catholic mission.[59] By the middle of the nineteenth century the days of makeshift chapels in private houses were largely gone, and Catholics in most places were taking their place alongside other dissenting denominations as an established element of East Anglian society.

The years between emancipation and the restoration of the hierarchy were a period of mixed success for the Church in East Anglia. On the one hand an East Anglian seminary was established and new missions were founded, but on the other hand the seminary turned out to be an expensive white elephant in a territory that did not produce enough vocations, and the new missions came late in the development of the new Eastern District. Bishop Wareing managed to extend the faith to Cambridge, Peterborough and the Fens, but the process was protracted and far from easy, not only on account of anti-Catholic hostility but also because of the district's parlous finances. Yet other missions continued to thrive, as the building works at Bury St Edmunds and Ipswich demonstrated, and the expansion of the Catholic community, whilst slower than it might have been, was inexorable.

Notes

1   J. A. Lesourd, *Les Catholiques dans la société anglaise, 1765–1865: Évolution numérique, répartition géographique, structure sociale, pratique réligieuse* (Paris : Librairie Honoré Champion, 1978), p. 969. Despite being marred by numerous mistakes, such as confusion of 'Arundel' and 'Arundells', this work is a useful attempt to apply some of the methods of the French school of 'Les Annales' to English Catholic history.

2   'Online Historical Population Reports' (http://www.histpop. org/ohpr/servlet/), accessed 30 June 2015.

3   W. Mazière Brady, *The Episcopal Succession in England, Scotland and Ireland, A.D. 1400 to 1875* (Rome: Tipografia della Pace, 1877), vol. 3, p. 212.

4   Lesourd (1978), p. 601.

5   Gillow (1885–7), vol. 1, pp. 43–52.

6   B. Carter, 'Catholic Charitable Endeavours in London, 1810–1840, Part I', *Recusant History* 25 (2001), pp. 487–510, at p. 496.

7   Mason (1998), p. 106.

8   P. Leavy, 'Progress, Publicity and Protest: New Catholic Chapels in Nineteenth Century Britain', *Catholic Archives* 35 (2015), p. 48.

9   K. L. Morris, 'Kenelm Digby and English Catholicism', *Recusant History* 20 (1991), pp. 361–70, at p. 362.

10 N. Pevsner and B. Wilson, *The Buildings of England: Norfolk I: Norwich and North-East* (New Haven, CT: Yale University Press, 1997), p. 500.

11 E. Crouzet, *Slender Thread: Origins and History of the Benedictine Mission in Bungay 1657–2007* (Bath, Downside Abbey Books, 2007), pp. 46–51.

12 *Ibid.*, pp. 54–6.

13   B. Zon, 'Plainchant in the Eighteenth-Century English Catholic Church', *Recusant History* 21 (1993), pp. 361–80, at pp. 376–8.

14   F. Stapleton, *The History of the Benedictines of St Mary's Priory Princethorpe* (Hinckley: Samuel Walker, 1930), pp. 92–7.

15   T. F. Teversham, *A History of the Village of Sawston* (Sawston: Crampton and Sons, 1942–7), vol. 2, pp. 239–40, 255. In spite of its two volumes, this work is very economical with information concerning Catholic life at Sawston, not so surprising since Teversham was in fact the Anglican incumbent.

16   M. Bence-Jones, *The Catholic Families* (London: Constable, 1992), p. 141.

17   *Ibid.*, p. 152.

18   *Ibid.*, p. 154.

19   E. Castle (ed.), *The Jerningham Letters (1780–1843): Being Excerpts from the Correspondence and Diaries of the Honourable Lady Jerningham and of her Daughter Lady Bedingfeld* (London: Richard Bentley, 1896), 2 vols; with further letters from the same collection being published in Mason (1995), pp. 350–69; see also Mason (1998), pp. 89–122.

20   R. B. Camm, *Sister Mary of St Francis, SND, the Hon Laura Petre (Stafford-Jerningham)* (London: R. & T. Washbourne, 1913).

21   Gillow (1885–7), pp. 492–507.

22   B. Ward, *The Sequel to Catholic Emancipation: The Story of the English Catholics Continued down to the Re-establishment of their Hierarchy in 1850* (London: Longmans, Green & Co, 1915), vol. 2, p. 65.

23   A. Robertson, 'Railways in Suffolk', in D. Dymond and E. Martin (eds), *An Historical Atlas of Suffolk* (Ipswich: Suffolk County Council, 1988), pp. 108–9.

24   *Great Gothic Fane* (1913), pp. 80–1.

25   C. Fitzgerald-Lombard, *English and Welsh Priests 1801–1914: A Working List* (Bath: Downside Abbey, 1993), p. 60.

26   *Ibid.*, p. 73.

27   *Ibid.*, p. 148.

28   *Ibid.*, p. 79.

29   *Ibid.*, p. 147.

30   *Ibid.*, p. 213.

31   *Ibid.*, p. 161.

32   *Ibid.*, p. 159.

33   *Great Gothic Fane* (1913), p. 81.

34   Saward, Morrill and Tomko (2011), p. 386.

[35] *Great Gothic Fane* (1913), pp. 155–6.

[36] *Ibid.*, p. 82.

[37] *The Tablet*, 31 October 1840, p. 6.

[38] *The Catholic Directory and Annual Register for the Year 1838* (London: Booker and Dolman, 1838), p. 19.

[39] *Ibid.*, p. 39.

[40] *Ibid.*, p. 42.

[41] *The Present from our Past: The History of the Church of St Edmund King and Martyr Bury St Edmunds* (Bury St Edmunds: St Edmund's History Group, 2012), p. 7.

[42] *Ibid.*, p. 8.

[43] *Catholic Directory* (1838), pp. 101–2.

[44] *The Catholic Directory and Annual Register for the Year 1843* (London: C. Dolman, 1843) p. 131.

[45] *Ibid.*, p. 94.

[46] C. Jackson, 'The Mission in Cambridge: A Tale of Three Bishops and a Determined Priest', in N. Rogers (ed.), *Catholics in Cambridge* (Leominster: Gracewing, 2003), pp. 66–80, at p. 70.

[47] P. J. Gilbert, *This Restless Prelate: Bishop Peter Baines* (Leominster: Gracewing, 2006), pp. 219–20.

[48] *The Tablet*, 6 October 1840, p. 8.

[49] *The Tablet*, 5 March 1842, p. 6.

[50] *The Tablet*, 30 July 1842, p. 5.

[51] *Catholic Directory* (1843), p. 78.

[52] A Sister of Notre Dame, Sister Mary of St Philip (Frances Mary Lescher), 1825–1904 (London, 1920), p. 16.

[53] *The Tablet*, 30 September 1843, p. 7.

[54] *Ibid.*

[55] On the foundation of the Cambridge mission see Jackson (2003), pp. 67–75.

[56] Smith (1977), pp. 11–18.

[57] P. Waszak, 'The Revival of the Roman Catholic Church in Peterborough *c.* 1793–1910', *Peterborough's Past* 3 (1988), pp. 27–39, at p. 30. On the King's Cliffe mission see P. Waszak, 'The "Golden Ball" Chapel at King's Cliffe, Northamptonshire', *Midland Catholic History* 8 (2001), pp. 16–28.

[58] Waszak (1988), p. 31.

[59] *Ibid.*, p. 32.

5

East Anglia in the Victorian Diocese of Northampton, 1850–1901

John Charmley

I N 1851 THE POPE restored the Catholic hierarchy in England and Wales. This was taken as a triumphalist gesture by the British Prime Minister, Lord John Russell, whose hereditary anti-Catholicism was supplemented by his need to give a boost to his ailing administration, and to the accompaniment of widespread 'anti-papist' riots, he introduced legislation to prevent the Catholic bishops taking the titles of existing English sees. The protests and riots were a reminder of the fact that for three hundred years, Catholics had been harried, persecuted, fined and banned from public life for professing their faith; the removal of the last of the prohibitions in 1829 had made little difference to the popular temper. As the reaction of the established church to the Oxford Movement had shown, even in the highest quarters, Catholics were an object of suspicion.

All the talk of a 'restoration' of the hierarchy masked an unpalatable truth. Three centuries of state-sponsored persecution and discrimination had all but extirpated the Catholic faith from the land once called 'Mary's Dowry'. Edmund Burke had said that the old penal code was a 'complete system, full of coherence and consistency', whose 'vicious perfection' was well fitted 'for the oppression, impoverishment and degradation of a people'.[1] He was right. Out of a population of 17,927,600 in 1851, 60.8 per cent attended church, according to the religious census of that year—of which only 2.1 per cent, that is 383,630, were Catholics; we cannot be sure how many more Catholics did not go to church that Sunday, but the figure is not likely to be far away from registering the scattered remnant. It might also be borne in mind that by that date immigration from famine-stricken Ireland was in full swing. Its effect can be seen from the fact that 20 per cent of Catholic places of worship were in Lancashire, mainly in Liverpool and Manchester. In Norfolk attendance at a Catholic service represented 0.7 per cent of the population, where 52 per cent were Anglicans and 31 per cent Methodists.[2]

Where Catholicism survived the Elizabethan onslaught, it did so first in secret, and then in private. Where aristocratic and gentry families adhered to the old religion, their adherents tended to follow suit, which created small pockets of Catholic believers. They adapted to the persecution and eventual toleration by keeping themselves to themselves and by not evangelising; it was a recipe for stagnation and decline. By the beginning of the reign of George III in 1760, it is estimated that there were about 80,000 Catholics in England and Wales.[3] As Bd John Henry Newman commented, it was odd that so many Englishmen harboured a prejudice against Catholics, when so few of them had ever met one. That figure had grown to nearly 400,000 by 1850, but this was largely the result of mass immigration from Ireland — and East Anglia was not a favoured destination when Liverpool, Glasgow and London were all available.

In the newly founded Diocese of Northampton, which comprised the seven counties of Buckinghamshire, Bedfordshire, Northamptonshire, Huntingdonshire, Cambridgeshire, Norfolk and Suffolk, there were no more than 10,000 Catholics.[4] Surveying the situation in 1851, it could be truly said that for '300 years the area included in the bishopric had been a most desolate one from the Catholic point of view. When England broke away from the Church, in no part of it was the rupture so complete as in the eastern counties'.[5] The few Catholics remaining were scattered unevenly across its seven thousand or so square miles, and they were served by only twenty-seven priests and eighty-six churches and chapels.[6] It was an area untouched for the most part by the effects of industrialisation and urbanisation, and so had few incomers. The region had been strongly parliamentarian in the Civil War, nonconformity was strong in the agricultural countryside, and Anglicanism predominated in the cities of Northampton, Norwich and Cambridge. It matched Newman's sombre description in his sermon on the 'Second Spring', where he spoke not of the 'Catholic Church in the country' or even of a 'Catholic community',[7] but

> A few adherents of the Old Religion, moving silently and sorrowfully about, as memorials of what had been … not a sect, not even an interest, as men conceived it, not a body … but a mere handful of individuals, who might be counted, like the pebbles and detritus of the great deluge, and who … merely happened to retain a creed which in its day, indeed, was the profession of a Church.

Of the spiritual resources and personal heroism which
kept the faith alive in such circumstances, we have all
too little evidence: a Mass book here, a devotional work
there must suffice, for the conditions of 'cultural and
personal hostility'[8] which made Catholics hide their
presence from the law have also ensured their absence
from the historical record.

If the story has seemed to be one of recusant gentry
families suffering the diminution of their hereditary
fortunes and exile from public service for their faith,
that does not mean that there were not middle-class
Catholics, but it does mean they tended to survive in
the purlieus of the gentry, who deserve their position
centre stage because they were, indeed, the keepers
of the flame. They provided some protection, and
employment, for local Catholics, and it is not surprising that the location of Catholic communities maps
onto recusant households. These families had not particularly welcomed the 'restoration' of the hierarchy,
being somewhat Gallican in their sympathies, and,
from long experience, wary of anything which stirred
up the anti-Catholic prejudices of their fellow countrymen. Indeed, the premier Catholic peer, the Duke
of Norfolk, actually voted for Lord John Russell's bill
banning Catholics from taking the titles of English sees.[9]

Northampton had been the headquarters of the
Vicar Apostolic of the Eastern District, and was therefore the natural choice for the new diocese, although
from the start there were suggestions that, geographically, Cambridge would have been a better choice.[10] The
first bishop, the old Vicar Apostolic William Wareing,
found his new diocese unwieldy, and was not the man
to lead any great mission. Fr Gordon Albion wrote of
him that he 'left all but no mark in the history of the
restored hierarchy', and that his appointment to the

vicariate was part of 'the clearance at Oscott', needed to make room for Wiseman's appointment as president; he lasted eight years.[11]

We can get some idea of Wareing's plight from an early report he made to Rome in 1854, where he commented that he had no 'palace' or 'cathedral'; in fact he barely had a church, as St Felix's was a tiny place. It was difficult, he explained, to ensure that religious services were carried out properly because of the distances involved, and local hostility meant that it was unsafe to leave the Blessed Sacrament reserved in church. There was only one substantial city in the diocese, Norwich, once the second city in the country, but by this stage somewhat in decline, and even there it was reckoned there were scarcely a thousand Catholics;[12] in the second city, Northampton, there were, he reckoned, about six hundred.

His successor but one, Bishop Riddell, noted in his 1880 Advent Pastoral that the 'diocese was so poor and the faithful so few in number, only about 6000' that it would take the combined efforts of the bishop, clergy and laity, if the faith was to advance.[13] 'In all its history and associations Norfolk is profoundly Catholic',[14] commented *The Tablet* in 1911, remarking that 'in spite of its marked tendency towards Cromwellianism in the seventeenth century, the county has on the whole been a witness for Catholic and monarchical principles.' But in the '300 years [since the Reformation] the area included in the bishopric had been a most desolate one from the Catholic point of view. When England broke away from the Church, in no part of it was the rupture so complete as in the eastern counties'.[15] It was the old county gentry, with ancient names such as Jerningham, Bedingfield, Paston and Southwell, who preserved the flame of faith during the dark years, and as those names suggest, it was Norfolk where what remnants that did remain were most numerous.

The Jerninghams, out at Costessey Hall,[16] have been described as 'the architects of the survival of the Old Faith in Norwich'.[17] It seems likely that priests cele-brated Mass there throughout most of the penal years, and in 1841 the family built a new church, Our Lady and St Wulfstan, to cater to the four hundred Catholics living in the vicinity. The Howard dukes of Norfolk had kept a private chapel in the city of Norwich until the 1780s, and the Jesuits had had a presence in the city throughout most of the period of the penal laws, although there is some dispute as to the location of their chapel.[18] Thus it was that Norwich, once one of the glories of medieval Catholicism, had, by the begin-ning of the nineteenth century, only two small chap-els in the back streets (one in the St Swithin's district, the other at Maddermarket). St John's Maddermarket, founded in 1790, was the oldest church in the new dio-cese. In the 1820s the Jesuits decided to build the Holy Apostles and Jesus Chapel (1827–29), in Willow Lane, Norwich, with a grand classical façade.[19] In doing so they declared that Catholicism was no longer afraid to declare its presence; however, situated just off the main road into the city, it suggested it was not quite ready for the mainstream. The church opened with all the ceremony of a high pontifical Mass on 29 September 1829. Abandoned in the 1890s for the grander St John's Cathedral, it became a school and is now a solicitor's office; its former use is unmarked by any plaque.

By the 1820s, Catholicism in Norwich was strong enough to move beyond the protective embrace of the recusant gentry.[20] This was just as well, as the 'demo-graphic time-bomb', as Francis Young has called it, which would lead to the extinction of most of them, was already well evidenced by the 1820s, when the Timperleys of Hintlesham Hall, the Tasburghs of Flixton Hall, the Mannocks of Stoke-by-Nayland and the Sulyards of Haughley and Wetherden had all died out. They were soon to be joined by the Jerninghams of Costessey (who had also helped with the funding of the chapel built in 1790 in Norwich) and the Rookwood Gages of Stanningfield. Only the Bedingfields at Oxburgh Hall remained of the ancient recusant families whose devotion and sacrifices had kept the old faith alive in the darkest hours.[21]

The pockets of Catholicism noted by Wareing were those effectively curated by recusant gentry. In Norwich itself, the presence of the dukes of Norfolk had kept a Catholic presence alive. In the west of Norfolk, there was a presbytery and Catholic school in the small village of Oxburgh, but that owed everything to the fidelity and generosity of the Bedingfields at the 'great house', and it would not be until 1907 that the first Mass was said in the large market town of Swaffham a few miles down the road. There was a Jesuit mission in Yarmouth, which served sailors, but made little impact beyond the town. Indeed, on the eighty-mile coastline between Yarmouth and King's Lynn there was no Catholic presence at all.

Just across the border into Suffolk, the Tasburgh family of Flixton Hall had kept a Catholic chaplain, as well as providing the Church with a succession of priests, monks and nuns. In 1753 the estate was sold off, but the last of the Tasburgh women, Elizabeth Wyburne, provided money from her share of the proceeds to provide for a 'priest's house' in the village of Flixton, which was served, as the house itself had been, by the Benedictines.[22] This made the mission to Flixton one of the first to be independent of gentry patronage (although there was an entail on the estate to provide for the missioner's annuity).[23] From the Benedictine chapter books, we get some indication of a small group of middle-class Catholics in Bungay and Beccles, whose missioner also worked with communities in the Diss area, where the Havers family of Thelton (now Thelveton) Hall provided a stipend of £15 a year. In the early 1820s the congregation at Flixton decided to transfer the mission to the nearby market town of Bungay. Its two most prominent members, John Cuddon (a timber merchant, and the descendant of a recusant gentry family) and Richard Smith (a cloth manufacturer), petitioned the twelfth Duke of Norfolk for help in purchasing a suitable site. They settled on a piece of land next to the Anglican Church, which had once been the site of the Holy Cross Priory. On 18 June 1823, a chapel was opened on the site of the current St Edmund's church. With commendable ecumenical spirit, Richard Mann, one of the church wardens at St Mary's, next door, held off ringing the bells whilst the High Mass was being celebrated, and then rang 'merry peals' during the day in celebration.[24]

These areas were, however, the exception rather than the rule. By 1862 the Diocese of Northampton had twenty-five priests and thirty-four churches, chapels and mission stations, with four convents. In all these areas, it was the back marker in England and Wales:[25] in Northamptonshire itself, in addition to the pro-cathedral of St Felix, there were churches at Daventry, Peterborough and Weedon Barracks; Bedfordshire had a single church at Shefford; there were four in Buckinghamshire; in Cambridge there were two with priests, with churches in Ely and Newmarket served once a month from King's Lynn, and the one in March served monthly from Wisbech; Norfolk had six churches with

regular services, with two supplied from Bungay and
Wisbech, which along with Suffolk's nine churches,
showed where the predominance of Catholics in the
diocese was—if, that is, one can use that word about
such small numbers.[26]

Wareing's successor, Francis Amherst, was another
Oscott man, but cut of a very different cloth. Coming
from recusant gentry stock, he was a fox-hunting man
who wanted to be an engineer before he found his
vocation.[27] He had been serving quietly at the mission
in Stafford when, to his surprise and consternation, he
received a telegram from Mgr Talbot in Rome telling
him he was appointed to the see of Northampton. His
response was indicative of his feelings: *Si fieri potest
transeat a me calix iste* ('If it can be, let this cup pass from
me'). Despite a very mangled version of this reaching
Rome by telegram, Pius IX persisted, and Amherst
found himself the reluctant successor to Wareing.
Amherst described the diocese as 'in a most destitute
condition, fifty years behind the rest of England' and
in 'want of priests and money'; as his obituary notice
in *The Tablet* commented,[28]

> The Diocese of Northampton is not one in which
> it is very easy to make a display. Bishop Amherst
> had an amount of zeal which would have shown
> itself in a more brilliant way had he possessed
> a field for operations. In the Northampton
> Diocese, there are not two thousand Catholics
> in any one town.

For all his talents, Amherst was obliged to content
himself with 'steady but solid progress'. It was Amherst who paved the way for the partial rebuilding of
the mother church in Northampton, and who helped
secure its cathedral status in 1859, and who bought the

church of St John the Baptist in the town. But progress, such as it was, was slow and extremely patchy. The scarcity of Catholics meant there was much inter-marriage and what Wareing had called 'consorting' with non-Catholics, as well as a relative neglect of feast days and other ceremonies.[29] The gradual increase in the number of churches across the next half-century did something to ameliorate this situation, but even by the 1890s, Cardinal Manning could describe Northampton as the 'dead diocese'.[30]

Those words should not be taken as a reflection on the faithful, who lived their faith in an atmosphere of prejudice and incomprehension from their neighbours. The penal laws and two and a half centuries of Protestant propaganda had left their mark in many ways, not the least of which was an understated and private style of worship. What ordinary British people thought they knew about Catholicism did not recommend it to them, and should any of them have walked into a Catholic Mass they would, for the most part, have found it literally incomprehensible, as it was, of course, in Latin. More educated members of the congregation would have followed the service through a missal, but, as anyone who has seen one of the (scarce) late-nineteenth-century missals would confirm, they are not easy to follow. Usually in small print, the Introit, Gradual, Offertory and Communion prayers are in parallel Latin and English columns, with the Collect and Secret and Post-Communion prayers in English only, with the Lessons and the Gospels in English only at the back of the missal; the Ordinary and Canon of the Mass appear elsewhere. The Old Testament was scarcely read at Mass, and the cycle of readings was from the same Gospels and Epistles every year, so very little of the Bible was heard or preached upon.[31] In a strongly Nonconformist region of England, where biblical literacy was taken as a sure sign of being 'saved', and Sunday sermons of an hour and a half were not uncommon, such Catholic worship did not impress the locals as a Christian witness, serving rather to confirm than deny popular prejudices.

Almost untouched by Irish immigration, Northampton remained the back marker of the fifteen dioceses of England and Wales, and even a decade after the restoration of the hierarchy it had fewer priests and churches than any of the others.[32] Northamptonshire, Bedfordshire and Buckinghamshire between them mustered only eight churches, two of which were served from elsewhere; only one of Cambridgeshire's six churches had a resident priest; Norfolk and Suffolk remained the *loci* of most Catholics, with Norwich itself having about 1,700 by the 1870s.[33]

Thus, when Amherst's successor, Bishop Arthur Grange Riddell, was appointed in 1880, it was thought that 'his acceptance of the diocese was a courageous step', as diocesan missions were few and far between, and endowments were insufficient.[34] He was 'heavily handicapped at the first, a northerner amongst strangers', and it was probably a good thing he hailed from a long line of soldiers, because he faced a situation which would have daunted all but the strongest heart. Well aware of the scale of the task facing him in his new diocese, as well as the paucity of the tools at his disposal, Riddell knew that England had yet to 'shake off the shackles of apostasy' and the task of the ordinary Catholic was simple, but hard:[35]

> Meanwhile, what is our duty? It is to be thorough Catholics, Catholics in name and in deed; practical Catholics, fulfilling all our duties to God and to our

neighbour, praying, hearing Mass, frequenting the Sacraments, keeping the days of fasting and abstinence, avoiding sin, practising virtue, loving God; this is the way for us to assist in the conversion of England, and there is no other.

From the start he determined to start more missions to create 'new centres of life and grace' which would be 'the means under God of saving some Catholics from the loss of faith' and bringing others to it.[36] He pursued his campaign with all the efficiency and manoeuvrability of a Christian soldier. He thought that

the best way of bringing back the faith to the English people is to open missions and to erect churches of a moderate size but of good design in new centres; and where a large mission already exists to divide it and separate its various outlying districts into new independent missions. The raising of an altar and the placing of the Blessed Sacrament in a new home is the sure way of advancing the interests of God and of conveying the faith to our beloved countrymen.

He was convinced that 'where our Divine Lord resides' the 'light of faith' would be 'kindled' and that 'sinners' would be 'drawn to repentance and the charity of devout people ... increased'.[37]

Had faith itself been sufficient, then Wareing and Amherst would have left Riddell a better inheritance, but it needed to be accompanied by a plan of campaign — this he had, as he revealed in his first pastoral letter in 1880. He intended to be a church planter; he would start wherever there were Catholics, and work out from that base as the Lord provided the opportunity. Rather in the way Cardinal Manning refused to build a cathedral in London until the Church was well provided with schools, so Riddell refused to sanction new buildings until two-thirds of the cost had been raised privately. This explains the nature of the progress made by Riddell during his twenty-seven years at Northampton. Much depended on individual initiatives and the generosity of private donors, so it was, to that extent, a tactical, rather than a strategic plan, and there would be false starts and dead ends as well as some spectacular gains. But finally, there was real progress: twenty-five missions were opened between 1880 and 1906 (not all successful), most notably at Sudbury and Daventry in 1880, Lowestoft, Wellingborough and Lynford in 1881, then Luton in 1884, and Slough the following year; these were followed by Aylesbury (1888), Gorleston and Wycombe (1889), then Ely (1890), Kettering and Buckingham; eighteen stations (where Masses took place as opportunity presented) were set up, most of them in private residences, and a further fourteen chapels were opened as an earnest of hopeful future growth.[38]

There is, in such histories as there are of this period, a naturally Whiggish tendency to dwell upon the missions that successfully grew to be the centre of the parish system when it was re-established, but whilst not resisting such a narrative, there is something to be learned about the wider context in which priests and laity struggled, from a brief examination of one of the early failures—Woodbridge in Suffolk.

St Pancras church in Ipswich was built in 1861, and served the small Catholic community in a staunchly Protestant part of a very Protestant county. Indeed, the year after the church was opened, there were anti-papist riots and attacks on the church and businesses owned by Catholics in the town.[39] Fr Arthur Job Wallace, the convert son of the Rector of Hadleigh, gave money to build a school there, and, being in the habit of tramping the nine miles out to the village of Woodbridge to minister to the small number of Catholics there, he bought some land on which to build a church for them in 1871, which, again, he funded, it is said from the monies he received from his time serving as a Catholic chaplain with British troops in South Africa during the Ashanti wars. A splendidly eccentric character, he once concluded a homily by asking for 'three cheers for the Pope!' He worked hard with local Catholics, and in April 1881 a mission centre was opened there, which, after Wallace's departure, was served by Fr George Wilmot Mayne, who celebrated Mass daily at 8.30, and on Sundays at 8 and 11. But the congregation was small, and the collections never enough to support the mission, and after 1885 it was served from Ipswich on an occasional basis.[40] Similarly, the mission at Brampton, which had been attached to the school there, failed when the school closed. These setbacks apart, the strategy of establishing missions was, on the whole, more successful than not, with Norfolk and Suffolk benefiting from the holiday trade, with missions established at Cromer and Hunstanton in 1902 and 1903, and at Felixstowe and Southwold in 1889.

The pattern varied according to local circumstances, but the usual practice was that followed at Woodbridge (though with little success there), which was to rent a room for a priest, establish a small oratory and then try to secure enough donations to buy land to build a church. Individual generosity could make a huge difference to the success of the missions. Mrs Lyne Stephens (a former prima ballerina, who was the rich widow of the man who had made a fortune inventing moving dolls' eyes), who paid for the bishop's house in Northampton, also paid for the building of churches at Lynford, Shefford and Cambridge. With that sort of generosity, the situation encountered at Woodbridge could be avoided. By 1895 presbyteries had been built at Cambridge, Aylesbury, Beccles, Kettering, High Wycombe, Wellingborough and Norwich, with the Benedictines of Downside contributing to the one at Bungay. The Duke of Norfolk's generosity in helping the churches in Norwich was crowned in the 1890s by his funding a huge new church in the city (the future cathedral).[41]

In 1880 no Mass had been said anywhere between King's Lynn and Yarmouth, but with the coming of the railways in the 1870s and 1880s, and the arrival of holidaymakers and prosperity, that situation changed. As usual, much depended on the generosity and drive of individuals. Clement Scott, the drama critic of the *Daily Telegraph*, a convert, married to the sister of Daphne du Maurier, had a home in Cromer and fell in love with the area between it and Sidestrand, which he christened 'Poppyland'. In 1886 he wrote to Bishop Riddell, drawing his attention to the existence of a private chapel set up at Abbots Hall Farm, near Aylsham, whose owner was willing to help pay for a priest, if one could be had. Scott volunteered to help pay for this. Riddell, correctly, thought Aylsham too difficult of access for a mission to succeed, but directed Scott's attention to Cromer itself. Described by one contemporary as 'the most Protestant town in Europe', Cromer had become a target for Riddell's mission-planting with the arrival of the railways.[42]

It was easy enough, in a holiday resort, for Riddell's missioner, Canon Duckett of Norwich, to secure a base from which Mass could be said for Catholic visitors, which he did every summer between 1888 and 1891.

The mission was successful enough for the search for a plot of land to be intensified, but the local Protestants were not keen to sell their land to the Catholic Church. Finally, in 1894, the 5th Baron Suffield, the greatest landowner in the area, allowed the church to take out a ninety-nine-year lease on an acre of land near Overstrand, with the option to purchase it thereafter for £510. Duckett's summer missions had already attracted donations from local worthies, but it was, once more, the remarkable generosity of Mrs Lyne Stephens which provided the final £5000 necessary to purchase the land and build the mission chapel, which could, if things went well, serve as the nave of a larger church.[43] Thus it was that in 1895, the church of Our Lady of Refuge was opened at Cromer—within easy reach of the station. In 1900, the Bishop exercised the right to purchase the plot.

Bishop Riddell's commitment to mission ensured that by 1896 the number of clergy had risen from twenty-five to sixty-one, and the number of churches had gone from thirty-five to sixty-one, with another seventeen chapels and communities; there were also forty-one elementary schools, and a seminary.[44] Not the least of his many achievements was to make such progress 'without doing anything to embitter those holding equally conscientiously other religious views'.[45]

Placing this record against Manning's comment about Northampton being a 'dead diocese', it is possible to construct a counter-narrative in which Riddell's 'brilliant administration' and 'clear vision' produced 'steady growth'.[46] But, given the current state of research, a note of caution might be entered, as where we can penetrate beneath the figures, we see signs of what we might expect—which is more of an ebb and flow, with eddies, than a steady flowing stream. Just as the reality of the faith, which sustained these efforts, cannot be adequately captured in the bare figures, so too do they fail to illustrate the local struggles to plant the Catholic Church in some pretty unpromising soil.

At Bungay, where the Benedictines continued to supply the new church, and where the Catholic community was well established, the thirty years after 1800 had seen ninety-one confirmations, many of them converts.[47] But a series of indifferent missioners across the next thirty years, when there were ten incumbents, halted this promising start. Ambrose Duck, who was there between 1840 and 1846, was a good and pious man, but 'owing to a want of mental vigour & coherence' was, according to Dr Ullathorne (later Bishop of Birmingham) unfit to be left in sole charge of a congregation. Part of the problem was the isolation—it was sixteen miles to Norwich, the nearest Catholic centre, and when, as had been the case with Duck, relations with senior members of his own congregation had become strained, there was no source of moral support. The deaths of the two men most prominent in funding the church in Bungay, John Cuddon (1839) and Richard Smith (1842), had created problems on the financial front, and there was a falling off of numbers, from seventy-six Easter communions in 1842 to sixty-five in 1845. Ullathorne reported that the choir had ceased, and the school was 'in ruins'. But Duck's departure did not improve matters, and by 1866 the congregation was down to fifty-eight. It was not, the Benedictine historian of the church has written, 'a popular mission'. One missioner wrote back to Downside: 'I have no news of any kind. One day here is exactly like the preceding with the exception of the weather'.[48] An attempt by the Benedictines to hand the mission over to the diocese was foiled because Bishop Amherst had no priests to spare. Such insights are not to be had everywhere, but they suggest that behind the bare recital of figures of growth, there were individual struggles about which we would like to know more.

In fact, just when the fortunes of the church at Bungay were at their lowest ebb, the widow of the fourteenth Duke of Norfolk, Minna, made substantial donations, which allowed the building of a school and improvements to be made to the chapel. As so often in the story, one donation led to another, and Frederic Smith, grandson of one of the founders of the church there, who had been instrumental in helping found the school, formed a fruitful relationship with the priest appointed by Downside in 1885, Dom Ephrem Guy (1833–99). Guy, whose love of bold projects had got him into financial trouble at Downside, found in Smith a man with the resources and will to match his own vision. Thus, in August 1888 the foundation stone of an enlarged chancel was laid, with Bishop Riddell celebrating Mass at its opening on 9 January 1889. The offertory collection was devoted to a planned future mission in Beccles, where a chapel was opened in 1901.[49] Thanks to Smith's generosity, a new Lady Chapel and presbytery, and later a baptistry, were also built. In all, Smith contributed about £17,000 of his own money, ensuring that St Edmund's, Bungay, was one of the finest churches in the diocese, later listed as Grade 1 by the authorities.

St Edmund's showed what could be achieved where there was a Catholic community with a vigorous priest and generous donors, but, as with Norwich, Cambridge and Northampton itself, it was something of an oasis in otherwise stony soil. Writing in 1891, Bishop Riddell listed those missions which depended entirely upon his mission fund: Coldham, Sudbury, Gorleston-on-Sea, Huntingdon, Wolverton, Aylesbury 'all require special grants for the maintenance of the priest and the other ordinary expenses of the mission', he wrote, whilst 'Ely, Daventry, Luton, Aston-le-Walls, and High Wycombe need special assistance', to which list of struggling missions he thought Wellingborough, Kettering and Stowmarket 'might be added'. In the case of the last, the long-serving priest, Fr Francis Wormall, died in 1899, having, in his twenty-year mission, seen the congregation grow from six to fifty-five, and they had been able to move from worshipping in a small (24 x 12 foot) 'tin tabernacle' to a school house with a chapel above it, having raised £1,600. But with Wormall's death, the school had had to be closed because of lack of funds.[50] This illustrated one of Riddell's problems. His mission fund had no endowment, and there were only nine individuals who gave money regularly; for the rest everything depended on the generosity of small congregations—and that amounted to about £1 a year per church in the diocese; the Lord may love a cheerful giver, but his Lordship wished there were rather more of them.[51] Where, like Mrs Lyne Stephens and Frederic Smith, their generosity came without too many conditions, such donors allowed Riddell to use their money where he thought best, but there were times when, as the history of the chapel at Walsingham showed, donors could provide him with a headache.

In 1895 a wealthy Anglican convert, Miss Charlotte Boyd, offered the old Slipper Chapel at Walsingham to the Benedictines, having become an oblate of Downside. Unwilling to take on an obligation so far from their own centre of operations in northern Suffolk, the monks suggested she contact Riddell.[52] Once the last stage of the pilgrimage to the great shrine, the old Slipper Chapel had sunk into rural neglect, with a few houses built on its side, and the site itself being used as a barn. Miss Boyd conceived the idea of restoring it as a centre for Catholic pilgrimage. But such a visionary approach sat ill alongside Riddell's chosen method of mission planting, and seeing that he proposed to use it merely as a mission chapel, Miss Boyd withdrew her offer and gave it to Downside.

Riddell's focus over in the west of Norfolk had been on King's Lynn, where Pugin had designed a church, St Mary's, which had been consecrated in 1845. The church provided a focus for about a hundred and fifty Catholics, for which it was just about adequate. But when the future Edward VII purchased Sandringham, just up the road, the area became more fashionable. The Prince of Wales entertained many Catholic friends, and the little church seemed in need of expansion. Fr George Wrigglesworth, the local priest, persuaded the Prince to pay for a survey of the church, which revealed that its foundations were unsound. An appeal was opened to build a new church, to which the Prince contributed fifty guineas (about £10,000 in today's currency). With help from Riddell (using Mrs Lynne Stephens's generosity) a new church, dedicated to Our Lady of the Annunciation, was opened in 1897.[53] Pope Leo XIII had given permission for the Lady Chapel of the Church to be established as a national shrine to Our Lady, which was one of the reasons Riddell had been unable to agree to Miss Boyd's suggestion. However, as St Paul once noted, all things work to the good when the Spirit moves, and Fr Wrigglesworth led a pilgrimage from Lynn to Walsingham the day after the shrine was consecrated — the first time there had been such a thing since the Reformation. The *Eastern Daily Press* on 21 August 1897 recorded that 'a procession of some forty or fifty persons headed by a crucifix, flanked with burning tapers and led by a priest wended their way to the way-side chapel, where a short private service was held' —after which the public were admitted.

Miss Boyd commissioned an architect to restore the old Slipper Chapel, although the work was not finished for nearly thirty years after her death in 1906. By then, the diocese had accepted the gift of the chapel, and the foundations for the present national Catholic shrine were laid. Symbolically, the return of Our Lady to Walsingham was an important moment in the history of modern English Catholicism.

Another significant moment came from a more traditional source of support—the dukes of Norfolk.[54] In 1877, Fr Duckett of St John's in Norwich wrote to the fifteenth Duke, Henry Fitzalan-Howard, asking whether he would be willing to make a donation towards the cost of a new church. Both the church and the house at St John's Maddermarket had been giving cause for concern for some time. The workmanship on both was substandard, and Fr Duckett was looking to see if they could be replaced. The Duke was happy to subscribe up to £27,000 for this purpose, and after some searching the Old Gaol site at the junction of the Unthank and Earlham roads was chosen. Bishop Amherst was not keen on it because it was so close to the Jesuit church in Willow Lane. But the land was purchased, and with it seeming as though it was the Jesuits who now stood in the way of the building of a splendid new church, negotiations opened between the Jesuit Superior, Edward Purbrick, and the newly appointed Bishop Riddell about the terms on which the Jesuits would leave their mission to the secular clergy, and undertake work elsewhere in the diocese. Although the local congregation was unhappy at the idea, Riddell and the Duke saw it as a good way out of an embarrassing situation. The Jesuits reckoned that they had spent about £12,000 on the Willow Lane chapel, and a valuation of £5,175 14s was placed on the whole property. Purbrick was willing to hand over the property for £3,000, a figure close enough to the valuation put on it by the diocese for a deal to be concluded. On 27 January, the Jesuits left Norwich after at least 250 years. Work on the new church began in 1882, with the foundation stone being laid in 1884. In 1894 the nave was opened, and the church of St John the Baptist, designed by George Gilbert Scott and his brother, John Oldrid, was completed in 1910.[55] It was the largest parish church in England—a fitting seat for the new Diocese of East Anglia when it was created in 1976.

The year 1900 marked 'Good Bishop Riddell's' twenty-fifth anniversary. He had set out to 'bring the faith to the English people'. It was not, he wrote, 'for us to enumerate the missions that have been started, nor the churches, presbyteries and schools that have been erected',[56] but with nearly seventy priests, thirty-five parishes and fifteen Mass stations, with a congregation of 12,744, he could be said to have succeeded in his task.[57] However, he could, 'without boasting', point to 'churches, such as Norwich St John's, Cambridge, and Bungay with which few others in this country can compare', and it was 'with a heart full of gratitude we thank God and our earthly benefactors for the work that has been accomplished during the past years of our episcopate'.[58] Even in Norfolk, there were no more than 3,000 Catholics, all but five hundred of them in Norwich. There were still, of course, 'large tracts' of the diocese where the Church had no presence, and Riddell did not underestimate the challenges facing him and his successors.

It was typical of Riddell that, at a grand dinner to celebrate his silver jubilee as Bishop in July 1905, he should have disclaimed credit for the many achievements, preferring instead to give it to his clergy and the generosity of the laity.[59] But by the time he retired in 1907, he could have said with St Paul that he had kept the faith and fought the good fight. The £600 raised for his silver jubilee went, needless to say, into further church planting. He had achieved far more than anyone thought would have been possible at the time of his accession, and by 1907 'the dioceses of Northampton and East Anglia had', their historian triumphantly records, 'gained nearly half their present shape.'[60] He was, of course, right to pay tribute to others, without whom what he achieved could not have been done, but tribute should be made to 'Good Bishop Riddell', as he came to be known, for fulfilling that mission to 'feed my sheep'.

Notes

[1]   D. Gwynn, *The Second Spring 1818–1852: A Study of the Catholic Revival in England* (London: Burns and Oates, 1942), p. 2.

[2]   I am grateful to Rowena Burgess for this information from the 1851 census.

[3]   E. R. Norman, *The English Catholic Church in the Nineteenth Century* (Oxford: Clarendon, 1984), p. 6.

[4]   Lance (2000), p. 2.

[5]   'Silver Jubilee of the Diocese of Northampton', *The Tablet*, 25 July 1905, p. 24.

[6]   G. A. Beck, *The English Catholics 1850–1950: A Century of Progress* (London: Burns and Oates, 1950), p. 118.

[7]   J. H. Newman, 'Sermon 10: The Second Spring' (http://www.newmanreader.org/works/occasions/sermon10.html), accessed 6 May 2015.

[8]   Norman (1984), p. 1.

9   V. A. McClelland, *Cardinal Manning: His Public Life and Influence, 1865–1892* (Oxford: Oxford University Press, 1962), pp. 5–6.

10 Lance (2000), p. 2, whence all the figures are taken.

11 G. Albion, 'The Restoration of the Hierarchy', in Beck (1950), p. 72.

12 Devany (2010), pp. 161–3.

13 C. A. Munkman, *The Catholic Revival in North Norfolk: Centenary of Our Lady Of refuge Church in Cromer 1895–1995* (Cromer: Parish Council of the Church of Our Lady of Refuge, 1995), p. 1.

14 *The Tablet*, 23 September 1911, p. 8.

15 *The Tablet*, 15 July 1905, p. 34.

16 See E. G. Gage, *Costessey Hall* (Norwich, 1991) for the history.

17 'Our Lady and St Walstan Church, Costessey', Norfolk Churches (http://www.norfolkchurches.co.uk/costesseyrc/costesseyrc.htm), accessed 9 May 2015.

18 Devany (2010), pp.159–60.

19 T. Holt, 'Catholic Chapels in Norwich before 1900', *Transactions of the Norfolk & Norwich Archaeological Society* 37 (1979), pp. 159–61.

20 *Ibid.*, pp. 153–4.

21 F. Young, 'Surviving the Reformation: Who were the Catholics?', Wuffing Education Study Day, Sutton Hoo, 29 March 2014.

22 Crouzet (2007) pp. 36–8.

23 *Ibid.*, pp. 38–9.

24 *Ibid.*, pp. 49–54.

25 *Ordo Recitandi Officii Divini* in *The Catholic Directory, Ecclesiastical Register, and Almanac, for the Year 1862* (London: Burns and Lambert, 1862), p. xvii.

26 *Ibid.*, pp. 131–3.

27 'Memoir of Bishop Amherst', *The Tablet*, 1 September 1883, p. 23.

28 *Ibid.*

29 Lance (2000), p. 2.

30 *The Tablet*, 21 February 1953, p. 9.

31 J. Rockett, *Held in Trust: Catholic Parishes in England and Wales 1900–1950* (Brockley: St Austin Press, 2001), p. 34.

32 *Catholic Directory* (1862), p. xvii.

33 *Ibid.*, pp. 131–4; Holt (1979), p. 169.
34 'Silver Jubilee of the Diocese of Northampton', *The Tablet*, 15 July 1905, p. 24.
35 *The Tablet*, 12 March 1887, p. 35.
36 Munkman (1995), pp. 1–2.
37 *The Tablet*, 16 December 1905, p. 14.
38 *Ibid.*, p. 2; Lance (2000), p. 24 has the full list.
39 'From the Church Archives', St Pancras' Church, Ipswich (http://www.stpancraschurch.org.uk/Church_History/Archives/archives.html), accessed 20 May 2015.
40 *A History of the Catholic Church of St Thomas of Canterbury, Woodbridge* (Woodbridge, 1987), pp. 3–4.
41 Munkman (1995), pp. 3–5.
42 *Ibid.*, p. 15.
43 *Ibid.*, pp. 17–18.
44 *The Catholic Directory Ecclesiastical Register and Almanac, for the Year 1896* (London: Burns and Oates, 1896), p. 215.
45 *The Tablet*, 15 July 1905, p. 24.
46 Lance (2000), p. 57.
47 Crouzet (2007), p. 55.
48 *Ibid.*, pp. 58–9.
49 *Ibid.*, p. 70; Lance (2000), p. 25.
50 Lance (2000).
51 *The Tablet*, 5 December 1891, p. 35.
52 P. Rollings, *Walsingham: England's Nazareth* (Walsingham: National Shrine of Our Lady of Walsingham, 1998), p. 20.
53 'The Annunciation, King's Lynn', Norfolk Churches (http://www.norfolkchurches.co.uk/lynnannunciation/lynnannunciation.htm), accessed 9 May 2015.
54 G. M. Fitzalan-Howard, *Henry FitzAlan-Howard, fifteenth Duke of Norfolk* (Oxford: Oxford University Press, 1917).
55 Holt (1979), pp. 164–5.
56 *The Tablet*, 16 December 1905, p. 14.
57 Lance (2010), p. 57.
58 *The Tablet*, 16 December 1905, p. 14.
59 'Silver Jubilee of the Diocese of Northampton', *The Tablet*, 15 July 1905, p. 24.
60 Lance (2010), p. 57.

✛ 6 ✛

From Idea to Reality: Towards a Diocese for East Anglia, 1901–1976

Michael Edwards

HEN, ON 2 JUNE 1976, in the church of St John the Baptist, Norwich, Alan Clark was installed as the first diocesan Bishop of East Anglia, an idea was given concrete reality which had been in existence for well over a hundred years. As early as 1860 Bishop Amherst, the second Bishop of Northampton (1858–79), was (perhaps not too seriously) considering the idea that Norfolk, Suffolk, Cambridgeshire and Essex could become an episcopal see, with Ipswich as its cathedral town. The unifying element of this 'dream diocese' would be the Great

This chapter is based on the first part of an article by the late Michael Edwards entitled '1976–2001 — Twenty Years a Diocese' which appeared in the diocesan ordo of the Diocese of East Anglia for 2001. The text of the article is reproduced here by kind permission of the Diocese of East Anglia. Michael Edwards acknowledged with thanks the assistance of Margaret Osborne, Diocesan Archivist of Northampton, Rev. Derek Lance, Rev. John Warrington, Dora Cowton and Sheila Monahan, Associate Archivists of the Diocese of East Anglia, the clergy of St John's Cathedral, and Ann Milton, Archivist of the National Shrine of Our Lady, Walsingham.

Eastern Railway system. 'It traverses the whole length, like a backbone sending out ribs in all directions'.[1]

Bishop Amherst's real Diocese of Northampton was in fact something of an anomaly. It is said that when, in preparation for the re-establishment of the Catholic hierarchy in 1850, diocesan boundaries were being discussed, there was little difficulty in establishing some ten of them: Beverley, Birmingham, Clifton, Hexham, Liverpool, Nottingham, Plymouth, Salford, Shrewsbury and Southwark—but that when all was done there were left, untouched and unprovided for, two great areas of the country, sparsely populated, with a minimum of Catholics and few prospects of an immediate revival: Wales in the west, and, in the east, all that tract of country comprising Norfolk, Suffolk, Cambridgeshire, Northampton, Huntingdon, Bedfordshire and Buckinghamshire: apart from Lincolnshire, in fact, the entire territory of the old Eastern Region. Of these two areas the first was disposed of by creating the Diocese of Newport and Menevia, and the second, for which no adequate provision seemed possible, was lumped together under one title, as the Diocese of Northampton.[2] The problem was, as Bishop Amherst himself expressed it in 1875, 'Seven large counties, and only six thousand Catholics!'[3]

The beginning was indeed hard, and it has been handsomely documented by Derek Lance in *The Returning Tide, Northampton Diocese 1850–2000*. The Diocese of East Anglia must always gratefully remember that it shares a century and a quarter of its history with the 'mother diocese' of Northampton. Chapter 5 of *The Returning Tide*, entitled 'Moving Out—Moving On (1976–2000)', describes how

Some priests, across the counties in our Eastern Region, on waking up on 14 March 1976, may well have echoed the words of Bishop Parker, 'We wonder where we are'. Practically overnight, they had been moved out of Northampton Diocese and into a new diocese called East Anglia, without taking a single step. What had been discussed for quite some time, had finally happened. The diocese had been divided. On 13 March 1976, by the decree *Quod Oecumenicum*, Pope Paul VI formed the Diocese of East Anglia, comprising the counties of Cambridgeshire, Norfolk and Suffolk. Priests now belonged to whichever diocese they happened to be stationed in at that time, although there was a period of grace, during which exchanges could be made, with the agreement of both bishops. Charles Grant remained Bishop of Northampton and Alan Clark was to become Bishop of the new Diocese of East Anglia. He was already a familiar figure there as he had been Auxiliary Bishop to Bishop Grant since 1969 and had had special responsibility for that eastern part of Northampton Diocese.[4]

Bishop Keating's 'Pastoral Letter for Advent 1917' has already been quoted. It is subtitled 'Is the diocese too large? Or too small?' He begins:

The annual appeal for the maintenance of our poor Missions offers a convenient opportunity for adverting to a matter of vital interest to the diocese, which has been discussed, with amazing and unprecedented freedom, in the correspondence columns of a Catholic newspaper.[5]

His closing words are:

Least of all could we endure to be compelled, by the depletion of our Poor Mission Fund and

other diocesan resources, to reduce the pittances
granted to our Clergy, to sacrifice, as Bishop
Wareing had to sacrifice, all hope of breaking
fresh ground, and to watch the mutilated remnant
of a diocese perish of inanition.[6]

In referring to the Poor Mission Fund both at the beginning and at the end of the letter, the Bishop clearly
shows that money was the problem. 'The real difficulty in administration arises, not from the fact that
the diocese is too large in area, but from the fact that
it is too small in numbers and resources.' In spite of
'the immensity of our territory' he estimates the total
Catholic population of the diocese at 15,000. 'Could
any sane person, knowing the situation, propose to
weaken it still further by division?'[7]

Give us some unsuspected source of wealth, such
as the discovery of oil-springs; or some great
commercial enterprise, such as the manufacture
on a grand scale of beet-sugar; or let agriculture
resume its place as the chief industry of our
country; let Catholic families come flocking to
us, as they have flocked hitherto into London,
Liverpool, and Manchester: in quite a short time,
we shall be as busy as our Brethren.'[8]

Bishop Keating's argument, however passionate it
may have been, was not against the inherent suita-
bility of a separate East Anglian Diocese, but against
the economic possibility of its realisation in 1917. The
underlying unrest of certain East Anglians, which in
1917 had manifested itself 'in the correspondence columns of a Catholic newspaper', surfaced again some
two decades later in *The Tablet* with the publication
of 'A Plea for an East Anglian Diocese'. The author,
who identifies himself simply as 'one who comes from

an old Norfolk family', acknowledges that 'Northampton remains the largest and most unwieldy of
the English dioceses, the poorest, and with the least
number of clergy to serve the greatest area *per capita*
(in fact 150 priests to serve seven counties, comprising four-and-a-half-million acres, or well over seven
thousand square miles)'. He goes on to argue that,
apart from questions of size and numerical strength,
'a diocese was originally, and still should be, where
circumstances permit, a geographical unit'.[9] He goes
back to the mid-seventh century, when Sigebert, as
king of East Anglia, had enabled St Felix to set up his
'see-centre' at (supposedly) Dunwich. He then traces
the vicissitudes of the diocese—or dioceses, for at
one stage there were two, for the 'North folk' and the
'South folk'—via Elmham and Thetford to Norwich,
the true capital of East Anglia, in 1094. But even under
the Normans

> East Anglia, isolated from the rest of England
> by the fens and wild moors, remained a
> distinct district, aloof from all others, in spite
> of the constant passing to and from of pilgrims
> from far and wide, to visit the great shrines of
> Walsingham, Bury and Bromholm. All those who
> came from outside its borders, East Anglia dubbed
> 'furriners', and 'furriners' they remain until this
> day. Conservative, loyal, stubborn, with intense
> pride of county, the East Anglian is hard to change.
> [...] Northampton, beyond the fens, had no sort
> of association with him at all.[10]

Our East Anglian admits that, against the division of
the diocese

> There would seem to be one great reason, and
> that is finance. [...] The diocese is not sufficiently

well off to divide. [...] Great rural districts, few
large industrial towns, widely scattered people,
tiny missions, lonely priests face to face with
fearful odds of which city folk, in prosperous
Catholic strongholds have small idea: these are
the factors which make any idea of division
nothing more than a pleasant dream. But
somehow the present writer (being a 'Norfolk
man') has a feeling that the Church in England
has accomplished so many things seemingly
'impossible' in the past century, and goes on
grappling with other problems equally immense,
that even this seeming impossibility of an East
Anglian Diocese may be achieved.[11]

Little more than a year later came the Second World
War—and East Anglia became one vast airfield. There
were evacuee children from London. There were all the
challenges of life in wartime. Norwich was bombed,
and the great church of St John—the future cathedral—
was damaged, though fortunately not too seriously.
Clearly, no changes to diocesan boundaries were going
to take place until the war was over, and in 1945 the economic situation of the East Anglian counties remained
much as it had been in 1939. Change, however, was
on the horizon. Over the next thirty years prosperity
blossomed in East Anglia. The population grew in size.
Though agriculture remained the principal industry,
other businesses grew and flourished, especially in
the towns and cities. East Anglia gradually ceased to
be a backwater.

In the meantime Pope John XXIII had galvanised the
Catholic Church by calling the Second Vatican Council,
the consequences of which have had, and continue to
have, the most profound effects throughout the life of
the Church. Among the Council's other decrees came

Christus Dominus, promulgated on 28 October 1965, 'On the Pastoral Office of Bishops in the Church'. It contains a section on diocesan boundaries (nos. 22–4). After the Council had closed, this decree was followed up by a *Motu Proprio* of Paul VI, *Ecclesiae Sanctae*, of 6 August 1966, on the implementation of *Christus Dominus* and other decrees. *Christus Dominus* had laid down that 'a prudent revision of diocesan boundaries should be undertaken as soon as possible' (no. 22). Three elements were to be taken into account: 1. The 'composition of the People of God', with the civil boundaries, and the special characteristics—psychological, economic, geographical or historical—of peoples and regions; 2. The size of the diocese, which should be appropriate for government by a single bishop; and 3. Adequate provision of priests and resources (no. 23). *Ecclesiae Sanctae* advocated the setting up of a special commission, where necessary, by each episcopal conference, to secure a proper revision of diocesan boundaries in its territory (no. 12).[12]

The bishops of England and Wales duly set up a Commission for Diocesan Boundaries in 1966, and each diocese submitted maps and figures. This led to the institution in 1967 of a National Committee for Population Study, which submitted its findings to the Bishops' Conference in 1969. It was decided, however, to postpone any review of existing boundaries until the details of the Local Government Act 1972 had been published. When this had taken place, the Committee for Population Study met with the standing committee of the Bishops' Conference on 14 December 1972, and its name was changed to the Committee for the Review of Diocesan Boundaries. Northampton was represented by its Vicar General, Mgr F. Diamond. A first draft scheme was submitted in October 1973, and a revised draft in Low Week 1974. This was published for general discussion under the title of *Ground Plan*.[13]

Ground Plan proposed, under the general heading 'London and the Home Counties (North) and East Anglia', a reduced Diocese of Northampton (Diocese 7) and a new diocese consisting of Cambridgeshire, Norfolk and Suffolk (Diocese 6).[14] At the request of Bishop Charles Grant of Northampton, a document was now prepared, and issued in November 1975, entitled *Proposals and Recommendations concerning the Division of the Diocese of Northampton*. Its purpose was to determine the practical steps necessary for the implementation of the recommendations of *Ground Plan* insofar as they concerned the Northampton Diocese.

> As a result of the publication of *Ground Plan* a systematic process of consultation was conducted in the Diocese of Northampton.[15] The Bishop instructed each Deanery Conference to discuss the proposals; views from the Deaneries were reported to the Senate of Priests for further discussion, and the resulting opinions were summarised and circulated to all the clergy. The matter was also considered on more than one occasion by the Cathedral Chapter, which submitted its views to the Bishop. At a subsequent meeting of the Senate of Priests a resolution was passed, with no dissentient voice, asking that the separation of the Eastern part of the diocese to form a new diocese should be asked for without delay. Further discussion in the Deaneries and by the Senate was called for using prepared 'Guidelines', and the Bishop announced the appointment of a small Committee to prepare a recommendation, after looking at the practicalities of the situation, for submission to the Holy See. It is as a result of this process of

consultation, and after consideration of views collected also from parish pastoral councils and from individual laity, including comments sent in to the chairman of the Bishops' Committee for the Review of Diocesan Boundaries, that this present paper is now submitted.

It is clear to all who consider it that the present Diocese of Northampton is too large, involving great distances, and that it has no intrinsic logical justification. The diocese has remained as it was originally set up in 1850, and there has never been any clear reason for this large and unwieldy territory other than that it was there as a remainder after the other more rational units had been arranged. There seems indeed to be no administrative or sociological bond, other than the Catholic diocese itself, which groups together such unrelated regions as the Fens and the Vale of Aylesbury, Suffolk and the Chiltern Hundreds. Northampton has never seemed a centre to which the large towns in the East such as Norwich, Ipswich, Cambridge or Bury St Edmunds would naturally relate. Dissatisfaction has been felt and expressed for a long time in the Eastern part of the diocese about the geographical remoteness of the episcopal See, and the formation of an 'East Anglian' diocese has been talked of for many years. Until recent times it has generally been judged impracticable because of the weakness of the Catholic community and its resources, in the diocese as a whole and especially in the rural eastern counties. The situation has however changed gradually as this part of England became involved in the sociological phenomenon known as 'the drift to the South-East'—the general growth in population and prosperity of the counties grouped around London. This has caused great development in the whole diocese in the last thirty years in its material fabric, Catholic population and activity. In fact, the rate of growth in the Northampton Diocese has been greater than in any other English diocese.

It is to be noted that the size of the diocese has been held to justify the appointment of an Auxiliary Bishop for the last fifteen years, and it seems that the normal functioning of the diocese, in its present form, would always demand it. Pastoral care in the Eastern half of the diocese is exercised in general through the Auxiliary Bishop, residing there. Inevitably the presence of the Auxiliary Bishop living and working in 'East Anglia' increases expectation of the formation of a new diocese, and fosters the growth of a local Catholic identity, so that there is a general eagerness to see the separate diocese established and to face the challenge of responsibility.[16]

The Auxiliary Bishop mentioned—and the future Bishop of East Anglia—was Alan Clark, formerly parish priest of St Mary's, Blackheath, who was consecrated Bishop of Elmham by Charles Grant on 13 May 1969. Almost immediately, Clark was appointed by the Holy See as co-chairman of ARCIC (Anglican/ Roman Catholic International Commission). He played an important part in drawing up the 'Agreed Statement on the Eucharist' (Winter 1971), the 'Agreed Statement on Ministry and Ordination' (Canterbury 1973), and later the 'Agreed Statement on Authority', all of which have become landmarks in relations between the Anglican and Roman Catholic Churches. In 1970 the Episcopal Conference elected him chairman of the National Commission for Ecumenism, which became the Department for Mission and Unity. He was also nominated to represent the Conference on the Council of the Conferences of European Bishops. In 1974

Bishop Clark was invited to address the General Synod of the Church of England—the first Catholic bishop ever to do so.[17]

Proposals and Recommendations goes on to deal in detail with the Diocese of Northampton as it then was, and as it would be after the division (and after the possible creation of the proposed Thames Valley Diocese—a possibility that in the event was not to come about). Though considerably smaller in area, Northampton would still consist of seventy-four of the existing parishes, with Northampton itself, Corby, Wellingborough, Bedford, Luton and Slough as its major towns, and a total Catholic population estimated at 135,380. The text continues,

> **The proposed Eastern Diocese.** The new Diocese of the Eastern Counties [...] would be considerably larger in area and in total population [...] although it would be, at present, much smaller in Catholic population. It would consist of 65 parishes. It is a more rural area than the other, and most of the clergy are deployed in parishes manned by one priest only, covering a small town and several villages. There are however four large towns with populations over 100,000 each, and these each contain a number of churches and clergy. Beside the four large towns (Peterborough, Ipswich, Norwich and Cambridge) there are a number of smaller towns which are to receive a considerable expansion in the next few years, chiefly by receiving 'overspill' from London as part of the national housing policy. There is a long coast-line with a number of holiday resorts showing a considerable seasonal increase in both the general and the Catholic population, and there are fishing-ports at Great Yarmouth and

Lowestoft, trading ports at Felixstowe, Ipswich and Kings Lynn. Norfolk and Suffolk formed the ancient kingdom of East Anglia in the sixth and seventh centuries, and this name has for hundreds of years attached itself to the whole region. This is both an indication of regional identity and a help to strengthening it.

The Location of the Episcopal See. Two towns have been considered for the Cathedral See: Cambridge and Norwich. Cambridge has a fine church, imposing if not over-large; but against Cambridge is the fact that it has never been thought of as the principal town in 'East Anglia'—in fact, strictly speaking, it is just outside the territory which formed the ancient kingdom. It lies only a short distance from the boundaries of the adjoining Dioceses of Westminster, Brentwood and the proposed new Northampton. It is conveniently used at the present time as a meeting-place for clergy and others of the existing Diocese of Northampton; but it would not have that central position in a new Diocese of the East. Norwich, on the other hand, has for centuries been somewhat more than a County Town; it is a regional centre for East Anglia. The Catholic church of St John the Baptist, Norwich, is large and imposing and a dignified and spacious setting for ceremonies; in fact it is the largest parish church, non-monastic and non-collegiate, in Britain, if not in Europe. Already major episcopal ceremonies, other than those related to an individual parish, are held there—e.g. the Chrism Mass of Maundy Thursday, and important national occasions marked by an episcopal Mass, such as a special Requiem Mass for the deceased cardinal archbishop of Westminster, or the inauguration

Mass for the Holy Year. It is hard to see how this established practice of using St John's, Norwich, for important religious functions could be set aside in favour of any other church in the new diocese, and the general expectation points to St John the Baptist's church, Norwich, as the cathedral church of the new diocese.

The Name of the new Diocese. While there is a convergence of arguments in favour of Norwich and the church of St John the Baptist as the place from which pastoral rule is exercised and where the people of God will assemble round their Chief Shepherd, there is a difficulty about calling the new diocese simply 'the Diocese of Norwich'. It is to be noted that there is already an Anglican Cathedral and Bishop of Norwich, dating from the extinction of the Catholic See at the Reformation. In 1850, with the restoration of the Catholic hierarchy in this country, the Church avoided taking the title of any pre-Reformation See now in Anglican occupation. There is no precedent since then for the adoption of a title already used by an Anglican Bishop or diocese in this country, and it would be a notable break with the established practice if 'Norwich' were now taken as the designation of a new Catholic diocese, see or Bishop in England. A number of suggestions have been put forward as alternative titles; they tend to be cumbersome and unreal, and in fact so unreal as to call attention by implication to the very thing they avoid saying, and even to have a suggestion of falsehood. There is, however, one solution which increasingly commends itself: it is practical and truthful, conveys its meaning at once to all English people, and will be capable of rousing a regional loyalty. It is, in fact, a name that has been already used a number of times in this present paper as a normal way of designating the region: *East Anglia*. It is the explicit request of the Senate of Priests at its recent meeting that this be the title of the new diocese, and that we may be given a Diocese of East Anglia, with its Chief Pastor, the Bishop of East Anglia, governing his flock from the Cathedral church of St John the Baptist, Norwich. This title of the diocese would be seen by the Anglican Church as a tactful and delicate avoidance of any kind of conflict or rivalry.[18]

The paper then goes on to consider the financial implications of dividing the Northampton Diocese, the distribution of clergy, and the matter of cathedral chapters. It concludes:

In view of all the foregoing considerations which have emerged in a long and thorough consultation and study conducted within the Diocese of Northampton, and with the unanimous request of the Cathedral Chapter, the overwhelming desire of the clergy expressed through the Senate of Priests, and of parish pastoral councils and groups of laity, it is now recommended:

That the Holy See be immediately petitioned for the division of the Diocese of Northampton to form two new dioceses, taking no territory from any other diocese and leaving no part of the diocese outside either of the two new dioceses;

That the Diocese of Northampton should thenceforward consist of and be co-terminous with the Counties of Northamptonshire, Bedfordshire, Buckinghamshire, and the part of Berkshire which until April 1974 was part of Buckinghamshire;

That a new diocese be formed consisting of and co-terminous with the Counties of Cambridgeshire, Norfolk and Suffolk;

That the Cathedral church of the new diocese should be the church of Saint John the Baptist, Norwich;

That the new diocese should be entitled the Diocese of East Anglia, and that the Bishop should be the Bishop of East Anglia, governing the diocese from his See in Norwich;

That in each diocese a Chapter of Canons of the Cathedral should be erected, consisting of a Provost and five Canons;

That a Commission be established forthwith representing the two territories to decide an equitable and acceptable division of the general diocesan funds;

That the bishops of the two dioceses be recommended to consider and bear in mind the suggestion that some interchange of clergy be allowed at least for a few years.

It is further recommended that the Holy See be petitioned to allow the division and creation of the new diocese to be announced in advance of the date when it is to take place, with an interval of four to six weeks, so that due preparation and instruction of the people may take place and a public ceremony may be arranged with an inaugural Mass; and thereby the people of each diocese may have their thoughts and prayers turned towards the local Church in which the Universal Church is made present to them, and may express their loyalty to their own Bishop and Pastor.[19]

So end the *Proposals and Recommendations* of November 1975. Bishop Grant acted in accordance with the recommendations that had been made — though according to the preacher at his funeral Mass (Canon Noel Burditt) he needed 'quite a bit of pushing: the division must inevitably, one supposes, have seemed rather tragic to him, entailing the loss of a territory full of places and people to which he, more than most, was bound by many ties'. Indeed, in his foreword to the official booklet of Bishop Alan Clark's installation Bishop Grant writes: 'This is a most joyful occasion, although for me tinged with sadness since I lose that part of the country in which I was born and in which I was ordained priest. I am of course sorry to be losing you all, but I am sure you will forgive me if I single out as a special cause of sadness the fact that I shall no longer be the Bishop of the shrine of Our Lady of Walsingham'.[20]

However, he duly sent a petition to Pope Paul VI in the following terms:

> Most Holy Father, I, Charles Alexander Grant, Bishop of Northampton in England, humbly petition that Your Holiness divide the present Diocese of Northampton by separating from it the territory of the Administrative Civil Counties of Cambridgeshire, Norfolk and Suffolk to form a new Diocese of East Anglia with that title, the Cathedral church of which will be the church of St John the Baptist in the city of Norwich.
>
> The reasons for the request are as follows:
>
> 1. The size of the present diocese. It is territorially the largest in England and Wales. The Catholic population has grown since 1945 from less than 40,000 to more than 200,000 and is still growing fast. In these circumstances it is practically impossible for one bishop to be an adequate pastor of all the priests and people.
>
> 2. The disparate nature of the territory of the present diocese, which has no real natural unity.

3. The almost unanimous desire of the clergy, and of the people in so far as this has been discovered for this division.

I enclose a memorandum drawn up by a small committee which I established for this purpose which I hope contains the facts which the Holy See may require. It has my full approval. I would add that the Episcopal Conference of England and Wales in their meeting in November gave unanimous approval to the proposed division. My Auxiliary Bishop, Alan Clark, also fully approves of the proposals.

I would add to the facts in the memorandum the following:

Concerning the financial viability of the two resulting dioceses, the basic consideration is that for six years from the appointment of Bishop Clark until the death of my predecessor Bishop Parker at Easter this year, the diocese has been supporting three bishops. The amount that Bishop Parker's maintenance cost could easily support one or two priests extra for the administration of the new diocese. In addition I enclose a statement of the capital assets of the present diocese from which it will be seen that we are as fortunately placed as can be hoped for in these difficult times to finance the future large developments which we foresee.

The other matter of importance not covered in the memorandum is the supply of future priests. Here again we are in a comparatively fortunate position as we have 30 students in major seminaries. Of these 2 come from outside the present diocese, and of the rest about half come from each of the proposed new dioceses. We have no students in minor seminaries, but we have a considerable number of men who have been accepted as students for the priesthood. These are under the care of the local priests, and are gathered together twice a year for preliminary training.

If the Holy Father should approve this proposal for the division of the present Diocese of Northampton, I would strongly support the proposal in the last paragraph of the memorandum concerning the timing of the announcement. It would be a great help to the priests and people to enable them to see this act of the Holy See as a truly pastoral one, and not a mere administrative arrangement. It would be difficult to arrange such a preparation and ceremony during the holiday months when many people are away and the children are not in school. This is from July to September inclusive.

There has been some change of mind about Chapters for the two dioceses, and as a result I would prefer to leave the number of members of the new Chapters open for future consideration, perhaps after the division has taken place.

Details of the diocese's capital assets were added in an appendix to the petition.[21] Bishop Grant's petition was speedily granted, and on 13 March 1976 Pope Paul VI issued the decree *Quod Oecumenicum* erecting the new Diocese of East Anglia, with the church of St John the Baptist, Norwich, as its cathedral.[22] The decree was signed by the then Secretary of State, Cardinal Jean Villot:[23]

Having in mind what the Second Vatican Council laid down about the better ordering of the size of local churches to the Diocese of Northampton, it clearly seems the right time to divide it into two parts. Thanks to God the great eastern part of the diocese has grown in terms of Catholicism, and the hope is that it will grow still more in the future. So now, at the request of Our Venerable Brother, Charles Alexander Grant, Bishop of Northampton, having heard the opinion of the Episcopal Conference of England and Wales, We have decided to create a new diocese from the Diocese of Northampton, having taken into account the opinion of Our Venerable Brother, Bruno Bernard Heim, Titular Archbishop of Xanthiensis, and Our Apostolic Delegate in Great Britain, and by Our Apostolic Power, we decree and order what follows.

We have taken from the Diocese of Northampton the counties, called in English Cambridgeshire, Norfolk and Suffolk, and from these we create the diocese which is to be called East Anglia, within these county boundaries. The seat of the diocese is to be in Norwich, and the bishop's *cathedra* is to be in the existing church of Saint John the Baptist, and this is to be known as the Cathedral.

The decree went on to set out the legal and financial status of the diocese as a self-sustaining suffragan of the Archdiocese of Westminster. More fancifully, given the diocese's small Catholic population, the decree called for 'A seminary … to be built, in which boys and young men can be trained, bearing in mind the norms set up by the Second Vatican Council and the particular decrees of the Sacred Congregation for Catholic Formation'. Finally, the document dealt with the incardination of priests in the Dioceses of Northampton and East Anglia.

However, although the diocese had been canonically erected, no bishop had as yet been appointed. Bishop Alan Clark, titular Bishop of Elmham and Auxiliary Bishop of Northampton, was in residence, though Bishop Grant remained Apostolic Administrator, while the usual consultation was begun: Catholics of the new diocese were invited to make their recommendations to the Apostolic Delegate within two weeks from 12 March.

Again, Rome acted speedily, and the appointment of Bishop Clark as the first Bishop of the new diocese was announced on Tuesday 27 April. His installation in the new cathedral was to take place on Wednesday 2 June.[24] The installation duly took place with great solemnity. It was presided over initially by the Cardinal Archbishop of Westminster, to which Province the new diocese belonged, Cardinal George Basil Hume,[25] by Bishop Grant as Apostolic Administrator, and by the Apostolic Delegate, Archbishop Bruno Heim—and, of course, after his installation, by the new Bishop of East Anglia. Many other members of the English and Welsh hierarchy were present, as were representatives of the Irish and Scottish bishops, and many priests. The Anglican Bishop of Norwich was present, as were those of St Edmundsbury and Ipswich, and Peterborough. The chairmen of the Methodist District and of the United Reformed Church, East Anglia, and the president of the Norwich Baptist Association were present, as was the Layminister of the Norwich Hebrew Congregation. The Anglican cathedral was represented by its dean, vice-dean and precentor. Other distinguished guests included the Master of the (Anglican) College of Guardians, Walsingham, with his administrator, and the secretary of ARCIC.

The civil authorities were represented by the Lord Mayor of Norwich, the Lord Lieutenant of Norfolk, the chairman of the Norfolk County Council and the vice-chairmen of the Cambridge and Suffolk County Councils, and the Chief Executives of Norwich and of Norfolk. Professor Norman Sheppard, FRS, represented the Vice-Chancellor of the University of East Anglia. His Grace the Duke of Norfolk was also present, together with Lady Miriam Hubbard, Lady Winefrede Freeman, Lady Katharine Phillips, and Lady Rachel Pepys.

The Bishop was welcomed by the cathedral administrator, Canon Edward McBride. The Bull of Appointment was then presented by the Apostolic Delegate to the Chancellor of the Diocese, Canon Paul Taylor, who read it out to the assembled congregation. The Apostolic Delegate then presented the Bull to the Bishop Elect, who formally accepted his charge, and then exchanged a sign of peace with Bishop Grant, hitherto Apostolic Administrator of the Diocese, and with the Cardinal Archbishop of Westminster, as Metropolitan, and the other Residential Bishops of the Province.

The Bishop was then solemnly installed on his cathedra by the Cardinal and Bishop Grant. From the Cardinal he received the Book of the Gospels, and from Bishop Grant his crozier or pastoral staff. He was then formally welcomed by representatives of the clergy and laity of the diocese, and exchanged greetings with the local civic representatives and religious leaders, the Lord Mayor and the Bishop of Norwich replying. The Mass of St John the Baptist was then celebrated, with the new Bishop presiding.[26]

Notes

1   From a letter in the Jesuit Archives, Farm Street. Essex was at this time part of the Diocese of Westminster. It became the Diocese of Brentwood in 1917.

2   See 'A Plea for an East Anglian Diocese', *The Tablet*, 20 August 1938, p. 3. The anonymous article was later reprinted as a pamphlet.

3   F. W. Keating, *A Pastoral Letter by Frederick William, Bishop of Northampton, Advent 1917*, Northampton Diocesan Archives, Pastoral Letters 1908–1918, Book IV, no. 38, fol. 430.

4   Lance (2000), p. 81.

5   See Keating (1917), fol. 424.

6   *Ibid.*, fol. 435. William Wareing, having been Vicar Apostolic of the Eastern District from 1840, had become the first Bishop of Northampton in 1850. He retired in 1858 and died in 1865.

7   *Ibid.*, fols 425, 427.

8   *Ibid.*, fols 431–2.

9   'A Plea for an East Anglian Diocese' (1938), p. 3.

10 *Ibid.*, p. 5. Bromholm (or Broomholm) was a Cluniac priory, on the east coast of Norfolk, where a celebrated relic of the True Cross was venerated.

11 *Ibid.*, pp. 6–7.

12 See *Christus Dominus* in A. Flannery (ed.), *Vatican Council II, the Conciliar and Post Conciliar Documents* (Dublin: Dominican Publications, 1980), pp. 564–90, and *Ecclesiae sanctae, ibid.*, pp. 591–610.

13 *A Suggested Reorganisation of the Diocesan Structure of the Catholic Church in England and Wales, Offered for Consideration by the Catholic Bishops' Conference of England and Wales* (London: Catholic Information Office of England and Wales, 1974).

14 *Ibid.*, pp. 18–20.

15 The Northampton diocesan magazine, PACE, had played an important part in the consultation, especially of the laity.

16 *Proposals and Recommendations concerning the Division of the Diocese of Northampton* (Northampton: Diocese of Northampton, 1975), pp. [1]–[3].

17 Details on Bishop Clark are from the Diocesan Secretariat.

18 *Proposals and Recommendations* (1975), pp. [4]–[5].

19 *Ibid.*, p. [6].

[20] A typed copy of the homily is in the Northampton Diocesan Archives, and a photocopy in the East Anglia Diocesan Archives. Bishop Grant's Foreword is on p. 3 of the Installation booklet.

[21] From a typed draft in the Northampton Diocesan Archives. There is a photocopy in the East Anglia Diocesan Archives. In the event East Anglia was set up on the American model, without a Cathedral Chapter.

[22] See *Acta Apostolicae Sedis*, vol. 68 (Rome: Ex Typographia Polyglotta, 1976), pp. 311–12.

[23] Editor's note: I am grateful to Fr Russell Frost for allowing me to reproduce his translation of the original decree as part of this chapter.

[24] *Acta Apostolicae Sedis*, vol. 68, p. 351. The original Bull, *Qui Universum*, dated 26 April 1976, is in the East Anglia Diocesan Archives.

[25] This was Cardinal Hume's first public function after receiving his red hat.

[26] All the above details are from the 48-page booklet printed for the occasion, entitled *The Installation of the First Bishop of East Anglia Rt Rev. Alan C. Clark* (Norwich, 1976).

✣ 7 ✣

The Diocese of East Anglia:
The First Forty Years, 1976–2016

Tony Rogers

THE LABOUR PAINS which preceded the birth of the diocese were not altogether surprising. The first concerned the name of the new diocese. The consultations that had taken place revealed strong support for a simple and descriptive title, and 'East Anglia' seemed obvious. But when the name was submitted, the Congregation of Bishops, entrusted with the establishment of new dioceses, pointed out that a diocese was normally linked to the site of its cathedral—as in Northampton and Brentwood. Fortunately, there were counter-arguments from within Great Britain, with Galloway and Argyll and the Isles in Scotland and Menevia in Wales all well established. That particular battle was won. The second labour pain concerned the way in which the news of the decree *Quod Oecumenicum* was released. Strict embargoes were imposed on the press, so that the priests of the two dioceses could be informed at least some hours before the news went public. The present writer, then a curate in Cambridge, was having supper with the other curates, when the parish priest, Canon Paul Taylor, burst into the room declaring that 'we now get our information from *About Anglia* (the ITV regional news programme at the time) who have informed us that we are now part of a new diocese'. The guilty party was an independent local radio station in Ipswich (Radio Orwell) which had not observed the protocol on the embargo, thus giving permission for all other media outlets to go public ahead of schedule.

But the diocese was born, albeit a few hours prematurely, and, in the absence of any instructions from Northampton, speculation was rife about who would be bishop, and whether the priests would have any choice as to which diocese they belonged to. Uncertainty was cleared up quickly and it was no great surprise, some six weeks later, to learn that Alan Clark, already resident in Poringland, was to be our first bishop. Although he had been Bishop Grant's auxiliary since 1969, and lived in the eastern part of the Northampton Diocese, the two bishops had, between them, ensured that their presence and activity was not confined to east and west. Alan Clark was well known and established in East Anglia, but he was equally familiar in Northampton.

The great advantage that a bishop in East Anglia would have was identity with a geographical region, even if Cambridgeshire was not part of East Anglia proper. The scenery was noticeably different, so much so that in discussions in the early twentieth century, it had been suggested that the 'A1', 'the Great North Road' was a logical topographical boundary. But it straddled county boundaries and would have made for endless problems in terms of local authorities and parish boundaries.

Alan Clark had a great ability to galvanise the new diocese, and in no small way helped it establish a clear identity of its own very soon. More than once he remarked that Buckinghamshire, Bedfordshire and Hertfordshire, and a bit of Berkshire, were a less cohesive entity than East Anglia. The rather sedate and compact *Northampton Diocesan Magazine* was soon upstaged by East Anglia's own tabloid *Pace*, which, under the editorship of George Broughton, ensured that maximum coverage was given to parish activities across the three counties. This was the first of several styles of publication, but there have been few gaps between then and our current newspaper *Catholic East Anglia*. The diocesan year book was another story. The first issue in 1977 was produced on a duplicator, and like all first editions, is a prized possession, containing inappropriate but highly amusing typographical errors. Subsequent year books give a picture of a diocese that was growing. What had been the Northampton Diocesan Travelling Mission, in the care of Fr Bob McCormick, set up Mass centres in people's homes, in village halls and even in a pub. In some places, Mass would be celebrated once a quarter, but in others it would be monthly. These seeds that had been sown over the years had marked and coalesced the presence of Catholics across a scattered rural area. From these mission outposts developed weekly Mass centres under the care of the local parish, and in more than one case, a parish was founded from such origins.

Bishop Clark's own commitment to ecumenism and his co-chairmanship of ARCIC (the Anglican Roman Catholic International Commission) saw a flourishing at local level of co-operation. Local ecumenical projects, known as LEPs, often undertaken by denominations sharing a single building or engaged in a single mission, were established in Bretton (Peterborough), Bowthorpe (Norwich), Bar Hill (Cambridge) and Norwich Prison.

But perhaps the most significant evidence of ecumenism at work, particularly in rural areas, was in the very widespread use of Anglican village churches across the diocese as weekly or monthly venues for the celebration of Mass. The use of the same building, as well as being both a link with the past and a sign of generosity on the part of bishops, incumbents and parish church councils, had the practical effect of ensuring that on many Sunday mornings, one congregation leaving its own liturgy would meet another coming in. According to the year books, Anglican churches were in regular use as Mass centres. The withdrawal from this practice was not connected with a breakdown in ecumenical relations, but a gradual awareness that the shortage of priests made commitments of this sort increasingly difficult. In 1977, for example, the parish of Our Lady and the English Martyrs in Cambridge was on a weekly or a monthly basis using no less than six Anglican or shared churches. Another way in which the growth of the diocese was marked was by the building of churches and the creation of new parishes in Cherry Hinton (Cambridge) and Orton Malborne (Peterborough).

Because of his co-chairmanship of ARCIC, Alan Clark was well known beyond the diocese. The period during which he and Henry McAdoo, the Anglican Archbishop of Dublin, were at the helm was known as ARCIC 1, and their commission was responsible for three documents—on the Eucharist, ordination and authority in the Church. The Commission members discovered, almost to their surprise, that there was often a greater level of agreement in faith on these matters than might have been assumed. The differences tended to be highlighted in the terminology used within Anglicanism and Catholicism, and Alan Clark was proud of their common statements. But the authorities in Rome gave a relatively lukewarm reception to them, and this was a source of real sadness to Bishop Clark, because, although he and his family had become Catholics when he was very young, his Anglican background was important to him and his understanding of the communion and its workings was deep-rooted.

The national shrine of Our Lady of Walsingham is one of the treasures of the diocese, and along with the cathedral, it holds a special place in the hearts of East Anglian Catholics. But the fine and ever-improving facilities we know today are a relatively recent phenomenon. When Bishop Clark became auxiliary bishop of Northampton, the Marist Fathers had only recently taken over the administration of the shrine. The Slipper Chapel, with its history, was, in a sense, the focal point of the shrine. But it was, and remains, a very small chapel. Provision for larger pilgrimages was very limited, and a wooden structure, which was no more than a shelter and surrounded by chicken wire to ward off intruders, was popularly known as the birdcage. It was replaced for a few years by a much larger open air sanctuary which provided a modicum of shelter from the east wind and the rain, but was less than satisfactory. So work began in 1980 on the Chapel of Reconciliation which we know today. The design of the chapel was modelled on a traditional Norfolk barn, and was blessed by Cardinal Hume in 1981 and consecrated by Bishop Clark a year later. Bishop Clark's love for the shrine lay behind his request that his body be buried in the grounds of the Slipper Chapel.

Alan Clark's style of management was a trifle unpredictable. The way in which he moved his priests from one parish to another is part of the folklore of the diocese. He communicated the information to one priest during a Saturday afternoon confession session, tapping on the door of his confessional as one penitent left and another was ready to come in. Another heard of the news via an answerphone message, and kept the tape for future reference as evidence of an unorthodox style! But he was a warm and gregarious man, who lived life to the full, and loved the Lord, his mother Mary, and the priests and people of the diocese of which he had pastoral care.

He had been appointed auxiliary bishop of Northampton in 1969 at the age of fifty, and served the people of East Anglia in that capacity and as bishop of the diocese for almost twenty-six years. Prior to his ordination as a bishop, he had spent the greater part of his priestly ministry on the staff of the English College in Rome, serving for much of the time as its vice-rector. He was then appointed parish priest of Blackheath in south-east London. He celebrated the silver jubilee of his episcopal ordination in May 1994, just three months before his seventy-fifth birthday in August, when he duly offered his resignation to Pope John Paul II. This was accepted *nunc pro tunc*—with the understanding that he would continue to be Bishop of East Anglia until his successor was appointed. During his last few years in the diocese, though he was in pretty good health, things began to slow down. He was aware that it would not be too long before his successor was in place, and felt that it would be unwise to start initiatives that he would not be able to see through to the end.

Bishop Clark had been a priest of the Southwark Diocese, and so was the man who followed him. Peter Smith was Rector of the seminary at Wonersh, near Guildford, a canon lawyer whose name had been in circulation as a possible candidate. So, it was good news for Bishop Clark that he did not have to wait too long for the appointment to be made. The news was made public on 21 March 1995, and Mgr Smith was ordained bishop by Cardinal Basil Hume on 21 May 1995. As the second bishop of the diocese, Bishop Peter had to assimilate the spirit and ethos of a diocese that was very different from his own. But he also had to live close to his predecessor, who had built a retirement bungalow just outside the gates of the White House (the bishop's home). It did not help that Bishop Clark would stroll along the drive to the diocesan offices most mornings just to check if there was any post for him! Bishop Peter took it all in good humour and quickly endeared himself to the priests and people of East Anglia with his down-to-earth accessibility, curiously enhanced by his need to light up a cigarette and stand outside churches and halls before he went in for the bun-fight that invariably followed confirmations or a celebratory Mass.

But the 1990s were very different from the days when the new diocese had been established. The regular source of vocations which had been taken for granted, and ensured a small but steady trickle of ordinations in most years, was no more. This had repercussions on the workload of priests and people. Many priests who were accustomed to having an assistant to share the load found that they were now in one-man parishes, with responsibility for all the Masses, rather than half of them. Mass centres abounded when Bishop Peter came to East Anglia. In 1995, no fewer than twenty-eight Anglican (or other) churches were used each week, not to mention chapels of ease built in various parishes. There were sixty-one parishes, with seventy-three priests, some of whom were retired, to serve them. The time had come to begin thinking about 'rationalisation' of both numbers of Masses and venues for celebration, because it was obvious that the present level could not be sustained, and the following years saw a gradual reduction in both Masses and venues, even though the numbers of priests increased, as a result of a sizeable number of former Anglican clergy, some of whom were married, being ordained for the diocese.

Peter Smith was Bishop of East Anglia for six-and-a-half years, being translated to the Cardiff Diocese in December 2001, in the wake of a difficult time there in the latter days of Archbishop Ward. East Anglia had to wait about fifteen months for a new bishop, and although not known by many, the appointment of Canon Michael Evans was not a great surprise. Michael was the third Bishop of East Anglia, and like his two predecessors was a priest of the Southwark Diocese. With Peter Smith he shared the experience of many years on the staff at St John's Seminary, Wonersh, where a number of the more recently ordained priests of the diocese, including most of the former Anglicans, had been trained. He had the reputation of being something of a stickler for deadlines, and former students reported that if midnight on a certain day had been set as the time for a piece of work to be handed in, it was certain that he would still be at his desk at that time and would know precisely whose essays were in on time! He had served as vice-rector under Bishop Peter, but prior to coming to East Anglia, had been parish priest of Tunbridge Wells for nine years. Michael Evans was taken aback by the appointment, news of which came on a Monday morning, when, while helping to count the weekend collection, he was summoned to the Nunciature in Wimbledon, and told to be there by 11 o'clock—no mean feat around the M25 at that hour of the day.

Although he became totally committed to his work as bishop of a diocese which he did not know, it was clear that, as a relatively young bishop (he was fifty-one at the time of his appointment), Michael Evans had a long road ahead of him. On the day following his ordination to the episcopate (19 March 2003), he made the comment to one of the clergy that he had something like twenty-three years and five months to serve before he was eligible to hand in his resignation at the age of seventy-five. Little did he—or anyone else—realise that his tenure as bishop was to be cut short by so many years.

Born in south London, Bishop Michael grew up in Whitstable in Kent. He said that he owed his vocation in large measure to his mother's brother, Fr Pierre Barbier, also a priest of the Southwark Diocese, and stated that, as long as he could remember, he had wanted to be either a priest or centre forward for Leeds United. In the press conference following the appointment we learned that he loved chillies—the hotter the better, was an avid supporter of Leeds United, a devoted follower of the martyred Archbishop Oscar Romero, a man deeply committed to the cause of the Church in Cambodia, and an honorary member of the Taizé Community in France, which had for well over twenty years been the venue for both his annual retreat and his break from parish life.

Bishop Michael's rather off-beat humour took a bit of getting used to, and was not to everyone's taste. On his first visit to Cambridge, he told the congregation that he had last come to Cambridge at the age of seven, did not enjoy the visit, and was not quite sure why he was there now! Needless to say, some people found that the comment did not endear him to them.

But, very quickly, he made the diocese his own, drove himself everywhere, mispronounced the quirky East Anglian place names, and began to learn the reality of working in a scattered but thinly populated diocese. He let it be known soon after he arrived that he believed that any priest in a small to medium-sized parish should stay no more than seven years, and those in big parishes no more than ten. He soon discovered that administrative life was not as simple as that, and quickly became much more flexible in this regard.

But he was not a man to let the grass grow under his feet. The urgency of a plan for the future of the diocese was apparent to him if not to everyone else. The speed with which he began this process caused some alarm, even among those who understood its necessity. When accused by a reporter of being 'a man in a hurry' he made no attempt to deny it, but added, 'The hurry is not caused by me. We have to get away from the attitude that "it will happen one day"'. So, in a letter introducing 'Forward and Outward Together'—a consultation paper on parish and deanery review—Bishop Michael told the people of the diocese that he intended to 'throw some chilli peppers into your bland salad'. To those who had not seen him in action in their parishes and schools, it caused adverse comment. First impressions are important, and this perhaps ill-advised beginning would seem to have coloured some of the subsequent responses. Michael Evans, as well as being a pastor, was a theologian, and he wrote from a position of deep knowledge, love and understanding of the Church. He had the wisdom, in follow-ups to his original letter, to take a gentler and more conciliatory tone. So he wrote, 'People are realising the need to move forward and will make decisions based on what people are telling me'. But not everyone was mollified, and one priest, in an interview, likened him to an oncologist 'whose clear-sighted analysis of the need for radical treatment has blinded him to the side-effects which the patient will have to endure'. This was balanced by a comment from a priest who was able to welcome his pragmatism, who said, 'There may have been some kind of oversensitivity. I've found him totally accommodating when presented with anomalies and local difficulties'. The consultative process resulted in a diocesan pastoral plan—a blueprint for action as circumstances changed.

Bishop Michael worked phenomenal hours, and it was nothing to find an email from him, written in the early hours of the morning when he had just returned from a trip abroad and was anxious to clear his desk before finally going to bed. But this dynamism and drive looked as if it was going to come to an abrupt halt when, in 2005, just two years after his ordination, he was diagnosed with aggressive prostate cancer. The outcome was uncertain, and he underwent both radiotherapy and chemotherapy, but no surgery. The treatment took its toll on his energy, and he experienced a constant feeling of tiredness, none of which lessened his commitment, determination and workload in succeeding years.

Despite the fact that he was not a man who relaxed easily or had much in the way of outside interests, his focus on many different areas of Church life was evident. He was anxious to help the people and priests of the diocese be conscious of the bigger Church, and to that end, he set up a twinning programme with two very different places. Fr Paul Maddison, one of the diocesan priests, had established a very strong link with the Latin patriarchate in Jerusalem, and was anxious to strengthen the ties. So, with the support and encouragement of Bishop Michael, the Diocese of East Anglia entered into a partnership with the patriarchate. This involved the twinning of East Anglian parishes with parishes in the occupied West Bank, and reciprocal visits of clergy and parishioners. A similar relationship was established with the Apostolic Prefecture of Battambang in Cambodia, formalising and deepening Bishop Michael's existing link with that country since his days as a parish priest in Kent. Once again, parishes were twinned, and the Cambodian partnership has gone from strength to strength over succeeding years.

On the wider scene, Michael was a committed ecumenist, both in interfaith matters in his dialogue with Muslims, and as a member of the Catholic–Methodist International Commission. He often spoke of the great affinity he felt with Methodism, not least its ecclesiology, and he worked closely with local Church leaders of all traditions. He had a good and close friendship with Bishop Graham James of Norwich and his wife, and was delighted when, along with the Methodist chair of the East Anglia District, he was made an honorary canon of Norwich Cathedral.

As a theologian Bishop Michael came into his own in his teaching ministry, which he saw as central to his episcopate. Curiously enough, here was an area where he did not feel it right to delegate. He insisted, for example, that all those who had been trained in their parishes to become special ministers of the Eucharist should come to a day of recollection, which he would always conduct himself, and which ended in a Mass at which they were commissioned. Those who went reluctantly, not wanting to give up a precious Saturday, would invariably come back uplifted and fulsome in their appreciation of his ability to communicate and share his love of the faith in an accessible and authentic manner.

But it is those who, during Bishop Michael's ministry, were involved as members of parish or diocesan youth groups who have a very special memory of his great gifts with young people. Michael was no young trendy; indeed several people suggested that a change from the 'Austin Powers glasses' which he wore when he first came to East Anglia might help improve his visual image. But he had a great ability to engage with young people, perhaps born of his experience as a school and university chaplain.

Bishop Michael, as well as making his own annual visit to Taizé, was anxious that the young people of the diocese should get to know and love the community as he did, and for many who went with him, this was a life-changing experience. On the other hand, he struggled a bit when it came to the annual diocesan pilgrimage to Lourdes. His heart was clearly in Taizé, which he knew well, and Lourdes never quite hit the spot for him. The bishop hit the headlines on one occasion when, as a very long-standing member of Amnesty International, he felt he had no option but to resign because of a change in direction which the organisation took in relation to abortion. From a neutral stance, they moved to a pro-abortion position, and Bishop Michael, at that point, reluctantly parted company with the charity.

The illness with which he had battled seemed never to get the better of him, yet in the last months of his life, it was clear that it was beginning to take its toll. Having presided over the centenary celebrations of St John's Cathedral, he began, little by little, to withdraw from diocesan life. In an article in *The Eastern Daily Press* called 'Faith through Dark Times' he said 'Having been told I'm dying, I have no idea what the journey will be. I expect that, one day, I will simply not wake up'. A moving and sensitive interview, shortly before his death, with Stuart White on BBC's *Look East* revealed a humble man of faith and courage. He died on 11 July 2011.

The diocese had to wait another two years before Bishop Michael's successor, Alan Hopes, was installed at St John's Cathedral. During the interregnum, Fr David Bagstaff was the diocesan administrator, a task involving the day-to-day running of the diocese, with limited powers in terms of decision-making. It was relief all round when Bishop Hopes's appointment was announced. Our second Bishop Alan had spent almost the whole of his life in London, apart from his earliest years in Oxford, and a year at St Boniface College, Warminster, to complete his theological training before his ordination as an Anglican priest in 1968. Bishop Hopes became a Catholic in 1994 and was ordained a priest of the Diocese of Westminster in December 1995. After a period as an assistant priest at Our Lady of Victories in Kensington, London, he became parish priest at Holy Redeemer and St Thomas More, Chelsea, and was appointed vicar general of the Diocese of Westminster in 2001. In January 2003 he was ordained bishop as an auxiliary in the Diocese of Westminster. Bishop Alan was appointed to East Anglia on 11 June 2013 and installed as bishop in St John's Cathedral on 16 July of the same year. Bishop Alan's arrival in the diocese was in the same year that Pope Francis was elected, and conscious of the vigorous life of faith envisaged by him and his predecessor, Pope Benedict XVI, Bishop Alan has embraced wholeheartedly the focus on the New Evangelisation, with a three-phase implementation in our diocese, and a real living out of the Year of Mercy which began in late 2015. Shortly after his arrival, the Marist Fathers, who had care of the shrine of Our Lady at Walsingham, announced (following the appointment of the shrine director Fr

Alan Williams sm as the new Bishop of Brentwood) that they would no longer be in a position to look after the shrine. Bishop Alan grasped the nettle, being convinced that, because Walsingham is the national shrine of our Lady, the Bishops' Conference should, from their number, be prepared to find a priest who could replace Fr Alan. The shrine, the diocese and the country were fortunate that Bishop Alan Williams sm was willing to release Mgr John Armitage to take up the role of rector of the shrine, and lead it boldly forward into a new phase of development and outreach.

At the same time, Bishop Alan Hopes recognised that the finances of the diocese also needed to be put on a sound footing, so the Alive in Faith campaign programme was launched in 2015. This, together with a very heartening increase in the number of students training to be priests, points to an invigorated young diocese, which has truly matured and grown in the forty years of its existence.

APPENDIX 1

Notable East Anglian Catholics

A number of these individuals are mentioned in the text of the foregoing chapters, and many (but not all) can be found in *The Oxford Dictionary of National Biography* (2004). The ODNB also exists in an online version which is regularly updated with new lives, and some of those listed here did not appear in the original print edition. In the majority of cases these people were born in East Anglia, but some have been included on account of a later association with the area.

1. William Alabaster (1568–1640) was born at Hadleigh in Suffolk into a Protestant merchant family. Through the patronage of his uncle William Still, Bishop of Bath and Wells, he attended Westminster School and Trinity College, Cambridge, where he became a Fellow. Alabaster wrote Latin plays and began composing an epic poem in praise of Elizabeth I. In 1596 he accompanied the Earl of Essex on his raid against the Spanish port of Cadiz, during which the English soldiers desecrated Catholic churches and chapels. In 1597 Alabaster met the Jesuit Thomas Wright at Westminster, hoping to convert the priest, but the reverse happened. Rumours reached the Archbishop of Canterbury, Richard Bancroft, that Alabaster had converted to Catholicism and he was placed under house arrest. Early in 1598 he escaped from the Clink in Southwark and by November he was at the English College in Rome. In the summer of 1599 Alabaster was kidnapped by English agents at La Rochelle and brought back to the Tower, then moved to Framlingham Castle in 1601. James I pardoned Alabaster in 1603, and in 1604 he returned to the Continent, having agreed to spy on other Catholics for the government. In 1607 he published a controversial book, *Apparatus in Revelationem Iesu Christi* ('The equipping for the revelation of Jesus Christ'), which attracted the attention of the Roman Inquisition because it drew on the Jewish Kabbalah. The Inquisition condemned his book in 1610 and ordered him to stay in Rome, but Alabaster fled to Amsterdam and then to England, where in 1613 he returned to the established church. He was given the living of Little Shelford in Cambridgeshire and spent the remainder of his life writing Protestant theological works.[1]

2. William Eusebius Andrews (1773–1837) was born in Norwich, the son of two converts to Catholicism. He rose from printer's apprentice to editor of *The Norfolk Chronicle*. In 1813 he moved to London and began publishing *The Orthodox Journal*, the country's first Catholic periodical. Andrews attacked key figures in the Catholic establishment and promoted a more aggressive campaign for Catholic emancipation, which was backed by the Vicar Apostolic of the Midland District, John Milner. In spite of periods of confinements in a debtors' prison he continued publishing until the end of his life, and joined working-class radicals of other denominations in campaigning for greater civil and religious liberty.[2]

3. John Austin (1613–99) was born at Walpole in Norfolk and was educated at Sleaford Grammar School and St John's College, Cambridge. He never graduated, probably because he converted to Catholicism whilst at university. He became tutor to the Fowler family and may have travelled on the Continent, but in the 1650s he was a member of the Catholic literary circle of Thomas Blount, Thomas White, Christopher Davenport, John Sergeant, John Belson and Thomas Keightley in London. Austin published many controversial works under the name of William Birchley, in which he adopted a conciliatory attitude towards the Church of England, but he is best remembered for his prayer book *Devotions in the Ancient Way of Offices* (1668), which was reprinted innumerable times by Catholics and Anglicans alike into the eighteenth century. He was also responsible for many hymns.[3]

4. Alexander Baker SJ (1582–1638) was born in Norfolk and left England for Spain in around 1600, where he studied at Seville. He was ordained priest at Malaga in 1608 and entered the Society of Jesus at Louvain in 1612. He received a son of the celebrated lawyer Sir Edward Coke into the Catholic Church in 1615. He was sent to England as Superior of the Residence of St Stanislaus (the Jesuit mission in Devon) and arrested in 1625, but he was pardoned and released as a result of the intervention of the French ambassador. In 1629 he travelled as a missionary to Newfoundland and then to Maryland in 1634, where he spent eight months. On his return to England he worked in London for the rest of his life.[4]

5. John Ballard (d. 1586) was born at Wratting in Cambridgeshire and went to school at Elmdon in Essex before studying at three different colleges at Cambridge. He went to Rheims in 1579 and was ordained priest at Châlons in 1581. Ballard was sent to England a few weeks later where he met another priest, Anthony Tyrrell. Both men became implicated in the Babington Plot to assassinate Elizabeth I and replace her with Mary, Queen of Scots. In 1586 Ballard travelled to Paris and brought back letters for Mary from the Spanish ambassador. Ballard was arrested, imprisoned and tortured on his return, and executed with 'special cruelty' at Tyburn in September 1586.[5]

6. William Barker (*fl.* 1540–76) was probably born in Norfolk of humble parents, since he enjoyed the patronage of the Boleyn family and later served as MP for Great Yarmouth. However, after study at Cambridge he went to Italy in 1549 and settled in Tuscany. He returned to England on Mary's accession in 1553 and became secretary to the Duke of Norfolk in 1554. He was elected to Parliament three times, but in 1569 he was arrested during investigations into Norfolk's attempted East Anglian conspiracy against Elizabeth. In 1571 he was involved in the Ridolfi Plot but betrayed Norfolk in order to save himself; Barker was confined in the Tower but released and pardoned in 1574.[6]

7. John Barnes OSB (*c.* 1581–1661) was the son of humble parents from Norfolk and studied at Cambridge, before converting to Catholicism and entering the English College at Douai in 1601. Barnes was sent to Valladolid in 1603 but left to join the Benedictines of San Benito, Valladolid in 1604. He spent the next decade lecturing at the English Benedictine houses. In 1619 he opposed the amalgamation of the Spanish and Cassinese English monks with those clothed by Sigebert Buckley as the 'English Benedictine Congregation', claiming that no such body had existed before the Reformation. He joined with another monk, Francis Walrave, and the two men attached themselves to the Cluniacs. Barnes's argument that Cluny was the only true Benedictine congregation in pre-Reformation England was answered by Clement Reyner's famous *Apostolatus Benedictinorum in Anglia* (1626), the definitive statement of English Benedictine identity. In later life Barnes was confined in a prison of the Inquisition in Rome, and finally in a lunatic asylum.[7]

8. Joshua Basset (1641–*c.* 1720) was born at King's Lynn, the son of a merchant, and entered Gonville and Caius College, Cambridge, in 1657. He was ordained in the Church of England and was Dean of Caius between 1674 and 1681. By 1685 he had converted to Catholicism, and on 3 January 1687 James II appointed him Master of Sidney Sussex College by royal mandate. After resistance from the College and University, Basset was admitted as Master in March, and proceeded to establish a Catholic chapel in the Master's Lodge. In November 1688 Basset left Sidney and the chapel was ransacked and destroyed by a mob in November. Basset went to live in King's Lynn but was attacked by a mob there as well, and lived out the rest of his days in London earning a living by legal work.[8]

9. Edmund Bedingfield (1615–80) was the third son of Sir Henry Bedingfield and was born at Oxburgh Hall. He studied at St Omer and Liège and was ordained in Seville in around 1644. He became chaplain to the English Carmelite nuns at Lierre and later became a canon of St Gumar in Lierre. In 1651, Bedingfield attempted to exorcise two Carmelite nuns (who were also sisters), Elizabeth and Margaret Mostyn, and a detailed and vivid account of the proceedings survives.[9]

10. Frances Bedingfield CJ (1616–1704) was a daughter of Francis Bedingfield of Redlingfield, Suffolk (d. 1644). In 1632 she joined Mary Ward, foundress of the Companions of Jesus, in Rome, and was professed in 1633. Frances remained with Mary Ward until her death in Yorkshire in 1645. In the 1650s she was in Paris and Rome and was later appointed Superior of the mother house of the Institute of the Blessed Virgin Mary in Munich. She returned to England in 1667 as Superior of a new house of the order in Hammersmith. She moved to York in 1685 and, in 1686, purchased a house by Micklegate Bar which became a school for girls and the famous 'Bar Convent'. In 1699 she was recalled to Munich and died there, the last surviving member of her order to have had contact with the founder, Mary Ward.[10]

11. Thomas Bedingfield (*c.* 1540–1613) was a son of Sir Henry Bedingfield (*c.* 1509–83) of Oxburgh Hall in Norfolk. In the 1560s, under the patronage of Edward de Vere, Earl of Oxford, he translated some works of the Italian mathematician Girolamo Cardano, and Queen Elizabeth made him a gentleman pensioner. Bedingfield went on to translate a work on horsemanship by Claudio Corte and Machiavelli's *Florentine History*. It is possible (but not proven) that he was responsible for one of the earliest manuscript translations of Machiavelli's *The Prince*.[11]

12. Bd Arthur Francis Bell OFM (1591–1643) was born in Worcestershire, rather than East Anglia, but he was sent at an early age, in 1598, to be educated at his mother Dorothy Daniel's family home, Acton Place in Suffolk. He was later educated at St Omer and trained for the priesthood at Valladolid; he was ordained at Salamanca in 1618. Later that year he joined the Observant Franciscans at Segovia. In 1620 he was sent to the English Franciscan Priory of St Bonaventure at Douai and became confessor to the Poor Clares at Gravelines. He was appointed Superior of St Bonaventure's in 1630. By 1633 he was Provincial of Scotland, although he never visited that country. He arrived in England in 1634, working partly in the household of Mary Kitson, Countess Rivers at Colchester. In 1643 Bell was arrested by Parliamentarian soldiers at Stevenage on suspicion of being a Royalist spy and, when his identity as a priest was discovered, he was tried and executed on 11 December. He was beatified in 1987.[12]

13. Bd Thomas Benstead (1574–1600) was born in Norfolk and trained at Valladolid and Seville, where he was ordained in around 1593. He left for England in 1595 and was a prisoner in the Clink by 1599. From there he was sent to Wisbech Castle, from which he escaped in March 1600 with five other priests. The Jesuit Superior, Henry Garnet, sheltered Benstead in London and then sent him to Lincoln. During a hue and cry for an escaped criminal, Benstead was interrogated and unable to explain his presence in the city; he was arrested, tried and executed at Lincoln in July 1600. Benstead was beatified in 1987.[13]

14. Myles Blomefylde (1525–1603) was born in Bury St Edmunds in 1525 and seems to have remained a crypto-Catholic throughout his life, preserving miracle plays among his copious manuscripts. In the 1570s Blomefylde was brought before the courts for sorcery but by the end of his life he was a respectable alchemist and medical practitioner in Chelmsford.[14]

15. Dorothy Henrietta Boulger (1847–1923) was born Dorothy Havers at Thelveton Hall in Norfolk, the second daughter of the colonial administrator Thomas Havers (d. 1870). She was the sister of the artist Alice Mary Havers (1850–90) and a member of an ancient and distinguished Norfolk Catholic family. However, she lived in the Falkland Islands and Uruguay until her father's death in 1870. In 1871 she began contributing stories to magazines, and she published her first novel in 1874; her best-known work is *Pretty Miss Bellew* (1875). In 1879 she married the botanist George

Simonds Boulger, who converted to Catholicism.[15] Dorothy Boulger was a popular and prolific novelist of the late nineteenth century and wrote evocative descriptions of her time in the Falklands.

16. Catharine Burton OCD (1668–1714) was born at Beyton in Suffolk, the daughter of Thomas Burton. Her brother Christopher became a Jesuit and three of her sisters also entered religion. After the Revolution in 1688 her family's home became a refuge for Jesuits from the College of the Holy Apostles in Bury St Edmunds. She suffered from a severe illness for many years and, attributing her healing to St Francis Xavier, she left England in 1693 and entered the English Carmelite house in Antwerp, where she was professed as Sister Mary Xaveria of the Angels in 1694. She wrote a detailed autobiography, later edited by Thomas Hunter SJ, which amongst other things is an important source on what happened to the College of the Holy Apostles after 1688.[16]

17. Alban Butler (1710–73) was not a native of East Anglia (he was born in Northamptonshire), but acted as chaplain to Edward Howard, 9th Duke of Norfolk, between 1754 and 1766, when he was appointed Rector of the English College at St Omer. During this period he was based at the Duke's Palace in Norwich and acted as Vicar General in East Anglia for the Vicar Apostolic of the Midland District, John Joseph Hornyold. Butler was the author of the celebrated multi-volume work of scholarship and hagiography, *The Lives of the Saints*.[17]

18. John Caius (1510–73) was born in Norwich and was educated by the monks of Norwich Cathedral before entering Gonville Hall, Cambridge, in 1529, where he studied theology and showed a talent for languages. Caius was elected a Fellow in 1533 but in 1539 he left England to study medicine at Padua, where he shared a house with Vesalius and began editing the works of Galen. Caius returned to England in 1544 and was elected a Fellow of the Royal College of Physicians in 1547. On Mary's accession in 1553 Caius secured the patronage of Cardinal Pole (whom he had known in Padua) for the imposition of a new humanist Galenism on the universities, and he was first elected president of the Royal College of Physicians in 1555. In 1557 he secured a royal charter from Phillip and Mary re-founding Gonville Hall as Gonville and Caius College, with Caius as the first master. On Elizabeth's accession Caius collected vestments and sacred vessels, but in 1572 the university authorities raided his rooms and publicly burnt his vestments. He retired to London and died shortly thereafter.[18]

19. Edward Cary (d. 1711) was born into a recusant family at Long Melford, Suffolk, but was sent to Devon at a young age.[19] In 1635 he entered the English College at St Omer but returned to enlist in the Royalist army in 1640. In 1646 he was admitted to the English College, Rome, and was ordained in 1651. Cary returned to England and worked as a chaplain in Devon, but by 1675 he was in Paris, writing controversial works in support of the Oath of Allegiance of 1606 and his friend John Sergeant. In 1684 he became chaplain at Torre Abbey in Devon and he was appointed Vicar General of Cornwall in 1684. James II appointed Cary chaplain general to the Catholics in his army and he set up a chapel on Hounslow Heath. He fled at the Revolution in 1688 and later served as chaplain to the Poor Clares at Rouen and acted as a Jacobite courier.

20. Henry John Palmer Chapman OSB (1865–1933) was born at Ashfield, Suffolk, the son of Frank Robert

Chapman, Archdeacon of Sudbury. Chapman studied at Oxford and was ordained deacon in the Church of England, but in 1890 he converted to Catholicism and joined the Jesuit noviciate at Manresa. However, in 1892 he left the Jesuits and joined the Benedictine abbey of Maredsous in Belgium. Chapman was ordained in 1895 and sent to Erdington, Birmingham. In 1913, when he was Prior of Erdington, Pope Pius X asked him to serve as Superior of the Anglican monks of Caldey Island who had just come into communion with the Apostolic See. He served as a military chaplain in the First World War and afterwards worked on the revision of the Vulgate in Rome. In 1919 he moved to Downside Abbey, where he was elected abbot in 1929. He was a prolific biblical scholar and spiritual writer.[20]

21. Bd Edward Colman (1636–78) was the son of Thomas Colman (d. 1661), vicar of Brent Eleigh, Suffolk. He studied at Trinity College, Cambridge, and became a gentleman pensioner to Charles II in 1661. Shortly afterwards he converted to Catholicism, and actively encouraged the conversion of others at court, including the King's brother James, Duke of York (later James II). In 1673 James appointed Colman secretary to the Duchess of York, Mary of Modena. In 1674 he went to the French court on a private embassy for James seeking subsidies for Charles II, so that the King was not forced to rely on Parliament. However, other courtiers moved against Colman and he was dismissed as secretary to the Duchess in 1676. In 1678 he was arrested during the 'Popish Plot' scare and the letters documenting his dealings with France were discovered. Colman was tried and found guilty of high treason, and executed at Tyburn on 3 December 1678. He was beatified in 1929.[21]

22. Anne Cornwallis (d. 1635), Countess of Argyll, was the daughter of Sir William Cornwallis (*c.* 1551–1611) of Brome, Suffolk. A manuscript collection of sixteenth-century poems, including at least one by Shakespeare, was previously attributed to her but this attribution is no longer accepted by scholars. In 1609 Anne married Archibald Campbell, 7th Earl of Argyll (1576–1638), in London. In 1618 her husband, who was one of the most powerful men in Scotland, converted to Catholicism under her influence. The couple moved to the Spanish Netherlands, where Argyll entered Spanish service, but they returned to London in 1627. Several of her daughters entered religious life.[22]

23. Sir Thomas Cornwallis (1518/19–1604) was the son of Sir John Cornwallis (*c.*1491–1544), steward of the household of Prince Edward 1538–44, and Mary Sulyard. He entered Lincoln's Inn in 1539, and married Anne Jerningham of Somerleyton (the Cornwallis, Sulyard and Jerningham families would all later play a crucial role in East Anglian Catholicism). He was knighted in 1548 and participated in the suppression of Kett's Rebellion in 1549. In July 1553, as sheriff of Norfolk and Suffolk, he initially proclaimed Jane Grey as Queen in Ipswich before switching his allegiance to Mary and riding to meet her at Framlingham Castle. He was subsequently appointed to the Privy Council and elected an MP. Cornwallis put down Wyatt's Rebellion in 1554, and in the same year he was appointed treasurer of Calais. Cornwallis opposed the confinement of Princess Elizabeth to the Tower and voted against England's reconciliation with Rome, suggesting that he favoured a conservative religious settlement with Mary as Supreme Head of the Church of England. In 1557 he was appointed Comptroller of the Household, but he was popularly blamed for the loss of Calais in January 1558. On Elizabeth's accession he was stripped of his offices and returned to Suffolk, where he was arrested in 1569 on suspicion of complicity with the Duke of Norfolk's projected rebellion. He became a church papist in 1570 but in 1578 returned to recusancy, which he maintained to the end of his life.[23]

24. Thomas Cornwallis (*c*. 1605–1675) was born at Beeston or Burnham Thorpe in Norfolk and was a son of Sir Charles Cornwallis (*c*. 1555–1629), the English ambassador to Spain, and a grandson of Sir Thomas Cornwallis (1518/19–1604). In 1634 he sailed with two ships sponsored by Cecilius Calvert, the *Ark* and the *Dove,* to a territory in the New World granted to Calvert by Charles I and named Maryland, after Queen Henrietta Maria. Calvert intended Maryland to be a refuge for English Catholics. Together with Calvert's nephew, Leonard Calvert, Cornwallis governed the early colony as Captain General. In 1635 he defended the new colony in a number of naval engagements against the Virginian William Clayborne, who resented the new colonists. In 1643 Cornwallis led a campaign against the Susquehanna, but he was back in England when another Virginian, Richard Ingle, sacked St Mary's City in 1646 and abolished the colony's guarantees of religious toleration. By 1659, Cornwallis had become disillusioned with the colonial project and returned to England, where he lived for the remainder of his life.[24]

25. Ambrose Cuddon (*fl.* 1822–8) was born in Suffolk but his parentage is unknown. He was working as a printer and publisher in 1823 when he established a Catholic circulating library of 15,000 volumes in Charterhouse Square, London. In 1822 he began publication of *The Catholic Miscellany and Monthly Repository of*

Information until the task was taken over by his fellow East Anglian, William Eusebius Andrews. However, Cuddon remained proprietor of *The Catholic Miscellany* until 1826. Cuddon laid the groundwork for the polemical journalism of Andrews.[25]

26. Sir Thomas Dereham (1678–1739), 4th Baronet, was born at West Dereham Abbey, Norfolk, and educated at the Florentine court under the care of his cousin Thomas Dereham, the English ambassador to the Grand Duchy of Tuscany. In 1718 he moved to Rome and represented the interests of King James III (the 'Old Pretender') to the Pope. He was admitted a Fellow of the Royal Society in 1722 and translated the *Philosophical Transactions* of the Royal Society into Italian, as well as corresponding with members of the Society about scientific developments in Italy.[26]

27. Ven. Thomas Downes (alias Bedingfield, Mountford or Mumford) (1617–78) was born at Bodney Hall in Norfolk; his mother was a member of the Bedingfield family. He was educated at St Omer and Valladolid and entered the Society of Jesus in 1639. In 1671 he became a chaplain to the Duke of York (the future James II) and was requested by the Duke to serve on board his flagship in the Battle of Sole Bay against the Dutch off the coast of Southwold in 1672. Downes reportedly acted with great bravery. In 1678 forged letters, purportedly from the Jesuit Provincial, were sent to Downes at Windsor and intercepted. James showed them to Charles II and maintained Downes's innocence, but he was unable to prevent his chaplain's arrest and imprisonment in the Gatehouse Prison, where he died. He was later declared Venerable.[27]

28. Thomas Everard SJ (1560–83) was born at Pond Hall, Linstead Magna, Suffolk, the son of the convicted recusant Henry Everard (d. 1596). Everard studied at Jesus College, Cambridge. In 1590, along with his friend Anthony Rous of Dennington, he met the Jesuit John Gerard at Lawshall in Suffolk, and as a result of Gerard's influence Everard and Rous entered the English College at Rheims in 1591. Everard was ordained in 1592 and joined the Society of Jesus the next year at Tournai. He was sent back to England to assist Gerard in London, but after the Gunpowder Plot he was sent to East Anglia for greater safety, where he began a missionary campaign and met his old friend Anthony Rous, who had conformed to the Church of England, betrayed fellow priests and accepted the living of Sweeting in Norfolk. Everard reconciled Rous to the Church and returned with him to the Continent in 1613. Everard was an accomplished linguist and translated many spiritual works of the Counter-Reformation into English for the first time, including *The Mirrour of Religious Perfection* (1618) and *Meditations upon the … Sacrament* (1622) by Luca Pinelli, *The Paradise of the Soule* by Albertus Magnus (1617) and the compendium *A Treatise of Mental Prayer* (1617). Everard returned to England in 1618 and, in spite of banishment in 1620, he continued his missionary work in Suffolk.[28]

29. John Fenn (1535–1615) was born at Montacute, Somerset and was a chorister at Wells Cathedral before studying at Winchester College and New College, Oxford. He was Master of the grammar school at Bury St Edmunds during Mary's reign and was renowned for his learning and teaching, but on the accession of Elizabeth he went into exile and studied at the University of Louvain. He was ordained priest in 1574 and served as a chaplain to Sir William Stanley's regiment in the Spanish Netherlands, but it was chiefly as a translator that he distinguished himself. Fenn was responsible for, amongst other things, the first English translation of the Catechism of the Council of Trent. Recent research by Jade Scott of the University of Glasgow suggests that Fenn served as Latin secretary to Anne Percy, Countess of Northumberland in exile between 1572 and 1573.[29] He ended his life as chaplain to the English Augustinian Canonesses of St Monica's, Louvain, from 1609.[30]

30. Elisabeth Jean Frink (1930–93) was born at The Grange, Thurlow, Suffolk, the daughter of Ralph Cuyler Frink and Jean Conway-Gordon, and was brought up a Catholic. She spent her early years following her father, a cavalry officer, to different postings around the country, but at the age of sixteen she gained a place at the Guildford School of Art. She began painting in 1947 but soon moved over to sculpture, at which she excelled. She continued her studies at the Chelsea School of Art and visited Paris in 1951, receiving her first commission in 1952. This was for a figure of St John Bosco for the church of St John Bosco at Woodley, near Reading. She taught at various schools of art from 1953 and married the architect Michel Jammet in 1955. In 1962 she was commissioned to create an eagle lectern for the new Coventry Cathedral. She married a second time in 1964 and, throughout the 1960s and 1970s concentrated on sculpting nude male figures, including a statue of St Edmund next to St Edmundsbury Cathedral to commemorate the amalgamation of the counties of East and West Suffolk in 1974. Frink married her third husband in 1974 and was appointed CBE in 1969 and DBE in 1982. She was elected to the Royal Academy in 1977 and appointed a Companion of Honour in 1992.[31]

31. John Gage-Rokewode (1786–1842) was born at Hengrave Hall, Suffolk, the fourth son of Sir Thomas Gage, 6th Baronet (d. 1798), and Charlotte Fitzherbert. Gage-Rokewode studied at Stonyhurst College in Lancashire and was called to the bar in 1818, but never practised as a barrister. In 1818 he was elected a Fellow of the Society of Antiquaries, and became director of the Society in 1829, holding the position until his death. Gage-Rokewode drew on the rich repository of evidence on his own family and the manuscript collections of his brother Sir Thomas Gage, 7th Baronet, for two important antiquarian works, *The History and Antiquities of Hengrave in Suffolk* (1822) and *The History and Antiquities of Suffolk: Thingoe Hundred* (1838), which was intended to be the first of several volumes on the county. Gage-Rokewode also edited the chronicle of Jocelin de Brakelond for the Camden Society in 1840, laying a firm foundation for future research into the medieval abbey of Bury St Edmunds. On the death of his brother Robert Joseph Gage in July 1838 he inherited both Hengrave Hall and Coldham Hall in Suffolk, and received a royal licence to assume the surname Rokewode. Gage-Rokewode's antiquarian interests contributed to the survival and excellent preservation of the Hengrave Manuscripts. He died at Claughton Hall in Lancashire and was buried at Stanningfield.[32]

32. Stephen Gardiner (*c.* 1495–1555), Bishop of Winchester, was one of the leading conservative voices of the early Reformation era in England and presided over the restoration of Catholicism in the reign of Mary I. He was born at Bury St Edmunds, the son of the clothmaker John Gardiner and his wife Agnes. It is highly likely that he was educated by the monks at Bury before going to Cambridge in 1511, eventually graduating as Doctor of Canon Law in 1522. Gardiner was a member of the humanist circle at Cambridge around Erasmus. He was soon Master of Trinity Hall and held in plurality the archdeaconries of Taunton, Worcester, Norfolk and Leicester and was a prebend at Salisbury Cathedral. Gardiner served as the English ambassador to Rome during Henry VIII's divorce and lobbied for Cardinal Wolsey as successor to Pope Clement VII. In 1529 he became Henry VIII's principal secretary and was appointed Bishop of Winchester. However, by 1532 Gardiner's opposition to the breach with Rome meant that he fell out of favour with Henry. Gardiner was replaced as royal secretary by Thomas Cromwell. The following year, however, Gardiner defended both the royal supremacy and the execution of St John Fisher. Gardiner was appointed ambassador to France but he angered Henry again in 1537 by suggesting concessions to the Pilgrimage of Grace. Instructed by Henry to arrange the arrest of Cardinal Reginald Pole, Gardiner prevaricated and Pole was merely expelled from France. Gardiner returned to favour after the execution of Cromwell in 1540, when Henry's regime took a more conservative direction. Gardiner travelled in Europe, disputing with Reformed theologians. Gardiner also began seeking out heretics at the royal court and was very nearly accused of denying the royal supremacy. Throughout the reign of Edward VI he opposed religious changes and he was soon imprisoned in the Fleet. He was later put on trial and deprived of the See of Winchester in 1551. On Mary's accession in 1553 he was restored to his see and to the Privy Council and appointed Lord Chancellor. Gardiner presided over the restoration of Catholicism and married Mary to Phillip of Spain at Winchester Cathedral in 1554.[33]

33. George Gilbert (d. 1583) was probably born at Clare, Suffolk, the son of Ambrose Gilbert (d. 1554) and Grace Townsend. Gilbert was educated at Cambridge but, on the death of his father, inherited significant wealth and estates at a young age. Whilst on the 'Grand Tour' in Europe he met the Catholic Thomas Darbyshire in Paris and was received into the Catholic Church by Robert Persons at Rome in 1579. Returning to London, he formed an association of wealthy young men who pledged to put their fortunes at the service of the English mission and presided over a network that helped and sheltered missionary priests. In 1581 Gilbert returned to Rome, where he entered the English College as a gentleman pensioner and commissioned the paintings of British and English martyrs for the College chapel by Niccolò Circignani. He died of a fever but was received into the Society of Jesus before his death.[34]

34. Charles Alexander Grant (1906–89), eighth Bishop of Northampton (1967–82), was born in Cambridge and converted to Catholicism at the age of fourteen. He studied at Cambridge University and, after ordination, he served parishes in Cambridge, Ely and Kettering. He was appointed Vicar General of the Diocese of Northampton in 1955 and Auxiliary Bishop in 1961, succeeding Leo Parker as Bishop of Northampton in 1967. He contributed to the Second Vatican Council and presided over the creation of the Diocese of East Anglia from the Diocese of Northampton in 1976, even though it was with great regret that he entrusted the area in which he had been born to another bishop.[35]

35. Elizabeth Grymeston (1563–c. 1604) was born at Gunton, Norfolk, the daughter of the landowner Martin Bernye. In 1584 she married Christopher Grymeston, a Fellow of Gonville and Caius College, Cambridge (in spite of the fact that fellows were forbidden to marry). In 1604, after Elizabeth's death, her advice book to her son Bernye was published as *Miscellanea: Meditations, Memoratives.* This was the first of a new genre of spiritual advice books that became popular in the seventeenth century.[36]

36. George Gunton (1801–90) was born at Costessey, Norfolk, the son of the Catholic brickmaker, John Gunton, and Elizabeth Spaul. In the 1820s he was commissioned by Sir George William Jerningham to transform the humble Costessey Hall into 'Costessey Park', a crenellated neo-Tudor castle suitable for the new Baron Stafford. Gunton designed mouldings, windows, corbel-tables, pinnacles and chimneys himself and, after the completion of Costessey, he sold these designs and worked on other restoration projects such as Flixton Hall. Gunton invented 'Cosseyware', pre-made brick mouldings that could be applied with relative ease to give a Gothic or neo-Tudor appearance to any building, and thanks to the railways connecting Norwich to the rest of the country, the use of Cosseyware became widespread and the business expanded rapidly. It was taken over by Gunton's sons and grandsons and reached its high point in the Edwardian era, although production of Cosseyware finally ceased in 1939. One building adorned by Gunton's bricks was the church of St Walstan at Costessey itself, erected by F. C. Husenbeth in 1841.[37]

37. Robert Hare (*c.* 1530–1611) was born at Bruisyard Hall in Suffolk, the second son of Sir Nicholas Hare (d. 1557), Master of the Rolls in the reign of Mary I. Hare entered Gonville Hall, Cambridge, in 1545 and the Inner Temple in 1548, and may have travelled on the

Continent in the 1550s. In 1555 he bore a bannerol at the funeral of Anne of Cleves. He was appointed Clerk of the Pells in 1560 and elected MP for Dunwich in 1563. However, in 1570, probably as a consequence of his recusancy and the Duke of Norfolk's abortive rebellion, he resigned all of his offices and devoted himself to antiquarian research. He was listed as a recusant in 1577 but his beneficence to Cambridge University, to whom he donated manuscripts, led the University to petition against his arrest in 1601. In 1590 Hare presented the richly illuminated *Liber Privilegiorum et Libertatum Universitatis Cantebrigiensis* to the University, a compilation of charters and letters patent relating to Cambridge. In April 1611 he inherited Bruisyard Hall from his brother Michael, but died unmarried later that year. In his will he made his nephew Nicholas Timperley of Hintlesham his heir, and bequeathed his soul to 'our blessed Ladie St Marie the virgin Mother of Christe my Savyoure, to St Michael the Archaungell and to all the holie Aungells and Archaungells and to the Rest of the glorious Company of heaven', as well as insisting that manuscripts from religious houses should be restored to them in the event of a Catholic restoration.[38]

38. Bd Henry Heath OFM (1599–1643) was born in the parish of St John, Peterborough, and studied at Corpus Christi College, Cambridge, where he became librarian. As a result of reading the works of the Church Fathers and controversial literature he became convinced of the truth of the Catholic faith. He fled to London and was received into the Church by George Fisher. He left England to study at the English College in Douai but by 1623 he had entered the Franciscan friary of St Bonaventure where he assumed the name Paul of St Magdalen. He was elected Superior in 1632. In 1641, hearing of the capture of a fellow friar, Heath obtained permission to go to England, where he travelled in the disguise of a sailor. He was discovered by having Catholic writings sewn into his cap and executed at Tyburn in April 1643. As a result of his son's witness, Henry Heath's father John went to Douai at the age of eighty, was received into the Church and became a laybrother at St Bonaventure's. Henry Heath was beatified in 1987.[39]

39. Catherine Mechtildis Holland OSA (1637–1720) was born at Quidenham, Norfolk, the daughter of Sir John Holland, 1st Baronet, who was MP for Castle Rising and a client of the Howard family. Although her mother was a Catholic she was brought up as a Protestant and spent the Civil War at Bergen op Zoom in the Netherlands. In 1652 the family moved to Bruges and Catherine began secretly attending Mass and became friendly with the English Canonesses of the Convent of Nazareth. The Hollands returned to Bergen in 1656 and England in 1657; however, she returned to Brabant in 1659 and converted to Catholicism. Holland sought help from the Jesuits to help her escape to Bruges but eventually had to rely on the assistance of the Prioress, Mary Bedingfield. She entered the English Convent in 1662. Catherine Holland is chiefly known for her vivid and compelling autobiographical conversion narrative, which was partially published in 1925.[40]

40. Anatole Andreas Aloys von Hügel (1854–1928), Baron von Hügel, was born in Florence to an Austrian father and a Scottish mother. His family settled in Devon in the late 1860s, and following his father's death von Hügel was sent to school at Stonyhurst, where he became interested in ornithology. He travelled to Fiji in the 1870s and, on his return in 1883, donated his ornithological collection to the University of Cambridge's Museum of General and Local Archaeology, of which he was appointed curator. Von Hügel was the first Catholic to be appointed at Cambridge since 1688, and he began to campaign for Cambridge to allow the admission of Catholic undergraduates. In 1893 he presented Pope Leo XIII with a finely bound edition of J. W. Clark's three-volume *Architectural History of Cambridge University* and knelt before the Pontiff in an MA gown. As a result, the bishops of England and Wales agreed to lift the ban on Catholics studying at Cambridge, with the proviso that a Catholic chaplaincy should be created. In 1896 he persuaded the Duke of Norfolk to buy a house in Cambridge, which became St Edmund's House (now St Edmund's College). In 1914 von Hügel became a British subject and he was admitted as an honorary ScD of the University in 1922. Pope Pius XI made him a Knight of St Gregory in 1923.[41]

41. Frederick Charles Husenbeth (1796–1872) was born in Bristol, the son of a German father and a Cornish mother. Husenbeth was educated at the Catholic school at Sedgley Park, Wolverhampton. In 1814 he entered St Mary's College, Oscott, and was ordained priest in 1820. Immediately after ordination he was sent to Costessey in Norfolk, where he remained for the next fifty-two years. Husenbeth was the first priest at Costessey to live in his own house, and in 1827 he was appointed Grand Vicar for East Anglia within the Midland District. He opened St Walstan's church in 1841 and was made a papal Doctor of Divinity in 1850. In 1852 he was appointed provost of the Chapter of the Diocese of Northampton. Husenbeth was a keen antiquary who submitted 1,305 articles to *Notes and Queries*. He was a 'priest of the old school' and disliked the new devotional practices of the mid-nineteenth century, and always remembered the years before emancipation with affection.[42]

42. Elizabeth Inchbald (1753–1821) was born in Stanningfield, Suffolk, to Catholic parents, the farmer John Simpson (d. 1761) and Mary Rushbrook of Flempton (d. 1783). She was confirmed in 1768 and educated by James Dennett, the Jesuit Provincial, who was then chaplain at Coldham Hall. Elizabeth tried to join a Norwich theatre in 1770 but her family discouraged her acting ambitions, so she left home and headed for London in 1772. Shortly thereafter she married the actor Joseph Inchbald (1735–79) in a Catholic ceremony. In the late 1770s she began work on a novel, and tried unsuccessfully to get it published in 1779, the year of her husband's death. Inchbald submitted her first plays to theatres in 1781 and she enjoyed her first success with the farce *I'll Tell You What* (1785). By 1789 she was able to give up acting, and nineteen of her plays were performed between 1784 and 1805. Inchbald held radical opinions and her play *The Massacre*, a commentary on the French Revolution in the guise of a play about the St Bartholomew's Day Massacre, was never performed. Her ground-breaking novel *A Simple Story* (1791) was set among the Catholic gentry of East Anglia.[43]

43. Henry Jermyn (1636–1708), Earl of Dover, was born at Rushbrooke in Suffolk, the second son of Thomas Jermyn MP (d. 1659). Jermyn converted to Catholicism and spent the 1650s at the court of the Dowager Queen Henrietta Maria at St Germain-en-Laye outside Paris. By 1656 he was a member of the household of Charles II's brother James, Duke of York (the future James II), and was appointed James's Master of the Horse in 1659. Jermyn became embroiled in the scandals of the Restoration court but was deprived of his offices under the Test Act in 1673 and retired to Cheveley in Cambridgeshire. In 1675 he married Judith Pooley (d. 1726) of Badley, Suffolk. On the accession of James II in 1685 he was created Baron Dover and appointed to the Privy Council, as well as being Lord Lieutenant of Cambridgeshire. Lord Dover was tasked with ensuring the compliance of the Corporation of Bury St Edmunds with the election of an MP sympathetic to James's agenda of religious toleration in 1688, but his chapel at Cheveley was pulled down during the Revolution and Lord Dover fled with James II to France. James created him Earl of Dover in 1689 in Ireland. However, Dover was blamed for the poor conduct of James's Irish campaign. Dover obtained a royal pardon from William of Orange in 1691 and returned to his estate at Cheveley where he lived out his remaining days.[44]

44. Edward Jerningham (1737–1812), poet and playwright, was born at Costessey in Norfolk and was the third and youngest son of Sir George Jerningham, 5th Baronet. He received his education at Douai and St Gregory's College in Paris, where he acquired a taste for Voltaire and Rousseau. He conformed to the Church of England in the 1790s, and acted as a go-between for the Prince Regent and his Catholic mistress, Mrs Fitzherbert. Jerningham was a sentimental poet who wrote a few comedies, but his significance is based on the fact that he was 'a link from the artistic generation of Gray, Mason, and Walpole to that of Sheridan, Coleridge, and Byron'.[45]

45. John L'Estrange (1836–77) was born in Norwich, the son of a plumber and glazier, and subsequently lived in the village of Heigham. He was brought up a Catholic. He worked as a clerk in the Norwich stamp office, while the priest at Costessey, F. C. Husenbeth, introduced him to the study of history. L'Estrange transcribed court books, guild records, churchwardens' accounts and lists of freemen for Norwich, King's Lynn and Great Yarmouth. In 1872–3 L'Estrange edited *Eastern Counties Collectanea*, a successor to Samuel Tymms's *East Anglian Notes and Queries*, in twenty-four parts. In addition to numerous contributions to *Norfolk Archaeology* he wrote *Church Bells of Norfolk* (1874).[46] However, L'Estrange remained poor and in 1877 he was found guilty of forging the signature of Francis Gostling Foster, the distributor of stamps, to embezzle money and steal over £3000 worth of stamps. He was sentenced to seven years in prison. He died in prison after just a few months—he may have committed suicide. After his death many more of his works were published and his antiquarian work remains valuable to historians of Norfolk.

46. Mary Adela Lescher (1846–1927) was a daughter of Joseph Sidney Lescher (1803–92/3), a wholesale druggist based in Stoke-by-Nayland, Suffolk. In 1856 she was sent to study with the Benedictines at East Bergholt. In 1869 she entered the Institute of Notre Dame at Namur, Belgium, taking the name Mary of St Wilfrid. She was professed in 1871 and returned to England to teach at Clapham. She was appointed Superior of the Institute's Liverpool House in 1892. In 1895 she became the first Principal of the first training college for female Catholic teachers in Scotland at Dowanhill, Glasgow. Mary Lescher pioneered new methods in the teaching of science and Montessori education.[47]

47. John Anselm Mannock OSB (1677–1764), religious writer, was born at Giffords Hall, Stoke-by-Nayland, and joined the English Benedictine Congregation after accidentally killing his brother by letting a cannonball fall from a window. He served as chaplain at Foxcote Hall in Warwickshire and Kelvedon Hall in Essex. He is best known as the author of *The Poor Man's Catechism* (1752), an oft-reprinted staple of eighteenth-century recusant piety.[48]

48. Francis Edward Martyn (1782–1838) was born in Norfolk and educated at Sedgley Park school before entering St Mary's College, Oscott, in 1796. In December 1805 he was ordained by John Milner, the first Catholic priest to have received his entire training in England. He served missions in Warwickshire, Staffordshire and the Black Country and his missionary activities were publicised by his fellow East Anglian William Eusebius Andrews in *The Orthodox Journal*. He died at Walsall.[49]

49. Roger Martin (*c.* 1527–1615) of Long Melford trained as a lawyer at Lincoln's Inn in the reign of Henry VIII and served as churchwarden of Long Melford during Mary's reign. On Elizabeth's accession he was replaced but continued to annotate the churchwardens' accounts. In the 1580s he wrote a manuscript entitled 'The state of Melford church … as I did know it' which described the pre-Reformation ornaments and ceremonies of the church in great detail, and has become one of the key sources for the late medieval church. He remained a committed recusant throughout his life and suffered several periods of imprisonment at Wisbech and Framlingham.[50]

50. Sir Christopher Milton (1615–93) was the younger brother of the poet John Milton and was born in London.

Like his more famous brother he was educated at St
Paul's School and Christ's College, Cambridge. He was
admitted to the Inner Temple in 1632. By 1641 he and
his wife Thomasine were living in Reading. Unlike his
brother, Milton was a committed Royalist, and spent
the Civil War moving from place to place until returning to London. In 1652 he moved with his family to
Ipswich. At the Restoration in 1660 he was appointed
a Justice of the Peace and Deputy Recorder for the
County of Suffolk. It seems likely that he converted
to Catholicism in the 1670s or 1680s. In 1686 James II
appointed him Sergeant-at-Law and a Baron of the
Exchequer, as well as bestowing a knighthood. Milton
was appointed Justice of the Common Pleas in 1687. In
July 1688 he retired to Rushmere St Andrew.[51] There
is a tradition that he maintained a Catholic chapel in
Ipswich's Tacket Street, next to what later became the
Tankard public house.[52]

51. St Henry Morse SJ (1595–1645) was born at Brome,
Suffolk, a son of Robert Morse (d. 1612) of Tivetshall
St Mary. After study at Corpus Christi College, Cam-
bridge, he entered Barnard's Inn, but he converted to
Catholicism in 1614 and was admitted to the English
College at Douai. Morse returned to England but was
arrested and imprisoned for four years at Clerkenwell.
He was released in 1618 and finally ordained in Rome.
In 1624 he returned to England, but was arrested off
the coast of Newcastle in 1626 while trying to get to
Watten. He was imprisoned at York until 1630. He was
finally received into the Society of Jesus at Watten, and
returned to London in 1633, courageously working
through an outbreak of plague. He was arrested in
1636, tried and convicted but pardoned by Charles
I. In 1640 he was arrested again and brought before

Archbishop Laud, who let him go as a result of the influence of Queen Henrietta Maria and Lady Cornwallis. In 1641 he served as chaplain to Henry Gage's regiment in the Low Countries but returned to England in 1643. He was captured at Newcastle in 1644 and, after trial, executed at Tyburn on 22 January 1645. He was canonised as one of the Forty Martyrs of England and Wales in 1970.[53]

52. James Mumford SJ (*c.* 1606–66) was a native of Norfolk or Suffolk but his parentage is unknown. He joined the Society of Jesus in 1626 and was ordained in 1635. In 1648 he was appointed Rector of the Jesuit College at Liège. He is principally remembered for his popular controversial work *The Remembrance for the Living to Pray for the Dead*, which defended the Catholic doctrine of purgatory, and resulted in Mumford being embroiled in a theological controversy with the philosopher and priest Thomas White. In 1650 Mumford was sent to England and stationed in Norwich as a member of the College of the Holy Apostles; he seems to have been Rector by 1655, and therefore the leader of the Jesuit mission in East Anglia. In 1658 Mumford was arrested and paraded around Norwich in priests' vestments accompanied by soldiers with altar vessels dangling from their spears; he was taken to Great Yarmouth to be imprisoned, but managed to negotiate his return to Norwich. He was released from prison after some months and moved the base of the Jesuit mission away from the city centre, but continued to lead the College of the Holy Apostles until his death.[54]

53. Edward Paston (1641–1714) was born in Norfolk, the son of William Paston, who was high sheriff of Norfolk in 1637. He entered the English College at Douai in 1651 and was ordained in 1666 in Bruges. He assisted in founding St Gregory's College, Paris, and taught philosophy at Douai from 1670; in 1681 he was made a Doctor of Divinity. He moved to England on the accession of James II but in 1688 was elected president of the English College at Douai. Controversially, Paston attempted to impose Sulpician reforms on the College and he was accused of Jansenism. He died suddenly at the College whilst still in post.[55]

54. Miles Prance (*fl.* 1678–88), goldsmith, was the son of Simon Prance of March, Cambridgeshire, a convert to Catholicism. Two of Miles's brothers became priests and two of his sisters became nuns at Rouen and Lisbon. Miles Prance became Goldsmith-in-Ordinary to Queen Catherine of Braganza and was responsible for decorating the Queen's chapel next to St James's Palace. In 1678 Prance was accused of being present at the murder of the magistrate Sir Edmund Berry Godfrey. He falsely accused Jesuits of complicity in the murder, evidence which set in train the events of the Popish Plot scare of 1678–81. On the accession of James II Prance was found guilty of perjury and pilloried.[56]

55. Cyril Edward Restieaux (1910–96), seventh Bishop of Plymouth, was born in Norwich and studied at the English College, Rome. He was ordained in 1932 for the Diocese of Nottingham, serving as administrator of Nottingham Cathedral and then Vicar General of the diocese. He was consecrated Bishop of Plymouth in 1955 and served for thirty-one years before his retirement in 1986.[57]

56. St Bartholomew Alban Roe OSB (*c.* 1583–1642) was born in Bury St Edmunds and may have attended the grammar school there before studying at Cambridge. Whilst an undergraduate, Roe visited a Catholic prisoner in St Albans in the hope of converting him to the

Protestant faith, but ended up being converted to Catholicism himself. He entered the English College, Douai, in 1607, but was expelled for insubordination in 1610. In 1613 he joined the Benedictine Priory of St Laurence at Dieulouard in Lorraine, taking the name Alban of St Edmund. In 1615, after ordination, he was sent to found a daughter house in Paris, which became the Priory of St Edmund. Roe was then sent to England, where he was imprisoned between 1618 and 1623. He went to St Gregory's, Douai, on his release before returning to England, where he was imprisoned in the same prison at St Albans where he had been converted years earlier. In 1641 he was transferred from the Fleet to Newgate. He was put on trial on January 1642, found guilty of high treason and executed on 21 January. He was canonised as one of the Forty Martyrs of England and Wales in 1970.[58]

57. Ambrose Rookwood (*c.* 1578–1606) of Coldham Hall, Stanningfield, was educated by the Jesuits at St Omer before returning to Suffolk to breed horses on the Coldham estate. He was approached by Robert Catesby to provide horses and gunpowder for the attack on Parliament in November 1605 and was one of the first of the plotters to escape the capital after the discovery of the Gunpowder Plot. He was captured in Staffordshire, tried and found guilty of high treason, and hanged, drawn and quartered in Old Palace Yard on 31 January 1606.[59]

58. Ambrose Rookwood (1664–96) was the sixth son of Ambrose Rookwood of Coldham Hall, Stanningfield (1622–93), and the great-grandson of Ambrose the Gunpowder Plotter. He left England in 1688 to join the royal lifeguards of the exiled King James II at St Germain-en-Laye. In 1695 he returned to England with Brigadier George Barclay, who believed that he had received instructions from James to assassinate William of Orange. Rookwood's involvement in the Barclay Conspiracy resulted in his arrest, trial and execution for high treason in April 1696.[60]

59. James Rosier (1573–1609) was born at Winston, Suffolk, the son of a clergyman. In 1575 the family moved to Sproughton and Rosier was brought up in the house of a relative in Ipswich. He studied at Pembroke College, Cambridge, before entering the household of Sir Philip Woodhouse at Kimberley Hall, Norfolk, where he became a Catholic. Sir Thomas Arundell (later Baron Arundell of Wardour) persuaded Rosier to join a mission to establish a colony for English Catholics in the New World, and Rosier set out on an exploration of the coast of Maine between 5 March and 18 July 1605. However, the discovery of the Gunpowder Plot put paid to the idea of a Catholic colony and Rosier left England for Rome in 1608, where he was admitted to the English College and ordained in 1609. He died at Loreto on his way to the English mission.[61]

60. Joseph Rudderham (1899–1979), seventh Bishop of Clifton, was born in Norwich and educated at St Bede's, Manchester, St Edmund's, Ware, and Christ's College, Cambridge. He was ordained at the Venerable English College, Rome, in 1926 as a priest of the Diocese of Northampton. He served as curate at All Saints, Peterborough, 1927–32, where he then served as parish priest until 1943. In that year he was appointed administrator of Northampton Cathedral, as well as serving as Diocesan Inspector of Schools, 1941–9. He was consecrated Bishop of Clifton on 26 July 1949. He participated in the Second Vatican Council and oversaw the building of Clifton Cathedral, of which he took possession on 29 June 1973. He retired in 1975.[62]

61. Robert Gregory Sayer OSB (1560–1602) was born at Redgrave, Suffolk, to modest parents, and studied at Botesdale for seven years before entering Gonville and Caius College, Cambridge, in 1576. The college refused permission to graduate on the grounds that he had converted other scholars to Catholicism, disputed against John Jewel's *Apology*, and been a friend of the college butler Bd John Fingley or Finglow (d. 1586/7). Sayer finally graduated from Peterhouse in 1581 and then proceeded to the English College at Douai, moving to Rheims in 1582. He was ordained in Rome in 1585 and returned to England in 1586, narrowly escaping arrest in Hackney. In 1589 he joined the Benedictines at Monte Cassino, the first Englishman to enter a monastery since the Dissolution. He was appointed Professor of Moral Theology at Monte Cassino before moving to San Giorgio Maggiore, Venice, in 1595. He was considered the pre-eminent moral theologian of the Counter-Reformation, and was the author of such works as *Clavis Regia Sacerdotum Casuum Conscientiae* (1605) and *Thesaurus Casuum Conscientiae* (1601). These works were reprinted in anthologies of moral theology as late as the nineteenth century.[63]

62. Bd Montford Scott (d. 1591) was born at Hawstead in Suffolk. He was educated at Douai from 1574 and returned to England, having been ordained subdeacon, in 1576. He was captured in Essex but, because he was not a priest, he was released and returned to Douai. He was ordained priest at Brussels in 1577 and returned to England a few days later. He was captured in Cambridge but was later released on bond, and went to Brockdish in Norfolk to stay with his cousin Richard Lacey, whom he tried to convert. In December 1590 he was captured at the house of William Kilbeck in his own home village of Hawstead, sent to London for trial, and executed on 1 July 1591. He was beatified in 1987.[64]

63. Richard Short (d. 1668) was the son of Thomas Short (d. 1631) of the parish of St James, Bury St Edmunds, and the brother of William Short, Rector of Euston. Nothing is known of Short's education but he probably attended the Bury St Edmunds Grammar School. In 1635 he married Margaret White at Euston; in 1640 he married his second wife, Ann Kennington, at the same church. Short wrote a Laudian pamphlet, *A discourse concerning the fitnesse of the vesture necessary to be used in taking the Bread & Wine* in 1642. He published another pamphlet, *The Highway to Peace*, in 1647, and in 1656 he published his only medical work, which tells us that he was a Doctor of Medicine by this time. *Of Drinking Water* was an attack on the fad for recommending water and vociferously defended Galenic medicine against any innovations. It is likely that Short had converted to Catholicism by 1654, which was when he sent his son Richard to study at the English College, Douai.[65]

64. Richard Short (1641–1708) was born at Euston, Suffolk, the son of Dr Richard Short (d. 1668) and his second wife, Ann Kennington. He was sent to study at the English College, Douai, in 1654. He obtained the degree of Doctor of Medicine at some point after 1681, probably by royal mandate because he was a Catholic. In 1688 he was at the centre of a dispute between the Crown and Magdalen College, Oxford, since James II tried to impose him on the College by means of Letters Patent and the College resisted. The case served to define the opposition to the royal prerogative that led to the Revolution later that year. Meanwhile Short was elected to the Corporation of Bury St Edmunds. He fled to Douai in November 1688 and subsequently spent time at Montpellier and in Italy and Paris before returning to England. In his later years Short became the leading advocate in England of Continental Jansenism and corresponded with the prominent Jansenist Pasquier Quesnel. He died in Bury St Edmunds.[66]

65. Thomas Short (1635–85) was born at Euston, Suffolk, the son of a Church of England minister, William Short. Short studied at the grammar school in Bury St Edmunds before proceeding to St John's College, Cambridge. Short was evidently not a Catholic at this time as he graduated, but he was created a Doctor of Medicine by royal mandate in 1668. Later the same year he applied for membership of the Royal College of Physicians, but was not admitted until 1675. In 1679 he was summoned before the College following an order from Parliament to expel Catholic members, but no action was taken. Short was a celebrated physician in his time, and became famous after his death in 1685 when Gilbert Burnet, Bishop of Salisbury, spread a rumour that Short was poisoned because he was going to reveal that his co-religionists had poisoned Charles II.[67]

66. John Palgrave Simpson (1807–87) was born in Norwich, the son of the town clerk of the city of Norwich and treasurer of Norfolk. He studied at Corpus Christi College, Cambridge, and then travelled in Europe, converting to Catholicism at Munich in 1842. Pope Gregory XVI made him a Knight of St Gregory. In 1846 he published his first novel, *Second Love,* and regularly contributed to *The Times* and *Blackwood's Magazine* throughout the 1840s. Simpson moved to London and wrote around sixty plays between 1850 and 1885, as well as many novels.[68]

67. St Robert Southwell (1561–95) was born at Horsham St Faith, Norfolk, the third son of Richard Southwell (d. 1600) and Elizabeth Shelley. Southwell entered the English College, Douai, in 1576. In 1578 he left for Rome with the intention of joining the Society of Jesus. During his novitiate he acted as secretary to the Rector of the English College, Rome, Alphonso Agazzari. Southwell was ordained in 1584 and left Rome with Henry Garnet in 1586. He landed at Folkestone and successfully reached London where he went into hiding, serving the recusants of the capital and the Thames Valley. In a house provided for him by Anne Howard, Countess of Arundel and Surrey, he set up a printing press which printed many of his works. Southwell was captured at Bellamy House at Uxenden in February 1592. He was tortured in the house of Richard Topcliffe before being committed to the Gatehouse Prison and then the Tower, where he endured solitary confinement for two and a half years. He was finally brought to trial for high treason in February 1595, found guilty and hanged, drawn and quartered at Tyburn on 21 February 1595. Southwell was canonised as one of the Forty Martyrs of England and Wales in 1970, but he is best known today for his poetry, such as 'The Burning Babe' and his five lyrics on the nativity, which were set to music by Benjamin Britten in his *Ceremony of Carols*.[69]

68. Richard Rapier Stokes (1897–1957) was the son of Phillip Folliott Stokes and Mary Fenwick Rapier, the heiress of Richard Christopher Rapier (1836–97), one of the founders of Ransomes & Rapier, the important Ipswich manufacturer of railway equipment and cranes. After his studies at Downside School and Trinity College, Cambridge, Stokes joined his mother's family business. In 1938 he was elected Labour MP for Ipswich. He opposed the carpet-bombing of German cities during the Second World War and, in February 1945, his questions in the House of Commons about the bombing of Dresden led to a change in government policy. In February 1950 Stokes was appointed Minister of Works, the first Catholic to hold ministerial office since the Test Act of 1673. He later served as Lord Privy Seal and Minister of Materials but lost office after Labour's defeat in the 1951 General Election. In July 1957 he was involved in a road accident when his car overturned in London, and this may have contributed to his death of heart failure a month later.[70]

69. John Tasburgh (1617–92) was the fourth son of John Tasburgh (d. 1629) of Flixton, Suffolk. He was educated in Eye under a Mr Dormond, but on the death of his Protestant father his mother Lettice Cressy sent him to study at Douai in 1632. He was in France in 1645 and probably went into exile, along with several other East Anglian Catholics, on the outbreak of the Civil War. In 1654 he was living at East Wretham in Norfolk. Shortly afterwards John's brother Cressy bought Bodney Hall, which had once belonged to the recusant Downes family. When Cressy died without issue the property passed to John at some point before 1662. In 1667 John bought the abbey of Cong in Ireland. John first acted as the Earl of Arundel's (later Duke of Norfolk's) election agent for the borough of Thetford in 1660, arranging for the Earl's candidate, William Gawdy, to be elected. Thereafter Tasburgh began exercising patronage over benefices owned by the Duke of Norfolk. Gawdy died in 1669, triggering a by-election in Thetford while the Duke was at Tangier. Lord Arlington put forward his own candidate, against the Duke's, who was duly elected. Tasburgh then switched sides and began working for Arlington. However, Tasburgh was disappointed of the government office Arlington had promised him. He turned to promoting the cause of his Protestant friends instead, and campaigned relentlessly for a benefice for a young man named Wormley Martin. In 1673 the Test Act put an end to Tasburgh's ambitions of government office, and he subsequently retired from active involvement in local politics.[71]

70. William Maurus Taylor OSB (b. 1576/77) was born in Ely, Cambridgeshire, the son of Rombald Taylor and Anne Adam, and studied at Lincoln Grammar School and Lincoln College, Oxford, before migrating to Magdalen. Disappointed of a fellowship at Magdalen because of his Catholic sympathies, Taylor became a secretary to Henry Somerset, 4th Earl of Worcester. He converted to Catholicism at Raglan Castle and followed Worcester to London in 1600, before entering the English College in Rome. Taylor fell out with the college authorities in 1602 and entered the Cassinese Benedictine monastery of San Giorgio Maggiore, where he seems to have known Gregory Sayer for the last few months of his life; he later edited Sayer's works of moral theology. In 1607 he returned to England and drew up the instrument of aggregation by which Sigebert Buckley recreated the English Benedictine Congregation by clothing two monks. Taylor later attempted to set up a convent of nuns in Paris and became a trusted adviser of Bishop Richard Smith, who recommended him for a bishopric in the event of the restoration of Catholicism in England. In 1637 he was appointed Superior of the English Cassinese Benedictines. He died in Italy at some point after 1653.[72]

71. Charles Tilney (1561–86) was the son of Philip Tilney of Shelley Hall, Suffolk, and Anne Framlington of Crowshall, Debenham, Suffolk. Charles was a gentleman pensioner at the court of Elizabeth I who became involved in the Babington Plot to assassinate Elizabeth and replace her with Mary, Queen of Scots. He was executed for treason in 1586.[73]

72. Bd Thomas Tunstall (d. 1616) was not a native of East Anglia, having been born in Westmoreland. He was ordained in 1609 and returned to England in 1610, where he was incarcerated in Wisbech Castle. Having cut his hands on a rope while escaping, he sought help from the wife of Sir Hammond L'Estrange of Hunstanton, but L'Estrange discovered him and had him committed to Norwich Castle. In July 1616 he was found guilty of high treason on perjured evidence and hanged, drawn and quartered in front of Magdalen Gate in Norwich. At Tunstall's own request, his head was displayed on St Bennet's Gate because he had wanted to enter the Benedictine Order. He was beatified in 1929.[74]

73. George Turner (d. 1610) was born in Suffolk and studied at St John's College, Cambridge, before going to Venice to continue his medical studies. He was elected a Fellow of the College of Physicians in 1588. Turner acted as a royal physician and apparently experimented with alchemy, and royal favour ensured that, in spite of his Catholicism, he was made an elect of the College of Physicians in 1602 and treasurer in 1609.[75]

74. St Henry Walpole SJ (1558–95) was born at Docking Hall, Norfolk, the eldest son of Christopher Walpole and Margery Warner. In 1575 the family moved to nearby Anmer Hall. In 1566 or 1567 Henry entered Norwich Grammar School before going up to Peterhouse, Cambridge, in 1575. Walpole was certainly a crypto-Catholic at this time, even if he was not a recusant, and he was joined at Peterhouse by his cousin Edward Walpole and other East Anglian Catholics, including Edward Yelverton of Rougham, John Cobbe of Sandringham, Philip Paris of Pudding Norton, and Bernard Gardiner of Coxford Abbey. He did not graduate at Cambridge and entered Gray's Inn in 1578. On 1 December 1581 he witnessed the execution of St Edmund Campion, and some blood from the martyr splashed his clothes. He wrote a poem in praise of Campion, as a result of which he was forced to go into hiding back at Anmer Hall, and later made his way on foot to Newcastle, where he took ship for the Continent. He was admitted to the English College at Rouen in 1582 and later studied at Rome, Verdun and Pont-à-Mousson before his ordination as a Jesuit priest in 1588. He served as a military chaplain in the Spanish Netherlands and was arrested by English troops when they captured Flushing. His ransom was paid and he spent a number of years teaching at Tournai. In 1592 he travelled to Spain and spent time at Valladolid and Seville. In 1593 he left Spain for St Omer and then embarked for England, with the intention of continuing the mission of Fr John Gerard in East Anglia. However, Walpole's party was forced to land at Bridlington and they were soon captured and confined in York Castle. He was committed to solitary confinement in the Tower for two months before interrogation and torture by Richard Topcliffe. He was sent to York for trial and found guilty of high treason. He was executed on 17 April 1595 and canonised as one of the Forty Martyrs of England and Wales in 1970.[76]

75. Michael Walpole SJ (1570–1625) was born at Docking, Norfolk, and was one of the younger brothers of St Henry Walpole. He was educated at Norwich School and met John Gerard in 1588, accompanying him throughout his mission to East Anglia. In 1589 he delivered the ransom money to free his brother Henry from his English captors at Flushing. He entered the English College, Rome, in 1590 and the Society of Jesus in 1593. He was Prefect of Studies at the English College, Valladolid, in 1603. In 1606 he moved back to London as confessor to the Spanish missionary Luisa de Carvajal. He was arrested in 1610 and banished to Douai and wrote a number of controversial works. In 1613 he was appointed Superior of the English Jesuits and returned to London in the retinue of the Spanish ambassador. In 1619 he retired to the English College at Seville.[77]

76. Jane Wentworth (*c.* 1503–72?), the 'Maid of Ipswich', was a daughter of Sir Roger Wentworth of Gosfield, Essex. When she was twelve years old she began displaying signs of demonic possession which were relieved by a vision of Our Lady. In 1516 her parents took her to the shrine of Our Lady of Grace at Ipswich, where she was dramatically cured in the presence of many notables, including the Abbot of Bury St Edmunds. A few days later she delivered a harangue to the assembled crowds and a sermon was preached to mark the miracle. Wentworth subsequently entered the Poor Clare house at Bruisyard and moved to Framlingham after the Dissolution, where she was living in 1554. She made her will in 1572, in which she revealed Catholic sympathies.[78]

77. Thomas Whitbread SJ (*c.* 1618–79) was a native of Essex, who was educated at St Omer and entered the

Society of Jesus at Watten in 1635. He was ordained in 1645 and sent to England in 1647. He was twice elected Superior of the College of the Holy Apostles and worked for thirty-two years in East Anglia and Essex. He was often based at Fithlers near Writtle, belonging to the Petre family. In 1677 Whitbread was appointed Superior of the English Jesuits, during which time he refused Titus Oates admission to the noviciate. In 1678 he was arrested, in spite of the fact that he was then living at the Spanish embassy, and tried and found guilty of high treason. He was executed in June 1679.[79]

78. Edward Maria Wingfield (1550–1631) was born at Stoneley in Huntingdonshire. He was admitted to Lincoln's Inn in 1576 but became a soldier in Ireland and the Low Countries. He was commended for bravery at the Battle of Zutphen in 1586 but was back at Stoneley by 1600. He was a cousin of Bartholomew Gosnold and became involved in the Virginia Company. On arrival at the site of Jamestown, he was elected first president of the Virginia Colony on 13 May 1607. However, attacks by the local inhabitants, famine and disease led to his deposition and arrest by September. He returned to England in 1608 and was later exonerated of the charges against him, but never returned to the New World. In the late twentieth century a tablet was erected in Kimbolton church to commemorate the first president of the first successful English-speaking settlement in America.[80]

79. Robert Wingfield (*c.* 1513–*c.* 1561) was the son of Sir Humphrey Wingfield, Speaker of the House of Commons, and was probably born at Brantham Hall near Ipswich. He studied at St John's College, Cambridge, and held conservative religious views which resulted in his house in Tacket Street, Ipswich, being chosen to host Queen Mary on her way from Framlingham Castle to London in July 1553. Mary rewarded Wingfield with an annual pension of £20 and he wrote a manuscript life of the Queen, *Vita Mariae Angliae Reginae*. Wingfield fell from favour on the accession of Elizabeth and was forced to sell Brantham Hall before his death.[81]

80. Francis Yaxley (b. before 1528, d. 1565) was the son of Richard Yaxley of Mellis, Suffolk, a younger branch of the Yaxleys of Yaxley. He started work as a clerk in the signet office of the Privy Council in 1547, and served as Clerk of the Signet between 1555 and 1557, one of many East Anglian Catholics to participate in the regime of Mary I. He also served as MP for Dunwich, Stamford and Saltash during her reign. On Elizabeth's accession Yaxley was twice imprisoned in the Tower between 1561 and 1563, and in 1565 he went into exile in Flanders. Later the same year he moved to Scotland and entered the service of Mary, Queen of Scots. Yaxley travelled to Spain as Scottish ambassador and managed to obtain 20,000 crowns from Phillip II for the expulsion of the English from Scotland. However, his ship foundered off Northumbria in December 1565 and Yaxley was drowned, his body and the gold washing up on Holy Island. His body was returned for burial to Yaxley churchyard.[82]

Notes

1   F. J. Bremer, 'Alabaster, William (1568–1640)', *ODNB*; online edn, Oct 2007 [http://www.oxforddnb.com/view/article/265, accessed 4 Dec 2015].

2   B. Carter, 'Andrews, William Eusebius (1773–1837)', in *ODNB*, vol. 2, pp. 137–8.

3   J. Blom and F. Blom, 'Austin, John [*pseud.* William Birchley] (1613–1669)', in *ODNB*, vol. 2, pp. 993–4.

4   T. M. McCoog, 'Baker, Alexander (1582–1638)', in *ODNB*, vol. 3, pp. 358–9.

5   F. Edwards, 'Ballard, John (*d.* 1586)', in *ODNB*, vol. 3, pp. 591–2.

6   K. R. Bartlett, 'Barker, William (*fl.* 1540–1576)' in *ODNB*, vol. 3, pp. 899–900.

7   A. Bellenger, 'Barnes, John (*c.* 1581–1661)', in *ODNB*, vol. 3, p. 993.

8   Rogers (2003), pp. 41–4.

9   G. Anstruther, *The Seminary Priests: A Dictionary of the Secular Clergy of England and Wales 1558–1850* (Great Wakering: Mayhew McCrimon, 1975), vol. 2, pp. 20–1; F. Young, *English Catholics and the Supernatural, 1553–1829* (Farnham: Ashgate, 2013b), pp. 209–16.

10   Sheils (2004), vol. 4, pp. 783–4.

11   L. G. Kelly, 'Bedingfield, Thomas (early 1540s?–1613)', in *ODNB*, vol. 4, p. 786.

12   Cooper (2004), vol. 4, p. 906.

13   Anstruther (1969), vol. 1, p. 33.

14   R. M. Schuler, 'Blomefylde [Blomefield], Myles (1525–1603)', in *ODNB*, vol. 6, p. 255.

15   K. Flint, 'Boulger [*née* Havers], Dorothy Henrietta [*pseud.* Theo Gift] (1847–1923)', in *ODNB*, vol. 6, pp. 794–5.

16   P. Arblaster, 'Burton, Catharine [*name in religion* Mary Xaviera of the Angels] (1668–1714)', in *ODNB*, vol. 9, p. 11.

17   J. A. Hilton, 'Butler, Alban', in *ODNB*, vol. 9, pp. 115–16.

18   V. Nutton, 'Caius, John (1510–1573)', in *ODNB*, vol. 9, pp. 480–2.

19   L. Gooch, 'Cary, Edward (*d.* 1711)', in *ODNB*, vol. 10, p. 427.

20   D. D. Rees, 'Chapman, Henry Palmer [*name in religion* John] (1865–1933)', in *ODNB*, vol. 11, pp. 55–6.

21   Barclay (2004), vol. 12, pp. 760–1.

22   R. K. Marshall, 'Cornwallis, Anne, countess of Argyll (*d.* 1635)', *ODNB*; online edn, Oct 2008 [http://www.oxforddnb.com/view/article/68036, accessed 14 June 2015].

23   A. Weikel, 'Cornwallis, Sir Thomas (1518/19–1604)', in *ODNB*, vol. 13, pp. 486–7.

24   B. Wright Newman, *The Flowering of the Maryland Palatinate* (Washington, DC: Clearfield, 1961), pp. 126–8, 139–41, 188–9.

25   T. Cooper (rev. R. Mitchell), 'Cuddon, Ambrose (*fl.* 1822–1828)', in *ODNB*, vol. 14, pp. 556–7.

26   Findlen (2009), pp. 1–43.

27   J. M. Stone, 'Downes (alias Bedingfeld, Mountford and Mumford), Thomas', in *The Catholic Encyclopedia* (New York: Robert Appleton: 1907–12), vol. 5, pp. 148–9.

28   Rowe (2004), vol. 18, pp. 788–9.

29   Jade Scott, pers. comm. 24 November 2015.

30   Harris (2004), vol. 19, p. 295.

31   J. Collins, 'Frink, Dame Elisabeth Jean (1930–1993)', in *ODNB*, vol. 21, pp. 33–5.

32   T. Cooper (rev. J. M. Blatchly), 'Rokewode, John Gage (1786–1842)', in *ODNB*, vol. 47, pp. 605–6.

33   C. D. C. Armstrong, 'Gardiner, Stephen (*c.* 1495×8–1555)', in *ODNB*, vol. 21, pp. 433–45.

34   T. Cooper (rev. T. H. Clancy), 'Gilbert, George (*d.* 1583)', in *ODNB*, vol. 22, pp. 175–6.

35   Lance (2000), pp. 63–4.

36   B. S. Travitsky, 'Grymeston [Grimston; *née* Bernye], Elizabeth (*b.* in or before 1563, *d.* 1601×4)', in *ODNB*, vol. 24, pp. 157–8.

37   R. Lucas, 'Gunton, George (*bap.* 1801, *d.* 1890)', in *ODNB*, vol. 24, pp. 263–5.

38   E. Leedham-Green, 'Hare, Robert (*c.* 1530–1611)', in *ODNB*, vol. 25, pp. 259–60.

39   Cooper (2004), vol. 26, pp. 173–4.

40   V. Van Hyning, 'Holland, Catherine (1637–1720)', *ODNB*; online edn, May 2014 [http://www.oxforddnb.com/view/article/105823, accessed 14 June 2015].

41   P. W. Allott, 'Hügel, Anatole Andreas Aloys von, Baron von Hügel in the nobility of the Holy Roman empire (1854–1928)', in *ODNB*, vol. 28, pp. 600–1.

42   G. M. Murphy, 'Husenbeth, Frederick Charles (1796–1872)', in *ODNB*, vol. 28, pp. 971–2.

43 J. Spencer, 'Inchbald [*née* Simpson], Elizabeth (1753–1821)', in *ODNB*, vol. 29, pp. 222–5. A number of biographical errors in this article are corrected in Young (2013a) pp. 573–92.

44 Miller (2004), vol. 30, pp. 46–7.

45 Smith (2004), vol. 30, pp. 51–3.

46 J. M. Blatchly, 'L'Estrange, John (1836–1877)', in *ODNB*, vol. 33, pp. 487–8.

47 L. M. Richmond, 'Lescher, Mary Adela [*name in religion* Mary of St Wilfrid] (1846–1927)', in *ODNB*, vol. 33, p. 415.

48 P. Jebb, 'Mannock, John [*name in religion* Anselm] (1681–1764)', in *ODNB*, vol. 36, pp. 520–1.

49 T. Cooper (rev. G. M. Murphy), 'Martyn, Francis (1782–1838)', in *ODNB*, vol. 37, p. 55.

50 D. Dymond, 'Martin, Roger (1526/7–1615)', in *ODNB*, vol. 36, pp. 975–6.

51 G. Campbell, 'Milton, Sir Christopher (1615–1693)', *ODNB*; online edn, Jan 2008 [http://www.oxforddnb.com/view/article/18798, accessed 16 June 2015].

52 G. R. Clarke, *The History and Description of the Town and Borough of Ipswich* (London: S. Piper, Hurst, Chance and Co., 1830), p. 226.

53 Holmes (2004), vol. 39, pp. 363–4.

54 J. Rowe, 'Mumford, James (*c.* 1606–1666)', in *ODNB*, vol. 39, pp. 728–9.

55 T. Cooper (rev. D. Milburn), 'Paston, Edward (1641–1714)', in *ODNB*, vol. 42, pp. 985–6.

56 A. Marshall, 'Prance, Miles (*fl.* 1678–1688)', in *ODNB*, vol. 45, pp. 208–9.

57 'Bishop Cyril Restieaux dies', *The Tablet*, 2 March 1996, p. 33.

58 A. Allanson (ed. A Cranmer and S. Goodwill), *Biography of the English Benedictines* (Ampleforth: Ampleforth Abbey, 1999), p. 41.

59 Nicholls (2004), vol. 47, pp. 699–700.

60 Hopkins (2004), vol. 47, pp. 700–1.

61 D. R. Ransome, 'Rosier, James (1573–1609)', in *ODNB*, vol. 47, p. 787.

62 'Past Bishops: Joseph Rudderham', Diocese of Clifton [http://www.cliftondiocese.com/diocese/past-bishops/joseph-rudderham/], accessed 17 June 2015]

63 T. Cooper (rev. D. D. Rees), 'Sayer, Robert [*name in religion* Gregory] (1560–1602)', in *ODNB*, vol. 49, p. 161.

64 Anstruther (1969), vol. 1, pp. 303–4.

65 Young (2008), pp. 190–1.

66 *Ibid.*, pp. 192–3; Young (2015a), pp. 63–5.

67 N. Moore (rev. M. Bevan), 'Short, Thomas (1635–1685)', in *ODNB*, online edn [http://www.oxforddnb.com/view/article/25460, accessed 29 June 2015].

68 C. Kent (rev. D. Hawes), 'Simpson, John Palgrave (1807–1887)', in *ODNB*, vol. 50, pp. 703–5.

69 Pollard Brown (2004), vol. 51, pp. 711–17.

70 See C. Hazlehurst, S. Whitehead and C. Woodland (eds), *A Guide to the Papers of British Cabinet Ministers 1900–1964* (Cambridge: Royal Historical Society, 1996), pp. 347–9.

71 Young (*2011*), pp. 190–4.

72 Young (2015b), pp. 152–75.

73 P. Williams, 'Babington, Anthony (1561–1586)', in *ODNB*, vol. 3, pp. 76–9.

74 Ryan (2004), vol. 55, p. 557.

75 N. More (rev. R. Hutchins), 'Turner, George (*d.* 1610)', in *ODNB*, vol. 55, p. 619.

76 Ryan (2004), vol. 57, pp. 43–6.

77 A. Jessop (rev. P. Milward), 'Walpole, Michael [*pseud.* Michael Christopherson] (*bap.* 1570, *d.* 1625)', in *ODNB*, vol. 57, p. 65.

78 R. Rex, 'Wentworth, Jane [Anne; *called* the Maid of Ipswich] (*c.* 1503–1572?)', in *ODNB*, vol. 58, pp. 127–8.

79 J. Rowe, 'Whitbread [*alias* Harcourt], Thomas (*c.* 1618–1679)', in *ODNB*, vol. 58, pp. 529–30.

80 R. C. Siimons, 'Wingfield, Edward Maria (*b.* 1550, *d.* in or after 1619)', in *ODNB*, vol. 59, pp. 728–9.

81 D. MacCulloch, 'Wingfield, Robert (*c.* 1513–*c.* 1561)', *ODNB*; online edn, Sept 2010 [http://www.oxforddnb.com/view/article/47131, accessed 14 June 2015].

82 L. MacMahon, 'Yaxley, Francis (*b.* before 1528, *d.* 1565)', in *ODNB*, vol. 60, pp. 753–4.

Appendix 2

Some Historic Sites in East Anglia Associated with Post-Reformation Catholicism

ANMER, NORFOLK

Anmer Hall was acquired by Christopher Walpole (d. 1586) in 1575, and his sons St Henry Walpole and Michael Walpole, who both later became Jesuits, were brought up there. Anmer Hall is now the home of the Duke and Duchess of Cambridge.

BURY ST EDMUNDS, SUFFOLK

In the **Abbey Gardens** the ruins of the old Abbot's Palace, the site of the Jesuit College of the Holy Apostles 1685–8 can still be seen; they are to the right of the main path from the abbey gateway, opposite Alwyne House. The former Suffolk Hotel on Cornhill (now the Edinburgh Woollen Mill and Waterstone's bookshop) was originally the **Greyhound Inn**, which was the main base of the Catholic mission in the 1730s and 1740s. The **memorial to Mary Haselton** can be seen in the great churchyard on the wall of the Charnel House; the Haseltons were a Catholic family and Mary was killed by a bolt of lightning in 1785 while saying her prayers. Note the prominent emblem of the Society of Jesus on the memorial. At the west end of **St Botolph's Lane**,

on the right hand side of street, is the former entrance
to a secret chapel established by Fr John Gage in 1755.
Numbers **9, 10 and 11 Northgate Street** were formerly
the townhouse of the Gage family. On the right of the
church of St Edmund, King and Martyr (1836–7), in
Westgate Street is **Fr John Gage's house** (1761), now
the presbytery. The present Blessed Sacrament Chapel
is the original **Chapel of the Immaculate Conception**
(1761).

CAMBRIDGE, CAMBRIDGESHIRE

Reminders of Mary I's restoration of Catholicism can
be found in Cambridge, such as the wooden statue
of Our Lady in the church of **Our Lady and the English Martyrs** on Hills Road, which may have stood on
the high altar of Great St Mary's church before 1559.
Trinity College Chapel was also built during those
years, as was **Caius Court** in Gonville and Caius College (refounded 1557), in which Dr Caius' collection
of Catholic vestments was burnt in 1572. **Sidney Sussex College** was briefly the site of a Catholic chapel
between March 1687 and December 1688, during the
mastership of Joshua Basset (1641–*c.* 1720). The exact
location of the chapel is unknown but it was in the
Master's Lodge. It was destroyed by a mob in the 1688
Revolution.

CHEVELEY, CAMBRIDGESHIRE

Cheveley Hall was acquired by Henry Jermyn in
around 1674 and a Catholic chapel was constructed
which was torn down by a mob in 1688. Jermyn died
in 1708 but his widow Judith lived here until 1726 and
maintained a chapel. Cheveley Hall was demolished
in 1925.

COSTESSEY, NORFOLK

Costessey Hall was the home of the Jerningham family and was demolished in 1925. The site of the Costessey estate is now Costessey Park Golf Club, but the belfry of the house is still standing by the 18th fairway. In Costessey village, **St Walstan's church** was built in 1841 by Fr Frederick Husenbeth and contains furniture from the older chapel of Costessey Hall, which was demolished along with the house.

DOCKING, NORFOLK

Docking Hall was the birthplace of St Henry Walpole and his brother Michael. It is now a private house.

EAST BERGHOLT, SUFFOLK

In 1849 the Old Hall at East Bergholt was purchased by English Benedictine nuns, formerly at Brussels. In 1857 they opened St Mary's convent and school. This was the first settlement of nuns in East Anglia since the brief exiles of the Augustinian Canonesses of Bruges and Benedictine nuns of Montargis during the period of the French Revolution. Bishop William Wareing lived out his last days at the convent and was buried there when he died in 1865. The nuns left in 1940 but after the war the old convent was acquired by the Franciscan friars, who turned it into a house of studies until 1973.

ELMHAM ST PETER AND FLIXTON, SUFFOLK

St Peter's Hall is a thirteenth-century manor house which was improved by John Tasburgh in the 1540s using stone from nearby Flixton Priory. It is now a brewery and restaurant. Virtually nothing remains of the Tasburgh family's main home, **Flixton Hall**, whose first floor is now a shelter for animals. However, the

Priest's House that housed the Benedictine mission from the 1740s is still standing close to Flixton church.

ELY, CAMBRIDGESHIRE

The Bishop's Palace was the site of the imprisonment of thirty-two recusant gentlemen between 1588 and 1597. It was also where John Feckenham, Abbot of Westminster, was imprisoned between 1577 and 1580. The palace has undergone quite significant alterations but the east and west towers and long gallery are still standing as they were when the palace was a prison.

EUSTON, SUFFOLK

Euston Hall was the home of a branch of the Rook-wood family until, having been impoverished by recusancy fines, they were forced to sell it in 1655. It later became the home of the dukes of Grafton and was rebuilt by them. In 1578 Euston Hall was the scene of the humiliation of Edward Rookwood by Queen Elizabeth during her progress through East Anglia. Some Rookwood family brasses can be seen in the church.

FRAMLINGHAM, SUFFOLK

Framlingham Castle was where, in July 1553, Mary I raised her standard with the support of the East Anglian Catholic gentry, launching her successful bid for the throne against Lady Jane Grey. The castle was later used as a prison for priests removed from Wisbech Castle in 1600. Framlingham church contains the tomb of Thomas Howard, 3rd Duke of Norfolk (1473–1554), and other members of the Howard family.

HENGRAVE, SUFFOLK

Hengrave Hall was built between 1525 and 1538 by a merchant, Thomas Kitson. In 1553 Mary I stopped here on her way to Framlingham Castle. Sir Thomas Kitson the younger was a recusant in Elizabeth's reign and the property subsequently passed to a branch of the recusant Gage family, originally from Sussex. The Gages continued to live at Hengrave until 1767 when they moved to Coldham Hall, but they returned in 1843 and lived here until the death of the 9th and last Baronet in 1872. Hengrave was the home of the English Convent from Bruges between 1794 and 1802, and in 1952 it was bought by the Religious of the Assumption, who ran a school there until 1974. In 1974 Hengrave became an ecumenical religious community until its dissolution in 2006. The hall contains Thomas Kitson's oratory, with some of the finest medieval stained glass in a domestic chapel in England, and the church of St John Lateran (actually a mortuary chapel) contains many Gage family monuments. Hengrave Hall is now a privately owned venue for weddings.

HINTLESHAM, SUFFOLK

Hintlesham Hall, now a hotel, was the home of the Timperley family, who rose to prominence as clients of the Duke of Norfolk and were determined recusants. The last Timperley left in 1720 and the house was remodelled by subsequent owners, but parts of the original house can be seen behind the Georgian façade.

HORSHAM ST FAITH, NORFOLK

Horsham St Faith Priory, which is constructed around the former refectory of a Benedictine priory, was the birthplace of St Robert Southwell in 1561. It is now a private house.

IPSWICH, SUFFOLK

According to an unsubstantiated tradition, **Ancient House** in the Buttermarket contained a Catholic chapel constructed by the Sparrowe family. Anthony Milton maintained a chapel close by in the reign of James II, but Milton's house has since been demolished. The **parish hall of St Mary's church** in Woodbridge Road is the church built by Fr Louis Pierre Simon in 1838.

LAWSHALL, SUFFOLK

Lawshall Hall, built in around 1557, was the home of the Drury family and was visited by Queen Elizabeth on her East Anglian progress in 1578. John Gerard stayed at Lawshall Hall and nearby Coldham Hall between 1589 and 1591, whilst conducting an important East Anglian mission that made many influential converts. **The church of Our Lady Immaculate and St Joseph** ('Coldham Cottage') on the Bury Road, just outside the gates of Coldham Hall but in the parish of Lawshall, was developed from an earlier presbytery in 1870. Before then there was a chapel at a house called Barfords. There was a public chapel separate from Coldham Hall as early as the 1780s.

LONG MELFORD, SUFFOLK

Melford Place is a house located to the south of the village centre of Long Melford, on the west side of the road known as Little St Mary's (B1064) and opposite Southgate Green. Much reduced from its original size, Melford Place was originally the home of the recusant Martin family, who maintained a chapel of ease dedicated to St James on the other side of the road (no trace of this now remains). Until 1761 a chapel was maintained here where the Dominican John Martin said Mass. The chapel still survives behind the large brick window facing the street. Melford Place is now a private house.

KING'S LYNN, NORFOLK

The mission at King's Lynn was founded in 1811 and the first church opened in 1845, but the present **church of Our Lady of the Annunciation** was built 1896–97 and its historical significance rests on the fact that, between 1897 and 1934, it served as the shrine of Our Lady of Walsingham, which was revived by a rescript of Pope Leo XIII at the instigation of Charlotte Pearson Boyd.

NORWICH, NORFOLK

Norwich has a rich Catholic history. Nothing remains of the **Duke of Norfolk's Palace** in Duke Street, although an excavation of the area commenced in 2015. The Palace contained a Catholic chapel until 1786, which was subsequently converted into a waiting room for the Poor Law guardians' office and demolished in 1974 to make way for a multi-storey carpark. The buildings of the former Blackfriars now occupied by Norwich University of the Arts were the site of a Jesuit chapel during the reign of James II, although the exact location is not known. The **Maddermarket Theatre** on St John's Lane is the former Maddermarket Chapel (1791). The **Jesuit chapel on Willow Lane** is now occupied by Rogers and Norton Solicitors.

OXBURGH, NORFOLK

Oxburgh Hall, which is now owned by the National Trust, is the home of the Bedingfield family, the last of East Anglia's ancient Catholic families to survive to this day. The house contains a genuine priest-hole and is regularly open to the public. There is also a large chapel in the grounds constructed in 1829 after Catholic emancipation.

SAWSTON, CAMBRIDGESHIRE

Sawston Hall was built between 1557 and 1584 by the Huddlestone family, who sheltered Mary I on her way to Framlingham Castle in July 1553 and suffered the destruction of the original Sawston Hall by the Duke of Northumberland's soldiers as a result. Sawston Hall contains a number of priest holes (at least one of them constructed by St Nicholas Owen) and an eighteenth-century chapel within the house.

STANNINGFIELD, SUFFOLK

Coldham Hall was built in 1574 by Robert Rookwood and contains a number of priest holes, as well as a secret staircase built into a chimney. The house was ransacked in 1605 after Ambrose Rookwood's involvement in the Gunpowder Plot. In the late eighteenth century an internal chapel was added on the ground floor. John Gerard stayed at Coldham Hall and nearby Lawshall Hall between 1589 and 1591, whilst conducting an important East Anglian mission that made many influential converts.

STILTON, HUNTINGDONSHIRE

The Bell Inn in the village of Stilton, just south of Peterborough, was the home of the French priest Étienne Jean Baptiste Desgalois de la Tour between 1807 and 1814 while he was chaplain to the Norman Cross prisoner of war camp.

STOKE-BY-NAYLAND, SUFFOLK

Giffords Hall was the home of the recusant Mannock family and was later the Seminary of St Felix, 1842–4. The ruined thirteenth-century **Chapel of St Nicholas** in front of Giffords Hall may have been in use as a Catholic chapel as late as 1768, when a confirmation is recorded as having taken place there. The **church of Our Lady Immaculate and St Edmund** at Withermarsh Green was built in 1827 and has the oldest Catholic graveyard in East Anglia.

WALSINGHAM, NORFOLK

Little Walsingham is the site of the national shrine of Our Lady (also the diocesan shrine of East Anglia), which is focused on the Slipper Chapel (1340), purchased by Charlotte Pearson Boyd in 1897, although it did not replace the Catholic church in King's Lynn as the shrine of Our Lady of Walsingham until 1934.

WISBECH, CAMBRIDGESHIRE

Wisbech Castle was the site of the imprisonment of 111 priests and laypeople between 1580 and 1616. The castle was demolished during the English Civil War and the house currently standing on the site is the second to replace the castle keep. The edge of the castle bailey is marked by the eighteenth-century crescent that now surrounds the remains of the castle. All that remains of the original castle is a series of underground vaults. The churchyard of St Peter's church opposite is where John Feckenham, Abbot of Westminster, and Thomas Watson, Bishop of Lincoln, are buried.

WOOLPIT, SUFFOLK

The Lady's Well, a natural spring in a moated area to the east of Woolpit church, was originally the site of a popular shrine of Our Lady. Pilgrimage to the site may have been revived by the Jesuits of the College of the Holy Apostles in the 1680s and local people in the nineteenth century still remembered it as a pilgrimage site.

NOTES ON CONTRIBUTORS

JOHN CHARMLEY

John Charmley is Professor of History at the University of East Anglia (UEA), where he is head of the Interdisciplinary Institute for the Humanities (IIH). He is the author of eight books on nineteenth- and twentieth-century history.

MICHAEL EDWARDS

Fr Michael Bede Edwards (1926–2003) was educated at Magdalen College, Oxford, before serving in the Royal Navy during the Second World War, when he became a Catholic. After the war he joined the Carmelite Order in Ireland, and lived in Rome for some years. In 1977 he became a secular priest in the Diocese of East Anglia and served in the parishes of St George, Norwich, Newmarket, St Phillip Howard, Cambridge and finally Sudbury until his retirement in 1997. In 1990 he was responsible for setting up the diocesan archives.

TIMOTHY FENWICK

Timothy Fenwick was born in Suffolk and baptised at Withermarsh Green. He was taught history at Ampleforth by J. C. H. Aveling and then spent three years at Grove Park and Oscott, where he assisted G. F. Pullen in the Recusant Library. He subsequently studied at the Université Catholique de Louvain (then still in Leuven) under Roger Aubert, the historian of Pio Nono and Vatican I. He obtained a British Council scholarship to study in the archives of Propaganda, the Vatican and the Venerable English College before pursuing a career in business, chiefly in Benelux and Russia.

JOHN MORRILL

John Morrill recently retired as Professor of British and Irish History in the University of Cambridge. He has been a deacon in the Diocese of East Anglia since 1996, serving in the parish of Our Lady Immaculate and St Etheldreda, Newmarket.

TONY ROGERS

Fr Tony Rogers is a priest of the Diocese of East Anglia, ordained in 1971, and currently based in Aldeburgh, having previously worked in Cambridge, Norwich and Newmarket, as well as a brief spell immediately after ordination at Northampton Cathedral. He is currently Chair of the Diocesan Liturgy Commission.

JOY ROWE

Joy Rowe has been writing on the history of English Catholicism since the late 1950s and is the author of many articles, published in *Recusant History* and elsewhere, on post-Reformation Catholicism in East Anglia. She is a Fellow of the Society of Antiquaries.

FRANCIS YOUNG

Francis Young is volumes editor for the Catholic Record Society. He was born and brought up in Bury St Edmunds, gained his doctorate in history from the University of Cambridge and teaches in Ely, Cambridgeshire. He is the author of many articles on the history of East Anglian Catholicism and several books, including *The Gages of Hengrave and Suffolk Catholicism, 1640–1767* (Catholic Record Society, 2015) and

Rookwood Family Papers, 1606–1761 (Suffolk Records Society, 2016).

RACHEL YOUNG

Rachel Young is a native of Suffolk and holds degrees in Anglo-Saxon, Norse and Celtic (ASNaC) and theology from the University of Cambridge. She is an ordained minister of the Church of England and her particular interest is Anglo-Saxon Christianity in East Anglia.

Bibliography

Manuscripts

Archives of the Diocese of East Anglia, Norwich
MS draft of Bishop Grant's petition to Pope Paul VI to divide the Diocese of Northampton, 1976
The Installation of the First Bishop of East Anglia Rt Rev. Alan C. Clark (Norwich, 1976)

Cambridge University Library, Cambridge
MS Additional 10079
MS Hengrave 76/2/20

The National Archives, Kew
State Papers 15/25 no. 19 (charge no. 36)

Northampton Diocesan Archives, Northampton
Homily by Bishop Grant at the installation of Alan Clark as Bishop of East Anglia, 2 June 1976
Pastoral Letters 1908–1918, Book IV, no. 38

Books and Articles

A. Adolph, 'The Catholic Havers of Thelveton Hall, Norfolk', *Catholic Ancestor* 7 (1999), pp. 144–60
——'The Bonds of Bury St Edmunds and their Family Connections', *Catholic Ancestor* 9 (2002), pp. 61–4
A. Allanson (ed. A Cranmer and S. Goodwill), *Biography of the English Benedictines* (Ampleforth: Ampleforth Abbey, 1999)
P. W. Allott, 'Hügel, Anatole Andreas Aloys von, Baron von Hügel in the Nobility of the Holy Roman Empire (1854–1928)', in *ODNB*, vol. 28, pp. 600–1

G. Anstruther, *The Seminary Priests: A Dictionary of the Secular Clergy of England and Wales, 1558–1850* (Ware: St Edmund's College, 1969–77), 4 vols

P. Arblaster, 'Burton, Catharine [*name in religion* Mary Xaviera of the Angels] (1668–1714)', in *ODNB*, vol. 9, p. 11

C. D. C. Armstrong, 'Gardiner, Stephen (*c.* 1495×8–1555)', in *ODNB*, vol. 21, pp. 433–45

'Assisted Catholic Emigrants from Cambridgeshire to Australia 1840–1879', *Catholic Ancestor* 4 (1993), pp. 198–9

J. C. H. Aveling, *The Handle and the Axe* (London: Blond and Briggs, 1976)

A. Barclay, 'The Rise of Edward Coleman', *The Historical Journal* 42 (1999), pp. 109–31

—— 'Colman [Coleman], Edward (1636–1678)', in *ODNB*, vol. 12, pp. 760–1

K. R. Bartlett, 'Barker, William (*fl.* 1540–1576)', in *ODNB*, vol. 3, pp. 899–900

G. A. Beck, *The English Catholics 1850–1950: A Century of Progress* (London: Burns and Oates, 1950)

W. Betham, *The Baronetage of England* (Ipswich, 1801), 2 vols

A. Bellenger (ed.), *English and Welsh Priests, 1558–1800* (Bath: Downside Abbey, 1984)

—— (ed.), *The French Exiled Clergy in the British Isles after 1789* (Bath: Downside Abbey, 1986)

—— 'Barnes, John (*c.* 1581–1661)', in *ODNB*, vol. 3, p. 993

M. Bence-Jones, *The Catholic Families* (London: Constable, 1992)

H. N. Birt, 'Recusancy and Catholicity in East Anglia', in *The Catholic Faith in East Anglia: Three Papers Read at the National Catholic Congress at Norwich, August 5, 1912* (London: Catholic Truth Society, 1912), pp. 3–25

G. Blackwood, *Tudor and Stuart Suffolk* (Lancaster: Carnegie, 2001)

J. M. Blatchly, 'L'Estrange, John (1836–1877)', in *ODNB*, vol. 33, pp. 487–8

J. Blom and F. Blom, 'Austin, John [*pseud.* William Birchley] (1613–1669)', in *ODNB*, vol. 2, pp. 993–4

L. Boothman and R. Hyde Parker (eds), *Savage Fortune: An Aristocratic Family in the Early Seventeenth Century* (Woodbridge: Suffolk Records Society, 2006)

J. Bossy, *The English Catholic Community, 1570–1850* (Oxford: Oxford University Press, 1976)

C. Brooke, *A History of Gonville and Caius College* (Woodbridge: Boydell, 1985)

Calendar of Letters and State Papers relating to English Affairs: Preserved Principally in the Archives of Simancas, ed. M. A. S. Hume (London: HMSO, 1892–99), 4 vols

Calendar of State Papers, Domestic Series, of the Reign of Elizabeth I, 1601–1603 with Addenda 1547–1565 (London: HMSO, 1870)

R. B. Camm, *Sister Mary of St Francis, SND, the Hon Laura Petre (Stafford-Jerningham)* (London: R. & T. Washbourne, 1913)

P. Caraman, *Henry Morse: Priest of the Plague* (London: Catholic Book Club [1957])

B. Carter, 'Catholic Charitable Endeavours in London, 1810–1840, Part I', *Recusant History* 25 (2001), pp. 487–510

—— 'Andrews, William Eusebius (1773–1837)', in *ODNB*, vol. 2, pp. 137–8

E. Castle (ed.), *The Jerningham Letters (1780–1843): Being excerpts from the Correspondence and Diaries of the Honourable Lady Jerningham and of her Daughter Lady Bedingfeld* (London: Richard Bentley, 1896), 2 vols

The Catholic Directory and Annual Register for the Year 1838 (London: Booker and Dolman, 1838)

The Catholic Directory and Annual Register for the Year 1843 (London: C. Dolman, 1843)

The Catholic Directory, Ecclesiastical Register, and Almanac, for the Year 1862 (London: Burns and Lambert, 1862)

The Catholic Directory Ecclesiastical Register and Almanac, for the Year 1896 (London: Burns and Oates, 1896)

'Catholics in Cambridgeshire', *Catholic Ancestor* 9 (2003), pp. 177–8

'Catholics in East Anglia, 1796', *Catholic Ancestor* 7 (1999), p. 250

'The Catholic Registers of Bury St Edmunds, Suffolk', *Catholic Ancestor* 8 (2000), p. 118

G. R. Clarke, *The History and Description of the Town and Borough of Ipswich* (London: S. Piper, Hurst, Chance and Co., 1830)

J. Collins, 'Frink, Dame Elisabeth Jean (1930–1993)', in *ODNB*, vol. 21, pp. 33–5

P. Collinson, *From Cranmer to Sancroft* (London: Hambledon Continuum, 2006)

——'Pulling the Strings: Religion and Politics in the Progress of 1578', in J. E. Archer, E. Goldring and S. Knight (eds), *The Progresses, Pageants and Entertainments of Queen Elizabeth I* (Oxford: Oxford: Oxford University Press, 2007), pp. 122–41

'Conformity in the Midlands and East Anglia 1590–1625', *Catholic Ancestor* 6 (1996) pp. 57–64

T. Cooper (rev. M. E. Williams), 'Bell, Arthur [*name in religion* Francis] (1591–1643)', in *ODNB*, vol. 4, p. 906

—— 'Heath, Henry [*name in religion* Paul of St Magdalen] (*bap.* 1599, *d.* 1643)', in *ODNB*, vol. 26, pp. 173–4

—— (rev. R. Mitchell), 'Cuddon, Ambrose (*fl.* 1822–1828)', in *ODNB*, vol. 14, pp. 556–7

——(rev. J. M. Blatchly), 'Rokewode, John Gage (1786–1842)', in *ODNB*, vol. 47, pp. 605–6

——(rev. T. H. Clancy), 'Gilbert, George (*d.* 1583)', in *ODNB*, vol. 22, pp. 175–6

——(rev. G. M. Murphy), 'Martyn, Francis (1782–1838)', in *ODNB*, vol. 37, p. 55

—— (rev. D. Milburn), 'Paston, Edward (1641–1714)', in *ODNB*, vol. 42, pp. 985–6

E. Crouzet, *Slender Thread: Origins and History of the Benedictine Mission in Bungay 1657–2007* (Bath: Downside Abbey Books, 2007)

F. J. Devany, *The Faithful Few: A History of Norfolk Roman Catholics, 1559–1778*, 2nd edn (Norwich, 2010)

Z. Dovey, *An Elizabethan Progress: The Queen's Journey into East Anglia, 1578* (Stroud: Sutton, 1996)

E. Duffy, *Saints, Sacrilege and Sedition: Religion and Conflict in the Tudor Reformations* (London: Bloomsbury, 2011)

D. Dymond and C. Paine (eds), *The Spoil of Melford Church* (Ipswich: Salient, 1989)

D. Dymond, 'Martin, Roger (1526/7–1615)', in *ODNB*, vol. 36, pp. 975–6

F. Edwards, 'Ballard, John (*d.* 1586)', in *ODNB*, vol. 3, pp. 591–2

N. Evans, 'The Tasburghs of South Elmham: the Rise and Fall of a Suffolk Gentry Family', *Proceedings of the Suffolk Institute of Archaeology and History* 34 (1980), pp. 269–80

M. A. Everett Green (ed.), *The Calendar of the Committee for Compounding with Delinquents* (London: The Public Record Office, 1889), 5 vols

D. Farmer (ed.), *The Oxford Dictionary of Saints*, 5th edn (Oxford: Oxford University Press, 2003)

P. Findlen, 'Founding a Scientific Academy: Gender, Patronage and Knowledge in Early Eighteenth-Century Milan', *Republics of Letters: A Journal for the Study of Knowledge, Politics, and the Arts* 1 (2009), pp. 1–43

C. Firth and R. S. Rait (eds), *Acts and Ordinances of the Civil Wars and under the Interrregnum* (London: HMSO, 1911), 3 vols

G. M. Fitzalan-Howard, *Henry FitzAlan-Howard, Fifteenth Duke of Norfolk* (Oxford: Oxford University Press, 1917)

C. Fitzgerald-Lombard (ed.), *English and Welsh Priests 1801–1914: A Working List* (Bath: Downside Abbey, 1993)

A. Flannery (ed.), *Vatican Council II, the Conciliar and Post Conciliar Documents* (Dublin: Dominican Publications, 1980)

K. Flint, 'Boulger [*née* Havers], Dorothy Henrietta [*pseud.* Theo Gift] (1847–1923)', in *ODNB*, vol. 6, pp. 794–5

H. Foley, *Records of the English Province of the Society of Jesus* (London: Burns and Oates, 1877–83), 8 vols

S. Foster, '"In sad want of priests and money": Bishop Amherst at Northampton, 1858–1879', *Recusant History* 25 (2005), pp. 281–93

E. G. Gage, *Costessey Hall* (Norwich, 1991)

J. Gage, *The History and Antiquities of Hengrave, in Suffolk* (London, 1822)

—— (ed.), 'Pedigree and Charters of the Family of Rookwood', in *Collectanea Topographica et Genealogica*, (London, 1835), vol. 2, pp. 120–47

M. Gandy (ed.), *Catholic Missions and Registers 1700–1800 Volume 2: The Midlands and East Anglia* (London: Catholic Family History Society, 1993)

——(ed.), *The Bishops' Register of Confirmations in the Midland district of the Catholic Church in England, 1768–1811 and 1816* (London: Catholic Family History Society, 1999)

'General Meeting—Shelley, Polstead, Boxford, Kersey, and Hadleigh: August 23, 1883', in *Proceedings of the Suffolk Institute of Archaeology* 6 (1886), pp. 321–5

J. Gerard (trans. P. Caraman), *The Autobiography of an Elizabethan* (London: Longmans, Green and Co., 1951)

P. J. Gilbert, *This Restless Prelate: Bishop Peter Baines* (Leominster: Gracewing, 2006)

J. Gillow, *A Literary and Biographical History, or Biographical Dictionary of the English Catholics* (London: Burns and Oates, 1885–1902), 5 vols

N. Goldie, 'The Last of the Norfolk Derehams of West Dereham', *Norfolk Archaeology* 18 (1914), pp. 1–22

L. Gooch, 'Cary, Edward (d. 1711)', in *ODNB*, vol. 10, p. 427

G. Goodwin (rev. S. J. Skedd), 'Howard, Charles, Eleventh Duke of Norfolk (1746–1815)', in *ODNB*, vol. 28, p. 327

A. Gransden, 'The Cult of St Mary at Beodericsworth and then in Bury St Edmunds Abbey to *c.* 1150', *The Journal of Ecclesiastical History* 55 (2004), pp. 627–53

M. A. R. Graves, 'Howard, Thomas, fourth duke of Norfolk (1538–1572)', in *ODNB*, vol. 28, pp. 429–36

D. Gwynn, *The Second Spring 1818–1852: A Study of the Catholic Revival in England* (London: Burns and Oates, 1942)

T. Harding, *A confutation of a booke intituled An apologie of the Church of England* (Antwerp, 1565)

P. E. B. Harris, 'Fenn, John (1535–1615)', in *ODNB*, vol. 19, p. 295

C. Hazlehurst, S. Whitehead and C. Woodland (eds), *A Guide to the Papers of British Cabinet Ministers 1900–1964* (Cambridge: Royal Historical Society, 1996)

J. A. Hilton, 'Butler, Alban', in *ODNB*, vol. 9, pp. 115–16

A History of the Catholic Church of St Thomas of Canterbury, Woodbridge (Woodbridge, 1987)

R. Hoggett, *The Archaeology of the East Anglian Conversion* (Woodbridge: Boydell, 2010)

P. Holmes, 'Morse, Henry (1595–1645)', in *ODNB*, vol. 39, pp. 363–4

G. Holt, 'Some Letters from Suffolk, 1763–80: Selection and Commentary', *Recusant History* 16 (1983), pp. 304–15

—— 'An Eighteenth Century Chaplain: John Champion at Sawston Hall', *Recusant History* 17 (1984), pp. 181–7

—— (ed.), *English and Welsh Jesuits 1650–1829* (London: Catholic Record Society, 1984)

——*The English Jesuits in the Age of Reason* (London: Burns and Oates, 1993)

T. Holt, 'Catholic Chapels in Norwich before 1900', *Transactions of the Norfolk & Norwich Archaeological Society* 37 (1979), pp. 159–61

P. Hopkins, 'Rookwood, Ambrose (1664–1696)', in *ODNB* vol. 47, pp. 700–1

C. R. Humphrey-Smith, 'The Walpoles and the Jesuits', *Catholic Ancestor* 6 (1997), pp. 230–1

T. Hunter, *An English Carmelite: the life of Catherine Burton, Mother Mary Xaveria of the Angels* (London, 1876)

C. Jackson, 'Glowing Embers: Catholic Life in Cambridgeshire in the Century before Emancipation', in N. Rogers (ed.), *Catholics in Cambridge* (Leominster: Gracewing, 2003), pp. 46–65

—— 'The Mission in Cambridge: A Tale of Three Bishops and a Determined Priest', in N. Rogers (ed.), *Catholics in Cambridge* (Leominster: Gracewing, 2003), pp. 66–80

'The Jailed Priests at Wisbech Castle', *Catholic Ancestor* 3 (1991), pp. 240–1

P. Jebb, 'Mannock, John [*name in religion* Anselm] (1681–1764)', in *ODNB*, vol. 36, pp. 520–1

A. Jessop (rev. P. Milward), 'Walpole, Michael [*pseud.* Michael Christopherson] (*bap.* 1570, d. 1625)', in *ODNB*, vol. 57, p. 65

J. Jewel, *Apologia ecclesiae Anglicanae* (London, 1562)

L. G. Kelly, 'Bedingfield, Thomas (early 1540s?–1613)', in *ODNB*, vol. 4, p. 786

A. Kenny (ed.), *The Responsa Scholarum of the English College, Rome* (London: Catholic Record Society, 1962–63), 2 vols

R. W. Ketton-Cremer, *Norfolk in the Civil Wars* (London: Faber and Faber, 1969)

P. Lake, 'A Tale of Two Episcopal Surveys: The Strange Fates of Edmund Grindal and Cuthbert Mayne Revisited', *Transactions of the Royal Historical Society* 18 (2008) pp. 129–63

D. Lance, *The Returning Tide (1850–2000): A History of the Diocese of Northampton over the last 150 years* (Northampton: Diocese of Northampton, 2000)

P. Leavy, 'Progress, Publicity and Protest: New Catholic Chapels in Nineteenth Century Britain', *Catholic Archives* 35 (2015)

E. Leedham-Green, 'Hare, Robert (*c.* 1530–1611)', in *ODNB*, vol. 25, pp. 259–60

J. A. Lesourd, *Les Catholiques dans la société anglaise, 1765–1865: Évolution numérique, répartition géographique, structure sociale, pratique réligieuse* (Paris: Librairie Honoré Champion, 1978)

K. Lindley, 'The Part Played by Catholics', in B. Manning (ed.), *Politics, Religion and the English Civil War* (London: Edward Arnold, 1973), pp. 127–76

R. Lucas, 'Gunton, George (*bap.* 1801, d. 1890)', in *ODNB*, vol. 24, pp. 263–5

T. M. McCoog (ed.), *English and Welsh Jesuits 1555–1650* (London: Catholic Record Society, 1994), 2 vols

—— 'Baker, Alexander (1582–1638)', in *ODNB*, vol. 3, pp. 358–9

V. A. McClelland, *Cardinal Manning: His Public Life and Influence, 1865–1892* (Oxford: Oxford University Press, 1962)

D. MacCulloch, *Suffolk and the Tudors: Politics and Religion in an English County 1500–1600* (Oxford: Clarendon Press, 1986)

L. MacMahon, 'Yaxley, Francis (*b.* before 1528, *d.* 1565)', in *ODNB*, vol. 60, pp. 753–4

P. McGrath and J. Rowe, 'The Recusancy of Sir Thomas Cornwallis', *Proceedings of the Suffolk Institute of Archaeology and History* 28 (1960), pp. 226–71

—— 'The Marian Priests under Elizabeth I', *Recusant History* 17 (1984), pp. 103–20

—— 'The Imprisonment of Catholics for Religion under Elizabeth I', *Recusant History* 20 (1991), pp. 415–35

F. MacLynn, *The Jacobite Army in England 1745: The Final Campaign* (Edinburgh: John Donald, 1988)

E. J. Mahoney, 'Gregory Sayers O.S.B. (1560–1602): A Forgotten English Moral Theologian', *Catholic Historical Review* 11 (1925), pp. 29–37

A. Marshall, 'Prance, Miles (*fl.* 1678–1688)', in *ODNB*, vol. 45, pp. 208–9

P. Marshall, 'Crisis of Allegiance: George Throckmorton and Henry Tudor', in Marshall, P. and Scott, G. (eds), *Catholic Gentry in English Society: The Throckmortons of Coughton from Reformation to Emancipation* (Farnham: Ashgate, 2009), pp. 31–68

M. J. Mason, 'Nuns and Vocations of the Unpublished Jerningham Letters', *Recusant History* 21 (1993), pp. 503–55

—— 'Nuns of the Jerningham Letters', *Recusant History* 22 (1995), pp. 350–69

—— 'Nuns of the Jerningham Letters … Benedictines at Bodney Hall', *Recusant History* 23 (1996), pp. 34–40

—— 'The Blue Nuns in Norwich 1800–05', *Recusant History* 24 (1998), pp. 89–120

W. Mazière Brady, *The Episcopal Succession in England, Scotland and Ireland, A.D. 1400 to 1875* (Rome: Tipografia della Pace, 1877), 3 vols

'Memorial Inscription at Bury St Edmunds', *Catholic Ancestor* 3 (1990), p. 54

J. Miller, 'Jermyn, Henry, Third Baron Jermyn and Jacobite Earl of Dover (*bap.* 1636, *d.* 1708)', in *ODNB*, vol. 30, pp. 46–7

V. H. Minor, *Passive Tranquility: The Sculpture of Filippo della Valle* (Philadelphia, PA: American Philosophical Society, 1997)

C. E. Moreton, 'The Walsingham Conspiracy of 1537', *Bulletin of the Institute of Historical Research* 63 (1990), pp. 29–43

K. L. Morris, 'Kenelm Digby and English Catholicism', *Recusant History* 20 (1991), pp. 361–70

C. A. Munkman, *The Catholic Revival in North Norfolk: Centenary of Our Lady of Refuge Church in Cromer 1895–1995* (Cromer: Parish Council of the Church of Our Lady of Refuge, 1995)

G. M. Murphy, 'Husenbeth, Frederick Charles (1796–1872)', in *ODNB*, vol. 28, pp. 971–2

P. Murrell, 'Bury St Edmunds and the Campaign to pack Parliament, 1687–8'; *Bulletin of the Institute of Historical Research* 54 (1981), pp. 188–206

[E. Neale], *Stray Leaves from a Freemason's Note-Book* (London: Richard Spencer, 1846)

P. R. Newman, *Royalist Officers in England and Wales 1642–1660* (New York: Garland, 1981)

M. Nicholls, 'Rookwood, Ambrose (*c.* 1578–1606)', in *ODNB*, vol. 47, pp. 699–700

E. R. Norman, *The English Catholic Church in the Nineteenth Century* (Oxford: Clarendon, 1984), p. 6

V. Nutton, 'Caius, John (1510–1573)', in *ODNB*, vol. 9, pp. 480–2

C. Paine, 'The Chapel and Well of Our Lady of Woolpit', *Proceedings of the Suffolk Institute of Archaeology and History* 38 (1993), pp. 8–12

Paul VI, *Qui Universum*, in *Acta Apostolicae Sedis*, vol. 68 (Rome: Ex Typographia Polyglotta, 1976), p. 351

—— *Quod Oecumenicum*, in *Acta Apostolicae Sedis*, vol. 68 (Rome: Ex Typographia Polyglotta, 1976), pp. 311–12

N. Pevsner and B. Wilson, *The Buildings of England: Norfolk I: Norwich and North-East* (New Haven, CT: Yale University Press, 1997)

[J. W. Picton], *A Great Gothic Fane: The Catholic Church of St. John the Baptist, Norwich, with Historical Retrospect of Catholicity in Norwich* (Norwich: W. T. Pike, 1913)

S. Plunkett, *Suffolk in Anglo-Saxon Times* (Stroud: Tempus, 2005)

N. Pollard Brown, 'Southwell, Robert [St Robert Southwell] (1561–1595)', in *ODNB*, vol. 51, pp. 711–17

J. H. Pollen (ed.), 'Bedingfield Papers', in *Miscellanea VI* (London: Catholic Record Society, 1906), pp. 2–4

[——(ed.)], *Bedingfield Papers, &c.* (London: Catholic Record Society, 1909)

The Present from our Past: The History of the Church of St Edmund King and Martyr Bury St Edmunds (Bury St Edmunds: St Edmund's History Group, 2012)

Proposals and Recommendations Concerning the Division of the Diocese of Northampton (Northampton: Diocese of Northampton, 1975)

M. Questier, *Conversion, Politics and Religion in England, 1580–1625* (Cambridge: Cambridge University Press, 1996)

——'Catholicism, Conformity and the Law', in P. Lake and M. Questier (eds), *Conformity and Orthodoxy in the English Church, c. 1560–1660* (Woodbridge: Boydell, 2000), pp. 237–61

—— *Catholicism and Community in Early Modern England: Politics, Aristocratic Patronage and Religion, c. 1550–1640* (Cambridge: Cambridge University Press, 2006)

D. R. Ransome, 'Rosier, James (1573–1609)', in *ODNB*, vol. 47, p. 787

J. Rastell, *A briefe shew of the false wares packt together in the named, Apology of the Churche of England* (Louvain, 1567)

'Record of the Catholic Missions of Norfolk before 1837', *English Catholic Ancestor* 1 (1984), pp. 1–15

V. B. Redstone, *The Ancient House or Sparrowe House, Ipswich* (Ipswich: W. E. Harrison, 1912)

D. D. Rees, 'Chapman, Henry Palmer [*name in religion* John] (1865–1933)', in *ODNB*, vol. 11, pp. 55–6

'The Registers of the Catholic Chapel at Haughley Park, Suffolk, 1807–1809', *Catholic Ancestor* 6 (1996), pp. 114–16

P. Renold (ed.), *The Wisbech Stirs (1595–1598)* (London: Catholic Record Society, 1958)

R. Rex, 'Wentworth, Jane [Anne; *called* the Maid of Ipswich] (*c.* 1503–1572?)', in *ODNB*, vol. 58, pp. 127–8

M. Reynolds, *Godly Reformers and their Opponents in Early Modern England: Religion in Norwich, c. 1560–1643* (Woodbridge: Boydell, 2005)

L. M. Richmond, 'Lescher, Mary Adela [*name in religion* Mary of St Wilfrid] (1846–1927)', in *ODNB*, vol. 33, p. 415

A. Robertson, 'Railways in Suffolk', in D. Dymond and E. Martin (eds), *An Historical Atlas of Suffolk* (Ipswich: Suffolk County Council, 1988), pp. 108–9

F. de Rochefoucauld (ed. N. Scarfe), *A Frenchman's Year in Suffolk* (Woodbridge: Suffolk Records Society, 1988)

J. Rockett, *Held in Trust: Catholic Parishes in England and Wales 1900–1950* (Brockley: St Austin Press, 2001)

N. Rogers, 'Popular Jacobitism in a Provincial Context: 18th Century Bristol and Norwich', in E. Cruickshanks and J. Black (eds), *The Jacobite Challenge* (Edinburgh: J. Donald, 1988), pp. 123–41

—— 'A Catholic Interlude: Sidney Sussex College, 1687–1688', in N. Rogers (ed.), *Catholics in Cambridge* (Leominster: Gracewing, 2003), pp. 38–45

P. Rollings, *Walsingham: England's Nazareth* (Walsingham: National Shrine of Our Lady of Walsingham, 1998)

A. Rossi, *Norwich Roman Catholic Cathedral: A Building History* (London: The Chapels Society, 1998)

J. Rowe, 'Roman Catholic Recusancy', in D. Dymond and E. Martin (eds), *An Historical Atlas of Suffolk* (Ipswich: Suffolk County Council, 1988), pp. 88–9

—— 'Suffolk Sectaries and Papists, 1596–1616', in E. S. Leedham-Green (ed.), *Religious Dissent in East Anglia* (Cambridge: Cambridge Antiquarian Society, 1991), pp. 37–41

J. Rowe, 'Roman Catholic Recusancy', in T. Ashwin and A. Davison (eds), *An Historical Atlas of Norfolk* (Norwich: Norfolk Museums Service, 1994), pp. 138–9

—— 'The 1767 Census of Papists in the Diocese of Norwich: the Social Composition of the Roman Catholic Community', in D. Chadd (ed.), *Religious Dissent in East Anglia III* (Norwich: University of East Anglia, 1996), pp. 187–234

—— '"The lopped tree": The Re-formation of the Suffolk Catholic Community', in N. Tyacke (ed.), *England's Long Reformation 1500–1800* (Abingdon: UCL Press, 1998), pp. 167–94

—— 'Everard, Thomas (1560–1633)', in *ODNB*, vol. 18, pp. 788

—— 'Kitson family (*per. c.* 1520–*c.* 1660)', in *ODNB*, vol. 31, pp. 843–46

—— 'Mumford, James (*c.* 1606–1666)', in *ODNB*, vol. 39, pp. 728–9

—— 'Whitbread [*alias* Harcourt], Thomas (*c.* 1618–1679)', in *ODNB*, vol. 58, pp. 529–30.

A. C. Ryan, 'Tunstall, Thomas (*d.* 1616)', in *ODNB*, vol. 55, p. 557

—— 'Walpole, Henry [St Henry Walpole] (*bap.* 1558, *d.* 1595)', in *ODNB*, vol. 57, pp. 43–6

G. H. Ryan and L. J. Redstone, *Timperley of Hintlesham: A Study of a Suffolk Family* (London: Methuen, 1931)

J. Saward, J. Morrill and M. Tomko (eds), *Firmly I Believe and Truly: The Spiritual Tradition of Catholic England. An Anthology of Writings from 1483 to 1999* (Oxford: Oxford University Press, 2011)

J. J. Scarisbrick, *The Reformation and the English People* (Oxford: Blackwell, 1984)

G. Scott, 'Three Seventeenth-Century English Martyrs', in D. H. Farmer (ed.), *Benedict's Disciples* (Leominster: Fowler Wright Books, 1980), pp. 266–82

R. M. Schuler, 'Blomefylde [Blomefield], Myles (1525–1603)', in *ODNB*, vol. 6, p. 255

W. J. Sheils, 'Bedingfield [Bedingfeld] family (*per.* 1476–1760)', in *ODNB*, vol. 4, pp. 782–5

R. C. Simons, 'Wingfield, Edward Maria (*b.* 1550, *d.* in or after 1619), in *ODNB*, vol. 59, pp. 728–9

S. A. Singer, 'Walsingham's Local Genius: Norfolk's "Newe Nazareth"', in D. Janes and G. Waller (eds), *Walsingham in Literature and Culture from the Middle Ages to Modernity* (Farnham: Ashgate, 2010), pp. 23–34

A Sister of Notre Dame, *Sister Mary of St. Philip (Frances Mary Lescher), 1825–1904* (London, 1920)

J. Smith, 'Jerningham, Edward (1737–1812)', in *ODNB*, vol. 30, pp. 51–3

S. Smith, *The Apostle to Ipswich: L'Abbé Louis Pierre Simon* (Ipswich: Wolsey Papers, 1977)

J. Spencer, 'Inchbald [*née* Simpson], Elizabeth (1753–1821)', in *ODNB*, vol. 29, pp. 222–5

D. Spittle, 'Gifford's Hall, Stoke-by-Nayland', *Proceedings of the Suffolk Institute of Archaeology and History* 30 (1965), pp. 183–7

M. Spufford, *Contrasting Communities: English Villagers in the Sixteenth and Seventeenth Century* (Cambridge: Cambridge University Press, 1974)

F. Stapleton, *The History of the Benedictines of St Mary's Priory Princethorpe* (Hinckley: Samuel Walker, 1930)

J. Stevenson, *Popular Disturbances in England, 1700–1832*, 2nd edn (Abingdon: Routledge, 1992)

J. M. Stone, 'Downes (alias Bedingfeld, Mountford and Mumford), Thomas', in *The Catholic Encyclopedia* (New York: Robert Appleton: 1907–12), vol. 5, pp. 148–9

C. Talbot (ed.), 'Recusants in the Archdeaconry of Suffolk', in *Miscellanea* (London: Catholic Record Society, 1961), pp. 108–11

T. F. Teversham, *A History of the Village of Sawston* (Sawston: Crampton and Sons, 1942–47), 2 vols

H. Thurston, *Stations of the Cross* (London: Burns and Oates, 1906)

T. B. Trappes-Lomax, 'Catholicism in Norfolk, 1559–1780', *Norfolk Archaeology* 32 (1958), pp. 27–46

B. S. Travitsky, 'Grymeston [Grimston; *née* Bernye], Elizabeth (*b.* in or before 1563, *d.* 1601×4)', in *ODNB*, vol. 24, pp. 157–8

G. Waller, *Walsingham and the English Imagination* (Farnham: Ashgate, 2011)

A. Walsham, *Church Papists: Catholicism, Conformity and Confessional Polemic in Early Modern England* (London: Royal Historical Society, 1993)

J. Walter, *Understanding Popular Violence in the English Revolution: The Colchester Plunderers* (Cambridge: Cambridge University Press, 1999)

B. Ward, *The Sequel to Catholic Emancipation: The Story of the English Catholics Continued down to the Re-establishment of their Hierarchy in 1850* (London: Longmans, Green & Co, 1915)

P. Waszak, 'The Revival of the Roman Catholic Church in Peterborough c1793–1910', *Peterborough's Past* 3 (1988), pp. 27–39

—— 'The "Golden Ball" Chapel at King's Cliffe, Northamptonshire', *Midland Catholic History* 8 (2001), pp. 16–28

A. Weikel, 'Cornwallis, Sir Thomas (1518/19–1604)', in *ODNB*, vol. 13, pp. 486–7

A. Whitelock and D. MacCulloch, 'Princess Mary's Household and the Succession Crisis, July 1553', *The Historical Journal* 50 (2007), pp. 265–8

A. Whiteman and M. Clapinson (eds), *The Compton Census of 1676: A Critical Edition* (Oxford: Oxford University Press, 1986)

P. Wickins, *Victorian Protestantism and Bloody Mary: The Legacy of Religious Persecution in Tudor England* (Bury St Edmunds: Arena, 2012)

A. Wilcox, 'The Seaman Family of Flixton, Suffolk', *Catholic Ancestor* 8 (2000), p. 12

'The Will of John Gooderiche of Bacton, Suffolk, Physician (1631)', *English Catholic Ancestor* 2 (1989), pp. 15–26

K. W. Woods, 'The Pre-Reformation Altarpiece of Long Melford Church', *The Antiquaries Journal* 82 (2002), pp. 93–104

E. S. Worrall (ed.), *Returns of Papists, 1767: Dioceses of England and Wales except Chester* (London: Catholic Record Society, 1989)

B. Wright Newman, *The Flowering of the Maryland Palatinate* (Washington, DC: Clearfield, 1961)

F. Young, 'Mother Mary More and the Exile of the Augustinian Canonesses of Bruges in England: 1794–1802', *Recusant History* 27 (2004), pp. 86–102

—— '"An Horrid Popish Plot": The Failure of Catholic Aspirations in Bury St. Edmunds, 1685–88', *Proceedings of the Suffolk Institute of Archaeology and History* 41 (2006), pp. 209–25

—— 'The Shorts of Bury St Edmunds: Medicine, Catholicism and Politics in the Seventeenth Century', in *The Journal of Medical Biography* 16 (2008), pp. 188–94

—— 'The Tasburghs of Bodney: Catholicism and Politics in South Norfolk', *Norfolk Archaeology* 46 (2011), pp. 190–8

—— 'The Tasburghs of Flixton and Catholicism in North-east Suffolk, 1642–1767', *Proceedings of the Suffolk Institute of Archaeology and History* 42 (2012a), pp. 455–70

—— 'How did Catholic Families survive and flourish under the Penal Laws?', *Catholic Ancestor* 14 (2012b), pp. 105–19

—— 'Elizabeth Inchbald's "Catholic Novel" and its Local Background', *Recusant History* 31 (2013a) pp. 573–92

—— *English Catholics and the Supernatural, 1553–1829* (Farnham: Ashgate, 2013b)

—— *Where is St Edmund? The Search for East Anglia's Martyr King* (Ely: East Anglian Catholic History Centre, 2014a)

—— 'The Bishop's Palace at Ely as a Prison for Recusants, 1577–1597', *Recusant History* 32 (2014b), pp. 195–218

—— *The Gages of Hengrave and Suffolk Catholicism, 1640–1767* (London: Catholic Record Society, 2015a)

—— 'From Ely to Venice: the life of William Maurus Taylor OSB (b. 1576)', *Downside Review* 133 (2015b), pp. 152–75

—— 'Papists and Non-Jurors in the Isle of Ely, 1559–1745', *Proceedings of the Cambridge Antiquarian Society* 104 (2015c), pp. 161–70

—— (ed.), *Rookwood Family Papers, 1606–1761* (Woodbridge: Suffolk Records Society, 2016)

B. Zon, 'Plainchant in the Eighteenth-Century English Catholic Church', *Recusant History* 21 (1993), pp. 361–80

UNPUBLISHED PAPERS

F. Young, 'Surviving the Reformation: Who were the Catholics?', Wuffing Education Study Day, Sutton Hoo, 29 March 2014

WEBSITES

'From the Church Archives', St Pancras' Church, Ipswich http://www.stpancraschurch.org.uk/Church_History/ Archives/archives.html)

J. H. Newman, 'Sermon 10: The Second Spring' http://www.newmanreader.org/works/occasions/sermon10.html

'Online Historical Population Reports' http://www.histpop.org/ohpr/servlet/

'The Annunciation, King's Lynn', Norfolk Churches http://www.norfolkchurches.co.uk/lynnannunciation/ lynnannunciation.htm

Oxford Dictionary of National Biography, online edition http://www.oxforddnb.com

'Our Lady and St Walstan Church, Costessey', Norfolk Churches http://www.norfolkchurches.co.uk/costesseyrc/costesseyrc.htm

'Past Bishops: Joseph Rudderham', Diocese of Clifton http://www.cliftondiocese.com/diocese/past-bishops/ joseph-rudderham

'Who were the Nuns?' project http://wwtn.history.qmul.ac.uk

INDEX

Individuals featured in Appendix 1 do not appear in the index unless mentioned elsewhere in the text.